The Keepers

The Keepers

PRISON GUARDS AND
CONTEMPORARY CORRECTIONS

Edited By

BEN M. CROUCH, Ph.D.

Department of Sociology and Anthropology
Texas A&M University
College Station, Texas

CHARLES C THOMAS • PUBLISHER
Springfield • Illinois • U.S.A.

Published and Distributed Throughout the World by
CHARLES C THOMAS • PUBLISHER
Bannerstone House
301-327 East Lawrence Avenue, Springfield, Illinois, U.S.A.

© *1980, by* CHARLES C THOMAS • PUBLISHER
ISBN 0-398-03970-4
Library of Congress Catalog Card Number: 79-19599

With THOMAS BOOKS *careful attention is given to all details of
manufacturing and design. It is the Publisher's desire to present books that
are satisfactory as to their physical qualities and artistic possibilities and
appropriate for their particular use.* THOMAS BOOKS *will be true to those
laws of quality that assure a good name and good will.*

Printed in the United States of America
V-00-2

Library of Congress Cataloging in Publication Data
Main entry under title:

The Keepers.

  Bibliography: p. 337
  Includes index.
  1. Prisons--United States--Officials and employees--
Addresses, essays, lectures. I. Crouch, Ben M.
HV9470.K43   365'.641'023   79-19599
ISBN 0-398-03970-4

For Nancy, Caren, and Amy

CONTRIBUTORS

LEO CARROLL, Associate Professor, Department of Sociology, University of Rhode Island, Kingston, Rhode Island.

NORMA MEACHAM CROTTY, Associate, Whiteman, Osterman and Hanna Law Firm, Albany, New York.

BEN M. CROUCH, Associate Professor, Department of Sociology, Texas A&M University, College Station, Texas.

MARY PATRICIA GREAR, Associate, Lord, Bissell and Brook Law Firm, Chicago, Illinois.

ANTHONY L. GUENTHER, Associate Professor, Department of Sociology, College of William and Mary, Williamsburg, Virginia.

MARY QUINN GUENTHER, Protective Services Coordinator, Social Services Agency, York County, Virginia.

GORDON HAWKINS, Professor, Institute of Criminology, Sydney University, Sydney, Australia.

JAMES B. JACOBS, Associate Professor, Department of Sociology and Law School, Cornell University, Ithaca, New York.

JAMES W. MARQUART, Doctoral Student, Department of Sociology, Texas A&M University, College Station, Texas.

EDGAR MAY, Free-lance writer, Springfield, Vermont.

DAVID G. MORRIS, Sociologist, Mid-State Penitentiary.

PAULINE J. MORRIS, Consultant to the Justice Department Commission, Vancouver, British Columbia.

HAROLD G. RETSKY, Chicago Wind Work Release Center, Chicago, Illinois.

EZRA STOTLAND, Professor, Department of Psychology, University of Washington, Seattle, Washington.

GRESHAM M. SYKES, Professor, Department of Sociology, University of Virginia, Charlottesville, Virginia.

G. L. WEBB, Program Evaluation Coordinator, Planning and Research Division, Harris County Juvenile Probation Department, Houston, Texas.

PREFACE

THIS book assumes that our understanding of the prison world will be enhanced by focussing on the man in the middle, the guard. He stands between the press of inmate demands below him and the dictates of administrative policy above. What he thinks and what he does are consequential for a wide range of prison outcomes. Yet, among "free world" persons, even students of prison, the guard remains a blurry figure.

The purpose of this book then is to bring the guard into sharper focus and place him in the context of a changing prison environment. Consequently, the materials presented deal almost exclusively with guards. Of course, the roles of guards and inmates are complementary, making it difficult to consider one without the other. But this is precisely what most traditional studies of prison life have done. Such studies, perhaps understandably, have primarily examined inmates, treating guards incidentally, if at all. The present anthology redresses this typical imbalance in the prison literature by highlighting the keeper instead of the kept.

I used two basic criteria in selecting papers to be included here. The first criterion was that papers focus in important and diverse ways on the problems of guard work. The second was that the papers reflect either the guard's point of view or provide a basis for better appreciating that point of view. In addition to drawing together writings from a wide range of publications, I have contributed three of my own previously unpublished papers.

The materials are organized into four sections, each examining a significant set of problems faced by guards. The introductory section contains a single essay intended as a backdrop for subsequent selections by presenting a macro analysis of prison change and its impact on guard work. Subsequent sections focus on (1) the process of becoming a guard, (2) the daily problems guards experience while dealing with inmates, (3) various ways guards accommodate to the changes and demands that characterize guard work today. Organized in this way, the selections generally take the reader from an overview of the guard's world through the stages of guard work an officer might experience: entry, formal and informal training, and exposure and adjustment to the routines and stresses on the job. Together the materials depict guards as rather ordinary men attempting to carry out one of society's "dirty work" assignments.

THE KEEPERS is intended for use by both students and researchers. Students in undergraduate and graduate courses in criminal justice and sociology will find it contributes to a better understanding of the dynamics of prison life and the role of security staff. The book can also be used as part of the training curriculum for new officers. Finally, corrections researchers, especially those interested in prison personnel, will find it helpful in developing questions and hypotheses for further investigation. A bibliography relevant to guard work is provided to facilitate this effort.

A comment is in order on the use of the term "guard" throughout the book. I am aware that prison administrators and line officers often disavow the term because it connotes a job that is both simple and closely linked to force. I chose to use the term, however, because it is conventional and most readily identifies the prison workers of which this book is about. Although I have called them guards, the papers in the book clearly indicate that officers engage in a complex set of tasks involving much more than simply "guarding."

I am grateful to many people who assisted in the preparation of the book. Geoff Alpert, Gary Webb, Elmer Johnson, and James Jacobs reacted to various materials I have developed for this volume. James Marquart has very helpful in preparing the comprehensive bibliography, while Connie Alexander graciously typed and retyped many parts of the manuscript. Many officers and staff within the Texas Department of Corrections regularly gave me frank feedback on my ideas and observations about guard work. Finally, my wife, Nancy, served as my personal editor and provided much needed encouragement throughout the project.

B.M.C.

CONTENTS

xiii

PART IV
RESPONDING TO CHANGE

The Keepers

PART I

INTRODUCTION

Chapter 1

THE GUARD IN A
CHANGING PRISON WORLD

Ben M. Crouch

> Over the years, (prison administrators) have
> relaxed the rules. Inmates have adopted a
> more daring attitude toward guards because
> they know they can use the slightest
> grievance — real or imagined — to get a
> guard on report. They're not afraid of
> punishment because punishment is lighter.
>
> *An Illinois guard at Pontiac Correctional
> Center* (quoted in Wiedrich, 1978b)

CORRECTIONAL institutions are a kind of
barometer of society's attitudes toward its offenders. The means
of detention, corporal, or capital punishment reflect society's
conceptions of just desert and effective deterrence (Rusche and
Kirchheimer, 1939; Rothman, 1971; Thomas and Williams,
1977). Although imprisonment is the dominant mode of punishment in twentieth century America, there is considerable
disagreement as to how prisons should function. Generally, in
the first half of this century, America's methods of incarceration went largely unquestioned. Most citizens probably had
little knowledge or concern about life behind prison walls.
Prisons were simply places where courts sent people found
guilty of felonies to "pay their debt to society"; what happened
to them there was probably deserved. As a result of these attitudes, prisons have traditionally been socially, and often physically, isolated from the mainstream of society. This isolation,
however, has changed dramatically in the past two or three
decades. Specifically, in this period, interest groups outside the
walls have called into question many traditional prison practices. For example, academics have urged, then challanged,
rehabilitation programs; civil rights activists have demanded

5

improvement in the legal position of inmates; and prisoners, especially those from minority groups, have employed the rhetoric of political exploitation to indict correctional systems. In addition to moving prisons into the glare of public attention, these external pressures in every case have required a response from prison officials, a response that typically altered or eliminated traditional practices. Not surprisingly, these responses have created turmoil and great uncertainty within prisons. In turmoil, prisons still reflect the broader society, since society today seems quite uncertain about how to define and react to its offenders.

In this essay I want to explore changes in the prison world from the point of view of a frequently overlooked staff member, the guard. Prison guards work at the very point in the system at which prisons try to translate into practice society's intentions, whatever they may be. At the same time, to inmates, guards are the most accessible and visible representative of the authority that locked them away. Guards are thus able to significantly influence the fate of institutional programs and policies while having an important impact on the kept (Glaser, 1969). Since these officers hold such an important place in the prison order, I want to examine how the changes prisons are currently undergoing affect them. This analysis not only makes the guard role stand out in sharp relief but provides a better understanding of current prison realities.

The essay that follows consists of three major sections. In the first, I consider three changes originating outside prison but having important consequences for institutional practices and, ultimately, for prison guards: (1) the rise of rehabilitation as an objective of imprisonment, (2) the entry of the federal judiciary into daily prison operation, and (3) changes in the size and composition of inmate populations. I describe first how each of these changes emerged and then consider the impact of each on the guard. The discussion of these changes is not intended to be an exhaustive account but rather an overview of the crosspressures impacting prisons. As such, each discussion of prison change provides a backdrop not only for the characterization of guard work in this essay but for each of the selections in this book. The second section presents a hueristic model of prison relations drawn from the race relations literature. The model is essentially a conceptual tool which both reflects the combined impact of prison change and suggests the direction in which prison relations are moving. In a final section, I review some alternatives the future may hold for prison organization generally and for guard work specifically.

IMPACT OF CHANGES IN THE PRISON ENVIRONMENT

The Rise of Rehabilitation

Eighteenth century jails in both Europe and America were largely places to hold miscreants prior to capital or corporal punishment. These jails typically combined offenders indiscriminately, and since they were often privately run for profit, an offender of means could increase his comfort significantly. By the beginning of the nineteenth century, however, a movement had begun to reshape American prisons by improving conditions and by adding an objective beyond punishment, namely rehabilitation. The impetus for this movement came from a group of Quakers in Philadelphia who in 1787 established the Society for Alleviating the Miseries of Public Prisoners. Their efforts laid the groundwork for the rational notion that incarceration, under specific conditions, could affect change in offenders for the better. Specifically, the Quakers stipulated that prisoners be isolated in their cells and cut off from all communication; they were to be left alone in the silence with only a Bible to help them become penitent.

Time soon began to erode the Quaker's original plans for rehabilitation and guided penitence. As nineteenth century America turned increasingly to institutions to handle her insane, delinquents and criminals (Rothman, 1974), prison populations grew accordingly. In the process the approach of isolating men throughout their sentences, as the early Pennsylvania reformers intended, became burdensome. Individual cells and exercise yards were expensive, and the inmates locked away in this manner could produce little in the way of useful work or goods to defray institutional costs. Thus, as prisons grew and concerns for economic realities mounted, the rhetoric of rehabilitation became largely window dressing while prisons became human warehouses.

This situation largely remained unchanged until after World War II. Until this time prisons were isolated in rural areas, receiving little in the way of public attention or legislative largess. Remedial programs were primarily limited to classification schemes which grossly separated various types of prisoners (Hippchen, 1975). After World War II, however, the goal of rehabilitation again became an important concern among prison reformers. Decades of inattention by society and efforts to maintain the inside *status quo* by prison administrators had produced atrocious conditions in prison by mid-twentieth century. These conditions, and the spate of riots in the fifties they ultimately sparked, prompted officials to ask outside scientists to examine the causes of the riots and to make recommendations. Their examinations rekindled theoretical interests in prisons and reinforced the feeling that prisons could and should be doing more than just keeping offenders locked away. Scientists felt that time "on ice" should be used actively to rehabilitate inmates, to treat the causes behind their errant behavior. Specific treatment efforts included individual and group therapy designed to modify the attitudes and personality structure of the offender and therapeutic communities in which every aspect of the offender's environment ideally contributes to the offender's improvement (Hippchen, 1975).

By the late 1960s and early 1970s, however, these same treatment efforts came under critical review. Although many studies examined the effectiveness of various treatment programs, the most frequently cited reports are those by Martinson (1974) and Lipton, Martinson, and Wilkes (1975). These writers conclude that rehabilitation efforts have no significant effect on recidivism. Although other writers suggest that the negative conclusion reported by Martinson and others are overdrawn (Palmer, 1975; Glaser, 1978), the criticism has undermined the once unquestioned goal of rehabilitation. The result, at this writing, is a general deemphasis of treatment programs in both federal and state institutions.

The introduction of rehabilitation and the various programs incorporated into prison routines to achieve this goal have certainly affected the guard role. Prior to the Quakers' efforts at prison reform, guards were simply jailers and, though they interacted with their charges, it is unlikely they actively or regularly sought to change prisoners into law abiding citizens. Even after the revolutions started by the Quakers' Pennsylvania approach to corrections, no one, administrators or guards, interacted with prisoners locked away in isolation. As prisons became human warehouses through the nineteenth and early twentieth century guards still had little to do with treatment. Prison managers expected guards to be concerned with security and control alone. If any rehabilitation was to be done, the job went to psychologists, ministers or parole counselors.

However, with renewed interest in rehabilitation after World War II, administration expectations of guards began to shift; guards were to become somehow active in the rehabilitation enterprise. For example, in those prisons where reformers tried the therapeutic community concept, all personnel, including guards, were expected to contribute to the treatment objective. Indeed, some programs during the mid-1960s urged guards to become "front-line therapists" and counsel with inmates (Craddick, 1964; Cavallin, 1967). At the very least, guards were told they must do whatever they could to support treatment efforts while maintaining strict security.

The rational introduction of rehabilitation as a legitimate prison goal and the subsequent expectation that guards support it create several types of conflicts that impact the guard role. One type of conflict frequently noted by prison observers involves the basic incompatibility of treatment and custody (Cressey, 1965). Treatment assumes that the behavior that brought inmates to prison and that threatens order inside has a cause that can be treated within a remedial, flexible environment. But such an environment makes security difficult, and daily control over inmates, which guards deem imperative, is hard to maintain. Even though the control or custody objective and the treatment objective may not be theoretically incompatible (Robinson and Smith, 1971), in practice, treatment and custodial staff members have often been at odds with little effective communication or cooperation (Piliavin, 1966).

A second type of conflict, stemming from the introduction of rehabilitation, involves the frustration that guards experience in trying to carry out the control and treatment aspects of the job at the same time. Not only are the guards typically called *correctional* officers but their employee manuals usually stress that they should actively facilitate treatment objectives. Indeed, some evidence indicates that despite reported conflict with treatment personnel, many guards support treatment as a legitimate goal. For example, when Jacobs (1978) asked a sample of Illinois guards what prisons are for, 46 percent answered "rehabilitation." Efforts by guards to mobilize positive feelings about treatment in their interaction with inmates, however, can lead to role conflict. In a survey of guards in a large southwest prison, I found that approximately six out of ten officers reported experiencing some degree of role conflict. Not only were the men untrained for any involvement in treatment, but, more importantly, prison organization and custodial demands preempted positive interaction with inmates toward that end (Crouch, 1976).

A final kind of guard conflict fostered by open and flexible rehabilitation programs is between custody-oriented guards and those who enter prison work with proinmate and protreatment attitudes. In many prison settings, guards with proinmate attitudes experience conflict between their personal inclination and the prevailing, custodial expectations for the job (Crouch, 1976). Over time, if they remain in prison work, those attitudes might fade in the face of expectations from the traditional guard subculture (Kercher and Martin, 1975). Or, finding their attitudes out of place, they may simply leave (Jacobs and Kraft, 1978).

If other like-minded officers are present, however, then proinmate attitudes may be reinforced thus creating conflict between two segments of the guard staff. Irwin (1977) suggests that this proinmate type of guard has been entering prison work in increasing numbers recently. Typically young, urban, and often nonwhite, this "new breed" of guard relates to inmates in ways that create conflict with the "old guard." Irwin writes:

> Some of the senior guards at Stateville have indicated in interviews that they believe that the new guards from urban settings are less loyal to the prison system, poor disciplinarians, too friendly with the prisoners and too often involved in

smuggling to prisoners. On the other side, several of the new guards have revealed that they do feel somewhat closer to the prisoners with whom they often share more in terms of culture and experience than they share with the older guards (1977, p. 37).

From these observations, treatment or rehabilitation objectives create tension and conflict for guards. Yet at least one writer, John Irwin (1977, p. 32), suggests that the recent trend toward dismantling the rehabilitation ideal places guards in a somewhat vulnerable position. Without the rehabilitation function, Irwin argues, the custody-punishment function of prisons stands out in sharper relief. Since guards are the most obvious and immediate symbols of this latter function, deemphasis of rehabilitation means guards lose the rhetorical buffer that softens the harsher side of the guard role. As a consequence, guard morale may decline.

Both of these positions — that guards suffer from the introduction of treatment efforts and that they will suffer from a reduction in those efforts — may have some merit. Yet it is difficult to judge accurately the position of most guards on the rehabilitation issue. Surveys may show guards feel rehabilitation is a very important and legitimate goal (Jacobs, 1978). A cynical interpretation of such a finding would be that guards say what they think prison administrators and researchers want to hear. Another likely interpretation is that guards indeed feel inmates should have prison experiences that would change them. However, guards may mean by treatment something quite different from what program-oriented administrators and researchers mean. That is, many of the so-called "old guard" may be as concerned for helping and changing convicts as the social worker, but the definitions of inmates and the techniques for achieving inmate change these guards subscribe to might be rather disconcerting to treatment personnel. So, without good data on how the rise and the fall of the rehabilitation ideology affects front-line officers, statements on the matter are not conclusions but hypotheses.

Entry of the Federal Judiciary

In addition to being isolated geographically and socially,

prisons and their wards have also been isolated from the courts. When a person was convicted and sentenced to serve time, courts traditionally adhered to what has come to be called the *hands off doctrine* (Goldfarb and Singer, 1973). According to this doctrine, courts felt they should not interfere in prison policies. As a result, a convicted person not only lost most of his freedoms as a citizen, but he was also subject to the often unquestioned and unsupervised dictates of prison authorities. Several writers have revealed how inmate punishment has often been cruel and guided by personal whims, while local political and economic arrangements shaped living conditions for inmates (March, 1978; Murton, 1969).

In the 1960s, however, courts reassessed the hands off tradition and began to review inmate petitions. This change in the courts' orientation toward prisons was part of a larger trend toward judicial review of many types of administrative discretion involving curtailment of citizen freedoms. Since their entry into corrections, the courts have defined, through review, four general categories of prisoner's rights (Singer and Keating, 1973). The first area of rights recognized by the courts involves the right of access by prisoners to the court to challenge convictions and the treatment they received during confinement. The second area of rights applies to the Eighth Amendment proscription of cruel and unusual punishment including initially physical torture and extended ultimately to include such conditions as overcrowding and isolation. A third area of court involvement in correctional policy concerns the procedural protections that must be present when correctional decisions significantly influence a prisoner's liberty. Courts have specified that those decisions involving discipline, transfer, and eligibility for parole must involve notice hearings and, in some cases, right to counsel. The final group of cases bringing the courts behind prison walls involves the First Amendment freedoms of religion, assembly, speech, and freedoms from racial discrimination and segregation.

In the courts, prisoners have found a new ally in their constant confrontation with their keepers. While there have always been "jail-house" lawyers, traditionally their concerns were limited to the evidence or sentence in their own or a fellow inmate's case. In the past two decades, however, these law-wise inmates, aided by the American Civil Liberties Union (ACLU) and National Prison Project (Gettinger, 1977, p. 8) attorneys, have turned their attention to the conditions and officials under which inmates live. The vehicle used by these legal activists to bring the federal court behind the walls is a Civil Rights Law passed by the United States Congress in 1871. This law contains a provision by which citizens who had been denied their civil rights by state officials could bring suit in federal courts. This provision, Chapter 42 U.S. Code Section 1983, was until recently, quite forgotten. However, it now figures as the basis for thousands of writs filed against prison systems and officials every year (Singer and Keating, 1973).

Resultant rulings by Federal District Court Judges have had far reaching consequences across the country. According to a recent survey by Gettinger (1977), the following state prisons have been declared unconstitutional: Alabama, Arkansas, Florida, Louisiana, Mississippi, Nevada, New Hampshire, Wyoming, and Rhode Island. Though not declared unconstitutional, prisons in Arizona, Minnesota, Ohio, Oklahoma, District of Columbia, Puerto Rico, and the Virgin Islands have come under still court orders. Moreover, jails in more than 100 cities and counties have been ruled by the courts to be unconstitutional.

Some latter-day prison administrators view such court order positively. They realize that conditions are poor and result, to a large degree, from the lack or mismanagement of state funds. They see the court rulings as a catalyst for improvement in their facilities.

However, a perhaps more widely shared reaction to the entry of the federal courts is to view that entry as unwanted or, at best, excessive intrusion (Estelle, 1977). From the point of view of many prison officials, federal judges have, in the interest of remedying unacceptable situations, caused additional problems. A prison is a system with many interrelated parts that, over time, work out dependent and accomodative relationships. But when courts order rapid changes in one part of a prison system, those changes produce problems unintended and unanticipated by the courts. Several examples can illustrate how the

organizational ripples set in motion by prison efforts to comply
with court orders affect daily prison operations, especially the
work of prison guards.

In 1977, the Parchman Prison in Mississippi was under court
order to close several of its "camps" or housing facilities. While
there was little question that the camps needed closing, efforts
to comply caused security problems. To close the camps,
Parchman officials arranged for rapid parole of all but clearly
ineligible men and women. This "skimming" of the inmate
population effectively removed many of the very persons who
could serve or were serving as trusties. And since prison personnel need inmates to fill many formal and informal positions, the skimming meant that less than desirable persons in
trusty roles. The custody staff also faced security problems
caused by increased density in noncondemned camps as inmates vacated those closed by the court. Specifically, since these
units were dormitories, housing men meant placing beds two
high in bunk fashion and moving them closer together. Because of the bunks themselves, the towels and clothes hanging
on them, security staff could observe very little of what occurred
in the dormitory.

Another consequence of court rulings for guards lies in the
fact that inmates have become increasingly knowledgeable in
using the law to their advantage. I have talked to officers in
several states who admit to an increasing concern about having
"writs" filed against them by inmates. Officers, in turn, become
hesitant in their dealings with inmates for fear of having their
action later ruled illegal (Gettinger, 1977). This concern is not
groundless since suits against correctional personnel are increasing (Mangrum, 1977). Inmates can also use court rulings
to advantage even without filing writs. Bob Wiedrich (1978a), a
Chicago Tribune reporter, relates an example of how Illinois
inmates manipulated court rulings and in the process created
security problems. In that state a federal court ruled that inmates in solitary cannot be denied commissary privileges, although, as a means of discipline, such privileges can be denied
inmates not in solitary. Because commissary is so important to
prisoners, they sometimes commit an act serious enough to
place them in solitary to regain commissary access lost earlier

for less serious transgressions. Thus, courts can indirectly cause trouble to occur.

The most fundamental concern about the federal courts guards seem to have, however, involves the loss of control and authority over inmates. From the guards' point of view, the court has become an external power base for inmates, while it has taken away from guards many of the mechanisms traditionally employed to control and discipline inmates. At one extreme, for example, these mechanisms include the strap and a device used as late as the early 1970s in Arkansas known as the *Tucker telephone*, an instrument that could send surges of electricity through wires attached to a man's genitals. While few lament the banning of such devices, many, especially old-line guards, do regret the loss of discretion in handling inmates. Like police chafing under court edicts regarding the street work only they fully understand, many guards feel that their decisions on the control and discipline of inmates would be more effective without court guidance (March, 1978, pp. 42-43; Jacobs, 1977a, p. 50).

For example, a high ranking security officer in the Texas Department of Corrections told me why he believed there was so much trouble in prisons today and, relatedly, why the inmate population was increasing so fast. He said that in the past, prior to the intrusion of the court, if a man committed a relatively minor offense, an officer would just "kick his ass, and that'd be the end of it." Today, he said, the officer not only cannot touch the inmate but that officer must file a disciplinary report that will bring the man before a prison court. My informant held that the filed report did not help the inmate straighten up nearly so much as the swift kick did, and, in the case of the latter punishment, no written record of his transgression remained to mar the file later reviewed by the Parole Board. When guard discretion can keep records clean in this way, he felt, more men would go home on parole thus reducing the population. The officer's argument reflects not so much an accurate thesis as a sentiment probably widely held. The federal courts' entry undermines the guard's authority, and the result is often a feeling of frustration and helplessness (Attica, 1972, p. 125). While few guards appear to practice excessive and unrea-

sonable control of inmates or even condone it, most officers
do feel that court ordered or influenced changes in prison relations make more difficult the already problematic guard
role. An officer in San Quentin related to me in September,
1978, "Hell, we don't have any control anymore; we're just
baby-sitting."

There is little question that guards often have negative
feelings about the intrusion of the courts. Because of this
feeling and because guards are in the front lines, it is possible
guards are the reason for slow or noncompliance with the court
rulings. However, Sullivan and Tifft (1975) argue that while
many reasons can be listed for the noncompliance of prison to
court orders, the primary problem lies not with guards but with
the managerial process within the prison organization itself.
They write:

> [I]n correction, prison guards . . . have been castigated for
> intervening in the lives of offenders without exhibiting ade-
> quate concern for their constitutional rights. Ironically, the
> same secretive, warehouse 'store 'em and forget 'em' ideology
> that has fostered arbitrariness by frontline correctional per-
> sonnel toward offenders . . . has also been used by correctional
> management to keep workers 'behind the line.' Will workers
> whose own constitutional rights are thwarted outright or by a
> managerial style that is inconsistent with due process norms
> be likely to demonstrate concern for the procedural rights of
> offenders? . . . No . . . (1975, p. 221).

Thus, if guard attitudes and behavior are not in accord with the
specific court orders or the general tenor of recent court rulings,
then those guard dispositions should not be examined apart
from the organizational climate of the prisons they work in.

Changes in the Inmate Population

While rehabilitation efforts and entry of the federal judiciary
have certainly influenced the guard role in important ways,
changes in the inmate population have probably had a more
immediate, tangible impact on that role. Over the past two
decades, the inmate population not only grew but the type of
inmate being sent to prison changed. In this section I will focus

on changes in the size and composition of the inmate population and the consequences of those shifts for guards.

Size

In recent years the problems associated with placing persons in penal institutions have been compounded as the number of men and women being sent to prison began to outstrip the available space. On January 1, 1976, America's adult prison population was 250,042; on January 1, 1977, that figure was 275,582, an increase of over 25,000 persons (Wilson, 1977). The population increase continued in 1978, although at a somewhat slower rate, with few state prison systems being immune to the pressure of overcrowding (Sherrill, 1978). Several factors account for the rise of inmate populations in the past decade (Sutherland and Cressey, 1978; Wilson, 1977; Flanagan, 1977). First, the "at risk" population has increased; the male twenty to thirty-four age group which contributes most prisoners has increased 48 percent over the past fifteen years. Second, also affecting males in this age group, is unemployment. Sutherland and Cressey (1978, p. 563) report that the incarceration rate is much more closely correlated with the unemployment rate than with the crime rate. The third reason for the rise in prison populations involves public and judicial attitudes. Public opinions seems to have shifted increasingly toward a "get tough" policy which emphasizes punishment. Judges, feeling this public attitude and noting the frequent failure of probation, have made even greater use of prison facilities. This general "beefing up" to deter crime more efficiently means that prisons, the final stop in the system, must accept and find a place for more and more inmates.

The growth of inmate populations has had a number of important consequences for the conditions under which guards work. One of these consequences is that guards may be less able to interact with prisoners as they could when prison populations were more stable. Older guards say, for example, that in years past they could name and had time to speak to most inmates. Today, they note, positive, informal relations between guards and inmates are less likely.

Population growth also causes changes in prison schedules, and these changes, in turn, create problems for both guards and inmates. Newly convicted felons cannot be sent back to the courts by prison officials; they must be accepted and placed somewhere. They must be fed, medicated, allowed to receive visits, provided with mail, and exposed to various prison programs. To provide even the necessary services to inmates, institutions must tighten or compress schedules to get everything done in one day. This tightening strains facilities, inmates, and security personnel. For example, prison food, well prepared and served, can be an important aspect of an otherwise bleak prison experience for inmates. However, when an institution designed to house and feed 1500 prisoners increases in size to 3000 or more, then pressures on food services becomes tremendous. The quality of meals goes down and inmates must eat at odd times through the day just so all will have a chance to pass through the food lines three times. In short, providing inmates meals or any other necessities requires greater regimentation when inmate numbers swell.

Another consequence of population increases for guard work involves the potential for violence and subsequent control problems. The programmatic activities that take inmates out of their cells such as work, recreation, and education clearly suffer under population growth. Limitations in time and supervisory staff restrict inmate participation in these activities; so, inmates spend proportionately more time in their cells. And when those cells, often designed for only two persons, contain three and even four prisoners, the situation becomes especially volatile. One possible control problem under these circumstances, of course, is collective violence: the prison riot (Travisano, 1978). Another problem involves inmate-inmate violence. Evidence indicates inmates homocide increases as prisons increase in size (Sylvester, Reed, and Nelson, 1975); prison population increases appear to be related to homosexual rapes as well (Wilson, 1977).

The tension and stress experienced by officers due to the problems of overcrowding may affect both their mental state and their dealings with inmates (Brodsky, 1977). Doctor Jack McCall, director of prison psychological services in North Carolina (quoted in Wilson, 1977), states that officers typically do not admit the stress, preferring to reflect a "John Wayne" image of competence. Yet, he notes, many miss work due to blood pressure related illnesses. Others finally come in for counseling and tranquilizers. In an effort to handle or release this tension on their own, some officers may tighten discipline and become repressive and punitive. Others may react by avoiding any interactions with inmates at all. Either type of reaction obviously makes already potentially unstable crowded conditions even more difficult for all concerned.

Although overcrowding in itself produces difficulties for inmates and staff, attempts at solutions have also brought problems. Several state prison systems, either on their own or in reaction to court orders to reduce overcrowding, have installed temporary housing facilities. The most common kind of temporary housing seems to be house trailers, mobile homes minimally adapted to shelter several inmates. While trailers offer some room to expand beyond the institution's regular cellblocks and dormitories, officers say they are hard to supervise and keep clean. Another institutional reaction to the increasing inmate population is to hire new correctional officers in a wholesale fashion. How this process can be problematic became apparent to me during an extended visit to the Angola prison facility in Louisiana in 1977. At that time Angola was receiving large numbers of inmates from court condemned parish jails. Traditionally, Angola, like most rural prisons, had hired local residents for security work. As the need for employees increased, available manpower dwindled and officials found themselves hiring many eighteen and nineteen-year-old youths as building security personnel. This move created tension among inmates who faced very young and quite inexperienced officers. One inmate, speaking of this new body of officers, told me that "its like walking on egg shells around here; you never know what they're going to do." At the same time, these young prison guards found themselves supervising men who were not only more "prison-wise" but in some cases quite hostile. These guards were thus especially subject to manipulation by prisoners.

Composition

Changes in the inmate population have not been limited to size, however. There has also been a gradual shift over the years in the type of inmate coming to prison. Inmates two and three decades ago generally did not question the fundamental legitimacy of the state or its right to employ imprisonment as a reaction to crime. The tendency was to view imprisonment as a response to crime alone and not as evidence of discrimination; prison was just the consequence of getting caught. The California Task Force on Violence notes that "the prisoner of 20 years ago upheld the political and economic system even as he was looting it" (1977, p. 254). Once in prison, most inmates sought to adapt to the coercive environment by accommodation and manipulation. Recognizing the fact that they were socially as well as physically isolated from the outside world, prisoners focussed their attention on "making it" behind the walls. Under such circumstances, most inmates sought to avoid confrontation with authorities because of the "heat" such contact could bring. In addition, prisoners, perceiving themselves in the same boat, so to speak, apparently reflected considerable solidarity. While there was certainly racial separateness and hostility among inmates twenty to thirty years ago, racial identity was much less apt to be the basis for collective action or politicalization than it is today (Jacobs, 1977a, p. 48).

Considerable empirical and impressionistic data, however, testify to the recent emergence of a kind of inmate with a quite different background and ideological characteristics. This new prisoner, for example, is more violent than those of a decade or two ago. Toch (1976) reports that in California in 1960, 17 percent of the inmate population were incarcerated for homicide and armed robbery; in 1972, the proportion of violent offenders like these had jumped to 33 percent. Over the same period the proportion of property offenders in the system fell from 40 to 20 percent. These changes are in part reflective of the greater use of community corrections, an important program designed to foster rehabilitation of less serious offenders. The result is, nevertheless, more violent inmates in prison.

Two other characteristics of this new breed of inmates involve minority status and age. Blacks and Chicanos have always been disproportionately represented in prisons. However, in recent years the degree to which minority inmates are overrepresented seems to have increased (Mattick, 1976, p. 537). Today's prisoners are also more apt to be younger. These particular changes are probably due in large part to unemployment and increases in the proportion of young persons in society generally. The careers of these young inmates often involve regular trips between the streets and probation offices, detention wards, jails, and prisons. These men, whom Irwin (1970) calls "state-raised youth," often survive on the streets of large cities with their gangs and, because many of their fellow gang members are also incarcerated, they can get along quite well when they go to prison. Inside, the gangs provide both a ready identity and the power of numbers. These gangs of young inmates are especially reflective of important shifts in prison demographics since prison gangs are very often, though not always, composed of minorities. Jacobs (1977a), for example, describes the significance of black and Chicano gangs in Illinois' Stateville prison. Similarly, Davidson (1974) suggests that Chicano gangs are a very important force in the operation of San Quentin.

Changes in the inmate population have not only been demographic, but they have been ideological as well. Essentially, inmates seem no longer exclusively concerned with exploiting the immediate prison environment for personal gain. Although this exploitation remains as a central part of prison life, there has been a relatively recent increase in inmate radicalization and sensitivity to the politics of prison (Browning, 1972; Baker, 1977). Many inmates have come to question the legitimacy of prison practices and personnel. This shift in how inmates define their situation is evident in the motivation of prison riots over the past twenty-five years.

Pallas and Barber (1973), in tracing the history of post World War II riots through three periods of struggle, reveal the connection between the increased numbers of young, nonwhites in prison, and the political radicalization of prisoners. The first period of struggle these writers identify involves the severe prison riots of the 1950s that were prompted by the poor living conditions inmates endured. Guided by tough, typically white inmate leaders, these riots were largely spontaneous uprisings. The second period of struggle is related to the rising influence of the Nation of Islam among lower-class blacks. Emphasizing a positive individual and racial identity while characterizing white society as the enemy, the Muslim philosophy was very attractive to young, lower-class blacks who had little hope of benefitting from assimilationist politics. As a result, the Black Muslims were able to recruit fruitfully not only in the urban ghetto but in prisons as well. Although the predominately white prison authorities opposed the Black Muslims, the decline of the movement in prison was not due, according to Pallas and Barber (1973), to this opposition. Instead, the decline was due more to internal splits that occurred in the early 1960s within the movement itself. Despite its decline, however, the Black Muslims did provide a model for racial identity and for the use of collective power against prison authorities. This model became the basis for increased radicalization of prisoners in the late 1960s and 1970s, the third stage of prison activism. The emergence of what Pallas and Barber call the "revolutionary prison movement" was a product of changes not just in prison but in the larger society. Events of the 1960s fostered many challenges to the political, economic and social *status quo*, challenges which were typically met by some level of repression. Obvious examples include the civil rights movement, antiwar efforts and even the efforts of deviant minorities such as gays to achieve relief from discrimination.

The political rhetoric and ideologies generated by these movements have provided many, especially minority, inmates (Jacobs, 1977b, p. 190) with a radical critique of prison. Thus, especially in those prisons with a history of political unrest, new inmates will be exposed to these critiques and become increasingly unwilling to accept the definitions of the prison experience offered by prison officials. Research by Faine and Bohlander (1978) indicates this radicalization of inmates does occur, especially among certain types of offenders. They found radicalization is most pronounced among inmates who are young, have friends already in prison (e.g. fellow gang members) and have little chance of postrelease success.

Over the past two decades then, a confluence of factors has produced a quite different inmate population. Traditionally there existed a general population marked by considerable solidarity cutting across race lines. While there were certainly racial hatreds, the deprivation and subordination of all convicts by authorities fostered a situation that pitted the cons against the officials. But the mobilization of the rehabilitation ideal and the entry of the federal judiciary combined to relieve some of that deprivation. At the same time prisons were called upon to house inmates who were increasingly nonwhite and young. Once inside, these inmates had access to radical ideas, ideas that provided a new way for inmates to view themselves and interpret their prison experience. These factors have eroded "convict solidarity and facilitated the emergence among prisoners of a fragmented social organization composed of numerous cliques with diverse normative and behavioral orientations" (Carroll, 1974, p. 9; Irwin, 1977, p. 33).

The entry of these new inmates and the erosion of convict solidarity has led to a lack of support for the informal and long established rules of prison life. Tenets of the inmate code involving doing one's own time, minimizing complications in the life of another convict simply because he is another convict, and avoiding staff confrontations that can bring "heat" are not particularly important to this new breed of convicts. Because the behavior of these young, tough, and sometimes gang affiliated inmates is so unpredictable in traditional terms, old school inmates feel threatened (Chambliss, 1972, p. 77). As one older inmate notes:

> "The new kinds of prisoners are wild. They have no respect for rules or other persons. I just want to get out and give it all up. I can't take coming back to prison, not with the kind of convicts they're getting now" (quoted in Irwin, 1970, p. 72).

The "kind of convicts they're getting now" also creates problems for prison guards. To the degree inmates do not subscribe to familiar accommodations between the keepers and the kept, guards find interaction with inmates increasingly uncertain. Being sued, injured, or even killed seems to guards more likely to happen today than in the past. This uncertainty stems in large part from changes in the means inmates use to secure power and to define the prison experience in ways favorable to them. These changes and how they relate to shifts in the inmate population just considered are discussed in a recent paper by Carroll (1977).

Carroll suggests that there are essentially three means inmates use to deal with officials: corruption of authority, censoriousness, and confrontation. First analyzed by Sykes (1956), *corruption of authority* refers to the informal, subtle process whereby inmates use the fact of guard dependence on them to maintain control and perform many prison tasks to gain extra freedoms; it compromises and erodes the authority officers have over inmates. Corruption of authority has been and will continue to be an important part of prison life. The other two forms of inmate response to subordinate status, however, are not only less covert but better reflect fundamental shifts in prison relations. *Censoriousness* refers to inmate criticism of officials for not following rules that are established as appropriate for the prison. This method of dealing with officials assumes some consensus between officials and inmates on norms and values. That is, inmates extend considerable legitimacy to the system generally, faulting it only as it fails to provide such things as good food or treatment programs. The final means open to inmates in dealing with officials is confrontation. *Confrontation*, by definition, denies legitimacy to the system; it also requires superior numbers, leadership, a target on which to focus the effort, and, perhaps most importantly, solidarity within a group of inmates.

According to Carroll's analysis, white inmates are more likely to employ corruption of authority and censoriousness. Because guard forces are predominately white, racial prejudice may prevent black inmates from getting close enough to white officers to manipulate this relationship to their advantage. Not only are white inmates thus better able to corrupt official authority, but white inmate leaders have a greater interest in maintaining the prison *status quo*. Less subject to discrimination inside and out of prison, white inmates have lacked the reason for the collective identity and solidarity needed for confrontation. And because they have been more willing than blacks, especially in recent years, to view prison as a legitimate enterprise, white inmates have traditionally employed censoriousness. Black and other minority inmates, however, have become increasingly inclined toward confrontation. They are more likely to perceive prison through the prism of political and racial discrimination and renewed racial identity. This shared perception provides the solidarity required for confrontation. Since these minority inmates do not view prison as legitimate, it makes little sense for them to pressure authorities to provide treatment programs. After all, treatment programs imply the reason for imprisonment lies with the prisoner himself and that the prisoner needs treatment (Jacobs, 1977b, p. 195). The more revolutionary position, held by many contemporary inmates, especially minority inmates, holds that the reason for imprisonment lies not with the convicted felon but with the criminal justice system and, ultimately, with society at large.

The use of confrontation as a means of interacting with officials, plus the general eroding of the guard's traditional authority, makes the role of keeper especially problematic. Jacobs offers a statement by a guard which illustrates some of this difficulty:

> "The inmate will say 'fuck you, Jack, I'm not going.' Then several members of his gang will gather around him. I've had to call a lieutenant. . . . Often one of the gang leaders will just come over and tell the man to go ahead" (p. 199).

Traditionally, such antistaff aggression and refusals to obey orders would likely be viewed by inmates as contemptuous as it might mean trouble for everyone. But today, notes Toch (1976, p. 56), inmates, especially younger ones, consider this behavior status conferring. For the prison guard, conditions such as these are certainly unpleasant and possibly dangerous. Although the likelihood of being killed or injured on the job may be relatively low compared to other occupations, safety is a real concern, especially in those prisons with increasing inmate activism. When Jacobs (1978) asked his officer respondents to indicate the main disadvantages of their job, the most frequently mentioned problem by far was danger. And some evidence suggests that this anxiety has some basis in fact. Mattick

(1976, p. 533), for example, notes that self-mutilations, suicides, and ambiguous deaths have decreased and the proportion of altercations between guards and inmates has increased. And the California Task Force on violence (1977) reports similar causes for concern among guards. This report notes that assaults on employees prior to 1970 were typically the unplanned results of escapes or other incidents that the staff was trying to control. Since 1970, however, violence against staff has had an increasingly deliberate, ideological character. Moreover, the hit-and-run tactics of guerilla warfare have replaced disturbances by large groups of inmates (Carter, McGee, and Nelson, 1975, p. 162). Finally, in a study of prison violence and victimization, Fuller and Orsagh report that " . . . a (guard) spending all his shift time with inmates has a 1.1 percent chance of being victimized in a three-month period. This rate is about twice the pure victimization rate experienced by convicts" (1977, p. 39).

A HUERISTIC MODEL FOR PRISON RELATIONS

To this point, I have reviewed several factors that have changed prisons generally and the guard role specifically. Clearly neither exists in a vaccum; important aspects of the social environment shape both prison organizations and their personnel. In this section, I will extend the above analysis by outlining how concerns for treatment, entry of the federal judiciary, and changes in the inmate population have combined to fundamentally alter the relations between the keepers and the kept. The intent is to offer a conceptual framework that both integrates the variables affecting prison relations and identifies the direction in which those relations are moving.

The conceptual framework employed here is adapted from a typology of race relations developed by sociologist Pierre Van den Berghe (1967). Van den Berghe suggests a continuum along which the quality of race relations in a given society may be placed. The continuum is defined by two polar, ideal types of race relations, "paternalistic" and "competitive." Applying this scheme to the United States, Van den Berghe argues that prior to the Civil War, the rules guiding racial interactions were paternalistic. That is, the status of blacks, slave and nonslave alike, was clearly and unequivocally inferior, a normative position supported by the legal system. From the Civil War to the present, however, the history of black Americans reveals uneven, but nonetheless real, progress toward equality. Political and social change altered the traditional, institutional arrangements that placed blacks in a predictably subordinate position in relation to whites. As legal and moral pressure against subordination grew, paternalistic relations gave way to competitive relations. The color line blurred allowing blacks to move into more equal relations with whites and thus vie for power. As a result of this shift, whites not only had difficulty dealing with blacks on an equal basis, but subsequent political, legal, and economic competition, not possible under paternalism, led to confrontation and conflict.

My argument is that relations between inmates and officials within prison institutions have also shifted from paternalistic toward competitive relations. Moreover, it seems possible to conceptually place various state systems along the continuum between the two extremes, because this general movement, wrought by external changes, is uneven. Some states such as Texas are still quite close to the paternalistic pole. And Jacobs' (1977a) excellent history of Stateville in Illinois implicitly describes that prison's shift toward competitive relations after the passing of Warden Ragen in 1961. The California system appears to qualify for advanced placement toward the competitive end of the prison relations continuum. The relevance of this scheme for the present concern for guards is that as prison organizations become more concerned with treatment and protecting inmate rights, inmates become increasingly equal to their keepers; such changes, here seen as the basis for competitive prison relations, place guards in a particularly vulnerable position inasmuch as their role, on a daily basis, still involves maintaining the traditional, dominant-subordinate *status quo*.

Applying a race relations model to prison is appropriate due to the striking parallels between the historical and present statuses of nonwhite Americans and of prisoners generally. Both occupy a subordinate position within an established *status quo*; both hold that status involuntarily, and the relations of both to their masters have been affected by changes outside that relationship. Although the two groups of subordinates are not mirror images, the race typology can nonetheless serve as a heuristic model for drawing conclusions about conditions in prison today. In the following paragraphs, paternalistic and competitive prison relations will be examined in turn.

Paternalistic Prison Relations

In a prison regime characterized by paternalism everyone knows his place; roles and statues are clearly defined. For example, certain areas of the building are off limits, and lines are drawn on the floor to dictate where inmates will walk and where staff will walk. More illustrative of the clear demarcation of status is the requirement that all inmates dress in the same state-issue clothing; the requirement that no personal clothing will be worn by inmates symbolizes very graphically the low, undifferentiated status of prisoners. When official dominance is clear and largely unquestioned, informal, even close, relations between officers and selected inmates are possible. That is, low social distance can be tolerated because of the unequivocal status difference. Thus, officers may routinely rely on inmates to carry out many prison tasks, ranging from bookkeeping and cooking to maintaining control over other inmates in the case of "goon squads" or "head strummers." In the extreme, selected inmates may even run the entire security system as was the case in Mississippi and Arkansas until recently (McWhorter, 1972; Murton, 1969).

Under paternalism the etiquette guiding inmate deportment before authorities is elaborate and the interactional rules well known. Officials may call inmates by their last name, a nickname or even a racial epithet while inmates must respond with *sir* and address the officials as *Mister*. In one quite paternalistic system, as a squad of inmates moved from one cotton patch to another, I observed all the men take off their hats in response to an order barked by one of their number. I asked about this practice and learned that tradition dictates that all inmates doff their hats as they pass by the captain in the field.

While paternalism certainly does not preclude aggression behind the walls, it does mean that trouble largely comes from the lower caste, the inmates. Thus, individual inmate aggression toward authorities involves escapes or personal vendettas and collective aggression such as strikes or riots over food and housing. The moral right of the state to incarcerate felons is not a primary issue. In the immediate post World War II period, the dominant mode of prison life in this country was paternalism, and the major riots of the 1950s suggest that the quality of aggression stems from that prevailing mode of prison relations. As I noted above, these early riots contested not the legitimacy of prison and the status of convicts, but the living conditions associated with that status (Pallas and Barber, 1973).

The paternalistic orientation also influences guard perceptions of inmates. Van den Berghe suggests that under this type of race relations, whites view blacks as "childish, immature, uninhibited, lazy, good-humored, fun-loving, inferior but loveable" (1967, p. 32). These adjectives, necessarily tempered, suggest something of the traditional attitudes held by guards towards inmates. Guards see inmates as capable of causing trouble and even being dangerous, but the danger tends to reside in individual maverick inmates and is typically situation specific. The stance toward inmates then is a kind of benevolent despotism.

The type of organizational structure that nurtures paternalism is either oligarchic or autocratic. In prison this typically means a definite bureaucratic hierarchy headed by a strong commissioner or warden who can infuse his staff with a sense of stability and power. Policies and orders move down from the top while information flows upward from lower ranks. Below the top administrator, whose word is final, are the guard ranks, which are themselves quite stratified. Guards always begin in the lowest rank and move up by demonstrating loyalty and the ability to "handle" inmates. Finally, inmates exist at the very bottom of the hierarchical chain. Jacobs' (1977a) account of Stateville, under the Ragen administration (1931 to 1961) well illustrates the administrative style and structure characteristic of paternalism. He writes:

> Joe Ragen's thirty-year rule of Stateville was based upon the
> patriarchal authority he achieved. In the vocabulary of both

employees and inmates, "he ran it." The "old boss" devoted his life to perfecting the world's most orderly prison regime. He exercised personal control over every detail, no matter how insignificant. He tolerated challenges neither by inmates nor by employees nor by outside interest groups. He cultivated an image which made him seem invincible to his subordinates as well as to the prisoners (Jacobs, 1977a, p. 29).

Although Ragen was demanding of his officers, they shared the same security and control objectives, and, thus, presented a united front to both inmates and the public. These objectives were fostered by a system of bureaucratic rules that ensured that inmates knew their place and stayed there. At Stateville, new inmates invariably worked in such lowly jobs as hauling coal from the pits or working the rock quarry. This general administrative system largely disappeared, however, with the passing of Ragen in the early 1960s; Stateville then began to move toward more competitive prison relations. By comparison, the Texas prison system that reflects many of the Stateville characteristics under Ragen is still quite paternalistic (Krajick, 1978).

Finally, under paternalistic conditions, prison inmates have a definite legal status, if only by implication. That is, the traditional stance of the courts defined inmates as legal or constitutional inferiors. The hands off doctrine of noninvolvement in prison affairs so rigidly held to by the courts until the mid-1960s in this country did more than cast inmates in an unequal legal position vis-à-vis their keepers; the doctrine also helped maintain the *status quo* of dominance behind the walls.

Competitive Prison Relations

The passing of paternalism means a change in the abject subordination of inmates as well as pressure on guards and other personnel to adjust to a changing definition of the situation. Thus, prison relations become increasingly antagonistic and marked by suspicion. Traditionally, inmates could be expected to engage in manipulative efforts to secure creature comforts and adhere to the convict code. Thus, though seldom devoid of some hostility, the interaction between guards and inmates was at least somewhat predictable. As this interaction becomes less predictable and even dangerous, officials become more concerned with maintaining both social and physical distance from inmates. For example, many guards especially more experienced ones, may seek assignments away from the inmate population in towers or outside work shops.

Changes in the prison world have undermined the castelike structure to the point where the dominant and subordinant roles are no longer so clearly defined. In many prisons the traditional symbols of subordinate status are gone. For example, instead of requiring all convicts to wear state-issue clothing, officials allow them to wear whatever they wish. Dressing in street clothes further symbolizes the changing status of inmates and the diminishing status gap between keeper and kept. In Louisiana's Angola prison, for example, inmates wear individualized clothing, although trousers are usually jeans. Because many treatment staff members (and in 1977, some security staff due to a shortage of uniforms) also wear jeans, it is not uncommon for a visitor to be confused as to who is and who is not an inmate. As external trappings of status differences fade, so too do the elaborate rules of etiquette that mark paternalistic relations and underscore the unquestioned dominance of prison guards.

Aggression, under competitive conditions, also takes on a different quality; rather than coming primarily from inmates, it may be initiated by both inmates and their keepers. As was noted earlier, the ideological changes that have fostered the shift to the competitive pole within prisons provide inmates with a radical critique of the whole idea and practice of incarceration. Thus, inmate incidents and riots begin to reflect a withdrawing of legitimacy and a concern for more than creature comforts (Carroll, 1977). At the same time, guards become increasingly concerned about maintaining authority and control as confrontations with racially and politically aware inmate groups become more likely. For this reason, elements of the predominantly white guard force may foment trouble between black and white inmates in an effort to diminish the power of minority inmates that appears to be threatening (Wright, 1973). Indeed, this is precisely what the Black Muslims feared as they came to prominence in the 1960s (Pallas and

Barber, 1973). Carroll (1977, p. 53) offers an example of a black guard who resigned in protest of an alleged conspiracy between white guards and inmates that permitted white inmates to assault black prisoners with impunity. While evidence of such instigations by guards is sketchy and the practice probably limited, it nonetheless becomes more probable under increasingly competitive circumstances.

According to Van den Berghe, as race relations shift from paternalism to competitive, there is a corresponding shift in society's form of government from autocratic and oligarchic to restrictive and pseudodemocratic. As the legal and social status of the lower caste improves, ruling bodies become somewhat more cognizant of lower caste claims. A similar shift appears at the organizational level of prisons as they move toward the competitive pole. As a consequence of the broad changes outlined in the first sections of this essay, new administrations gradually replace the paternalistic regimes that enjoyed little or no operational interference from outsiders and certainly none from prisoners. Accounts of prison change in Arkansas (Murton, 1969) and Illinois (Jacobs, 1977a) indicate, for example, that prison changes in administrations usually bring an increased sensitivity to both outside interests and pressure from prisoners. This sensitivity to the claims of inmates themselves at least gives the impression that the traditional solidary dominance over inmates by all prison authorities (guards and administrators) has weakened somewhat.

For their part, many inmate groups intend to heighten administrative openness to their claims by collective organizing and even unionization. Although efforts to form a union or some other inmate organization are not new (Baker, 1977), such efforts are particularly apparent in recent years. Writing on the attempt by Ohio prisoners to form a union, Huff observes:

> The increasing militancy of Ohio's prisoners has recently evolved from rioting and requests for better conditions to an increasingly sophisticated organizational effort in the form of a prisoner's union with the political rhetoric of demands. This kind of movement is not indigenous to Ohio, but is reflected in a number of other States and appears to be

strongest in the Scandinavian countries. The prisoners' union has been opposed by state corrections departments, largely on the basis of perceived threats to institutional order and security and (more latently) because of the pressure of the guards and unions representing guards (1977, p. 472).

Although prisoners in this country have not yet effectively organized through unions to counterbalance the power of prison officials, the many efforts by inmates in this regard indicate a keen awareness of the changing prison order.

It should be apparent that the key element in the shift from paternalistic toward competitive prison relations is the change in inmate power. The reason for the altered balance of power is a decreased dependence by inmates on their immediate keepers. This point is grounded in Richard Emerson's (1962) notion of "power-dependence" relations. Emerson suggests that "the power of A over B is equal to, and based upon, the dependence of B upon A" (1962, p. 33). When goals sought by B are believed to be only available through A, then B is dependent on A and A, to that extent, holds power over B. In prison, since inmates and guards depend on each other, neither holds anything like absolute power. However, under paternalism, in a clearly subordinate caste and largely isolated from society, inmates must depend on their keepers for every relief. Under such benevolent despotism, inmate power is limited and alternatives for remedying adverse situations behind the walls are few. That is, limited in power, inmates may seek relief from deprivation via the existing convict code and the manipulation and exploitation that code implies or they may resort to more extreme remedies such as escape, self-mutilation, or suicide.

In the past twenty years, however, the dependence of inmates on prison officials has been somewhat reduced. That is, with the emergence of the treatment ideology, the rise of political and racial awareness among significant members of prisoners, and the entry of the federal courts, inmates need no longer rely exclusively on institutional authorities to determine the quality of prison life. As inmates collectively gain power in this way, they became increasingly able to compete with their keepers in the daily process of defining prison situations. That is, what was once an unambiguous case of rule violation may now be interpreted by inmates as a case of racial disrespect or legal deprivation.

THE FUTURE OF GUARD WORK

The gradual shift of American corrections toward a competitive mode had essentially meant the raising of inmates as a class into a position more equal to that of guards. As the prison world moves into the political, social, and legal mainstream of society, inmates have become more like free world citizens in their ability to claim individual, collective, and constitutional identities. Changes in the prison world, however, have occurred largely in the inmate camp. That is, guards have generally remained in the same position within prison, charged with maintaining control on the one hand and misunderstood and poorly rewarded on the other. For this reason, the immediate future of guard work appears to involve confrontation and even conflict not just with inmates but with prison administrators as well.

In addition to the changes affecting guard-inmate relations that I sketched earlier, new developments in the criminal justice system may cause further strain in the near future. One of these developments is the use of diversion from incarceration into various community corrections programs (Klapmuts, 1977). Diversion, simply stated, refers to efforts to minimize offender exposure to the justice system, especially incarceration. The spread of community corrections means that more and more prisoners who might once have been locked up may now be treated in a setting more conducive to the reintegration of that person into society. But not all can be diverted; some, the chronic and perhaps violent offenders, will be placed behind bars.

A related, and equally important, development in the criminal justice system involves the length of time a convict might spend in prison. This development is the move toward determinate sentencing (Fogel, 1975; Sherrill, 1977; Gettinger, 1977; May, 1977). Efforts to make available to district courts specific length or "flat time" sentences stem largely from two related trends: disenchantment with prison rehabilitation results and a general "get tough" attitude that involves a renewed interest in deterrence as the primary objective of corrections.

The significance of these criminal justice developments for guards in the near future is that the inmates they supervise may be, on the average, more intractable than in past years. For example, an investigation of violence in California prisons reported that community-based correctional programs, including probation, had reduced from 30 to 10 percent the proportion of convicted felons actually sent to prison. That 10 percent includes, on the one hand, fewer property offenders and "first timers" and, on the other, more state-raised youth and chronic offenders (Task Force, 1974, p. 254). As California and other states move toward determinate sentencing, these more intractable inmates may be in prison longer due to fixed terms and limited parole. Clearly then, on the heels of other changes, an increasingly chronic offender population locked up longer could further complicate the guard role, especially if guards remain relatively poorly trained.

Current tensions between guards and prison administrators are also likely to continue into the near future. Those tensions stem generally from a weakening of the solidarity once projected by guards and their wardens or the central office. Although within paternalistic prison systems this solidarity was not always complete (Jacobs, 1977a), guards and the administration nonetheless shared a conception of prison that placed inmates in a lower caste to be controlled, managed, and used. However, with the advent of treatment programs and personnel and court ordered changes in policy, old administrators began to give way to replacements, often from completely outside the system. Frequently college educated, these replacements have at times seemed to the guards to be more interested in inmates than in employees. What has been occurring, and will continue as corrections lumber toward the competitive mode, is a change in informal alliances. Organizationally, the traditional hierarchy marked by guard loyalty to wardens is giving way to a kind of triangular configuration with each point representing a component of the system — the guards, the administration, and the inmates. In short, guards have increasingly found themselves alone with changes they are often unprepared to deal with occurring above as well as below them in the system.

The most apparent collective response by guards to this state of flux has been unionization (Wynne, 1978). There are many reasons why guards seek to establish collective bargaining through unions. In his study of guard labor relations in Ohio, Staudohar (1976) lists employee safety as a primary concern of striking guards. He writes that "the 1968 insurrections and continuing inmate restiveness caused tension and stress among guards that became a primary factor in their initial work stoppage" (1976, p. 182). Staudohar also suggests that guard activism stemmed from dissatisfaction with administrative behavior in supporting employees on the job. These kinds of concerns, found in many guard forces, serve to make other work-related problems such as low pay and long hours stand out in sharp relief (Cockerham, 1977; Staudohar, 1976; Jacobs, 1978).

My projections of a somewhat embattled guard force may be accurate in the near future. However, while there will always be some tension in prison, some of the tension that marks the guard's world may diminish somewhat as the composition of guard forces themselves change. One important change that can be expected is the entry into corrections work of more young and socially conscious people (Carter, Mcgee, and Nelson, 1975, p. 384). They will temper, if not replace, the "old guard" whose view of corrections may be more in tune with the paternalism that is slowly passing from the prison scene. Another, more specific, addition to guard forces will be women officers.

The entry of women into prison work, which began quite recently, will certainly increase. In some cases their addition to the guard force in men's prisons has been out of necessity. For example, Louisiana's Angola prison, located on an isolated, rural site, could not find enough local men to meet the demands of a rapidly growing inmate population. Administrators decided to take the men off the perimeter guard towers and replace them with women. Elsewhere, the use of women officers in male prisons has reflected a concern for providing equal employment opportunities. California, for example, had no female officers prior to 1973; today they number over 100 in a state security staff of approximately 3000 (Becker, 1975). After initial resistance by male officers and by inmates, women have been increasingly accepted, even to the point of working on the San Quentin special security squad that deals with the most recalcitrant inmates. Because women are proving they can do the job as well as a man and because they may even have a leveling or quieting effect on inmate aggressiveness (Morris, 1974, p. 109), the involvement of women in front-line prison work will grow.

A third change in the composition of guard forces is the use of ex-offenders. Extensive use of this resource has been little tried and those who have done time may never constitute a very large percentage of the prison staff. However, as Morris (1974, p. 109) suggests, ex-offenders could show inmates as well as themselves that it is possible to "make it." According to a recent survey by Smith, Wood, and Milan (1974), 85 percent of the correctional systems in this country, including the District of Columbia and the Federal Bureau of Prisons, employ ex-offenders in various positions including correctional officer. The practice is relatively new, however. Of those states reporting a date, the overwhelming majority began hiring ex-offenders only in the last ten to twelve years.

Finally, minority groups will be increasingly represented among security personnel. Today guard forces are overwhelmingly white, and often rural in background, even as the inmate population is urban and disproportionately composed of minorities. This racial imbalance was especially significant in the tensions that were part of the riot at Attica prison in New York (Attica, 1972). With recognition of the importance of race in prison and the general, societal trend toward open employment for minorities, the numbers of minority officers are increasing. There are problems, of course; black officers frequently feel they are treated unfairly by prison management (Beard, 1975, p. 8). But their general impact on other officers and on inmates appears to be quite positive. In his study of black correctional workers, Beard (1975, p. 16) reports that three out of four of the inmates interviewed felt that black officers were more effective than white officers in helping black inmates. Does this mean that bringing in more black guards will improve relations between the keepers and the kept? Research reported by Jacobs and Kraft (1978) indicates that this is not necessarily the case. These writers surveyed black and white guards in Illinois to determine which factor, the demands of the guard role or race differences, could better account for the tension and conflict in prison. They concluded that since the black officers differed very little from white officers in their attitudes toward prison, inmates, and the administration, the attitudes guards hold emerge more from the conditions of the work setting than from the race of the officers.

This conclusion by Jacobs and Kraft clearly argues that if attitudes and behavior of guards are to change, then the organizational structure of prison must change. And since most authorities argue that prisons will be around for a long time to come, changes in prison organization and their impact on guards become important issues. Carter, McGee, and Nelson (1975, p. 386-387), for example, suggest that the future holds two types of facilities. The first, designed specifically and unabashedly for punishment, will differ relatively little from the maximum security institutions of today. These facilities, though perhaps smaller than many of today's stone monoliths, will still be formalistic and authoritarian. Presumably little would be expected of guards except maintaining order and ensuring that inmates remain safe and in custody according to legal guidelines.

The other type of organizational structure that Carter and his associates envision will be grounded in the principles of participative management, mutual trust of officials and inmates, flexibility, and greater decision-making power among lower officials. Correctional institutions and programs so organized would focus on reintegration and deal with more retrievable, less serious offenders. Here the staff and inmates would collectively work toward returning inmates to a productive life. Somewhere between these two types of facilities lies the prison proposed by Norval Morris (1974). Morris describes a prison for dangerous, especially violent, offenders that seeks to treat inmates rather than punish them. Excluded would be offenders who are hard to reach such as the psychotic, those who are famous such as organized crime figures, and other dangerous types such as gang leaders and militant groups. These offenders presumably would be sent to prison for punishment. In Morris' scheme, front-line officers would be the linchpin of a treatment program that would require the integrated efforts of all personnel to help offenders.

It appears, except perhaps for small prisons designed simply for punishment, that future correctional facilities will move away from the authoritarian, bureaucratic structures of today. In the process, the roles of guard and inmate will be redefined. I argued above that the movement of prisons toward the competitive mode produces increases in inmate equality and power and threatens traditional subordinate/superordinate role definitions. But as the organization structure that legitimates such traditional role definitions fades, relations between the keepers and the kept may become less threatening. Carter, McGee, and Nelson (1975, p. 387) suggest that in time, the "we-they" dichotomy characteristic of guard and inmate attitudes toward each other may diminish. Similarly, these writers note that the traditional line between custody and treatment staffs will become increasingly blurred. "The reintegrative programs of the future will emphasize *teams* of individuals (staff and offenders) possessing varied competences and working together in an equalitarian context" (1975, p. 387). It was to such teams that the Presidents' Commission on Law Enforcement and the Administration of Justice (1967) referred when it called for "collaborative" institutions in which all components work together to help inmates.

If today's keepers are truly to move toward more systematic and significant involvement in the correctional enterprise, then current conceptions of guards, held by the public and by guards themselves, must change. One means of affecting that change is the professionalization of correctional personnel (Brodsky, 1974; Frank, 1966). Such a suggestion, of course, does not mean moving correctional work toward occupational parity with established professions such as medicine. More modestly, professionalization means changing the job so that it will attract and hold the best people available.

At least three changes in the keeper's job as currently defined would significantly alter prevailing, and often negative, conceptions of the guard role. The first, and most obvious, improvement is increased wages. Citizens, and more directly state legislators in charge of prison budgets, have traditionally viewed prisons as simple operations; prisons keep convicted felons secure and fed until their punishment is over. Correlated with this view is a conception of guard work that holds that anyone can do this relatively simple job. Consequently, pay has always been quite low. The changes I have reviewed in this essay, however, demonstrate that the work is quite complex, and if good people, capable of doing the job, are to be attracted, they must be better paid.

The second job improvement that would make guard work more professional is a rewarding career ladder. Too often officers in the entry rank find not only that they make relatively little money, but that their chances of moving up in the prison organization are limited. Traditional prison organizations feature many first-line officers but relatively few supervisory ranks. Once these upper ranks are filled, organizational mobility can stagnate and become very frustrating to aspiring correctional personnel. More attractive is an arrangement whereby personnel interested in self-development and advancement could move up within a given prison unit, move to another or even into other noninstitutional correctional programs within the state system (Morris, 1974, p. 111).

Finally, the current role of prison guard may become more professional if it is enlarged or expanded. Currently, guards who have the greatest impact on and access to inmates have very limited discretion in dealing with inmates. The typical prison division of labor casts them as controllers, with little else expected. It is little wonder then that at least half of all correctional employees (most of whom are guards) feel they have very little freedom on the job (Joint Commission on Manpower and Training, 1969, p. 15). A report by Brief, Munro, and Aldag (1976; Williams and Thomas, 1976) indicates that expanding the job of guard could make the job more attractive. These researchers examined the correlations between selected employee reactions to the job and certain characteristics of the correctional task. Results indicate clearly that as the job becomes more complex and allows greater freedom, employee's satisfaction and job involvement also increase.

Obviously, the changes in correctional work outlined here are closely interrelated. For example, with job enlargement comes diversity, which fosters the employee satisfaction and advancement now so lacking. Similarly, better pay first attracts good people and then rewards them for filling an important role. Equally clear is the fact that such changes cannot occur without fundamental shifts in traditional prison organization. Whether the above sketch of the future of guard work is accurate remains an open question. More certain is the fact that prisons have moved onto center stage, and society must pay attention. The tensions currently experienced by the keepers and the kept cannot continue indefinitely.

REFERENCES

Attica: *The Special Report of the New York State Special Commission on Attica.* New York, Bantam, 1972.

Baker, J. E.: Inmate self-government and the right to participate. In Carter, R., Glaser, D., and Wilkins, L. (Eds.): *Correctional Institutions,* 2nd Ed. Philadelphia, Lippincott, 1977.

Beard, E.: *A Study of the Attitudes and Perceptions of Black Correctional Employees as a Basis for Designing Recruitment and Retention Strategies.* Institute of Urban Affairs and Research, Howard University, 1975.

Becker, A.: Women in corrections: a process of change. *Resolution,* Summer, pp. 19-21, 1975.

Brief, A. P., Munro, J., and Aldag, R. J.: Correctional employees' reactions to job characteristics: a data based argument for jobs enlargement. *Journal of Criminal Justice, 4 (Fall):* 223-230, 1976.

Brodsky, C.: Long-term work stress in teachers and prison guards. *J Occup Med, 19 (February):* 133-138, 1977.

Brodsky, S. L.: A bill of rights for the correctional officer. *Federal Probation,* June, 1974.

Browning, F.: Organizing behind bars. *Ramparts,* February, pp. 40-45, 1972.

Carroll, L.: *Hacks, Blacks and Cons.* Lexington, Lexington, 1974.

———: Race and three forms of prison power: confrontation, censoriousness and the corruption of authority. In Huff, C. Ronald (Ed.): *Contemporary Corrections: Social Control and Conflict.* Beverly Hills, Sage, 1977.

Carter, R., McGee, R., and Nelson, E.: *Corrections in America.* Philadelphia, Lippincott, 1975.

Cavallin, H.: The case study: A clinical approach to the training of the correctional officer. *American Journal of Correction,* May-June, pp.

14-18, 1967.

Chambliss, W.: *Box Man a Professional Thief's Journey*. New York, Torch. Har-Row, 1972.

Cockerham, W. E.: Connecticut weathers 3-day guard strike. *Corrections Magazine, 111, 2 (June):* 37-41, 1977.

Craddick, R. A.: An approach to short-term training of custodial officers and staff in prisoner-counseling. *Canadian Journal of Corrections*, July, pp. 325-330, 1964.

Cressey, D. R.: Prison organizations. In March, J. G. (Ed.): *Handbook of Organizations*. Chicago, Rand, 1965.

Crouch, B.: *Role Conflict Among Prison Guards*. Paper presented before the Mid-West Sociological Society, St. Louis, 1976.

Davidson, R. T.: *Chicano Prisoners. The Key to San Quentin*. New York, HR&W, 1974.

Emerson, R.: Power-dependence relations. *Am Sociol Rev, 27, 1 (February):* 31-40, 1962.

Estelle, Jr., W. J.: Federal courts now write their own law. *Corrections Magazine, 4 (December):* i, 1977.

Faine, J. and Bohlander, Jr., E.: The genesis of disorder: oppression, confinement and prisoner politicalization. In Huff, C. R. (Ed.): *Contemporary Corrections: Social Control and Conflict*. Beverly Hills, Sage, 1978.

Flanagan, J.: Crisis in prison population. In Carter, R., Glaser, D., and Wilkins, L. (Eds.): *Correctional Institutions*. Philadelphia, Lippincott, 1977.

Fogel, D.: *We Are the Living Proof: The Justice Model for Corrections*. Cincinnati, W. H. Anderson Co., 1976.

Frank, B.: The emerging professionalism of the correctional officer. *Crime and Delinquency*, July, pp. 272-276, 1966.

Fuller, D. A. and Orsagh, T.: Violence and victimization within a state prison system. *Criminal Justice Review, 2, 2 (Fall):* 35-56, 1977.

Gettinger, S.: Cruel and unusual prisons. *Corrections Magazine, 111, 4 (December):* 3-16, 1977.

———: Three states adopt flat time: others wary. *Corrections Magazine, 111, 3 (September):* 16-30, 33, 36, 1977.

Glaser, D.: Counterproductivity of conservative thinking. *Criminology, 16, 2 (August):* 209-224, 1978.

———: *The Effectiveness of a Prison and Parole System*. New York, Bobbs, 1979.

Goldfarb, R. and Singer, L.: *After Conviction*. New York, Simon and Schuster, 1973.

Hippchen, L. J.: Changing trends in correctional philosophy and practice. In Hippchen, L. J. (Ed.): *Correctional Classification and Treatment: A Reader*. Cincinnati, W. H. Anderson Co., 1975.

Huff, C. R.: Unionization behind the walls. In Carter, R., Glaser, D., and Wilkins, L. (Eds.): *Correctional Institutions*, 2nd Ed. Philadelphia,

Lippincott, 1977.

Irwin, J.: The changing social structure of men's prisons. In Greenberg, D. (Ed.): *Corrections and Punishment*. Beverly Hills, Sage, 1977.

———: *The Felon*. Englewood Cliffs, P-H, 1970.

Jacobs, J. B.: Stateville: The Penitentiary in Mass Society. Chicago, U of Chicago Pr, 1977a.

———: Street gangs behind the bars. In Carter, R., Glaser, D., and Wilkins, L. (Eds.): *Correctional Institutions*, 2nd Ed. Philadelphia, Lippincott, 1977b.

———: What prison guards think: a profile of the Illinois force. *Crime and Delinquency, 24 (April):* 185-199, 1978.

Jacobs, J. B. and Kraft, L. J.: Integrating the keepers: a comparison of black and white prison guards in Illinois. *Social Problems, 25:* 304-318, 1978.

Joint Commission on Correctional Manpower and Training: *Final Report: A Time to Act*. Washington, U.S. Govt. Print. Office, 1969.

Kercher, G. A. and Martin, S.: *Severity of Correctional Officers Behavior in the Prison Environment*. Paper presented before the Texas Academy of Sciences, Huntsville Texas, 1975.

Klapmuts, N.: Community alternatives to prison. In Leger, R. G. and Stratton, J. R. (Eds.): *The Sociology of Corrections*. New York, Wiley, 1977.

Krajick, K.: They keep you in, they keep you busy, and they keep you from getting killed. *Corrections Magazine, 1 (March):* 4-8; 10-21, 1978.

Lipton, D., Martinson, R., and Wilks, J.: *Effectiveness of Correctional Treatment: A Survey of Treatment Evaluation Studies*. New York, Praeger, 1975.

McWhorter, W.: The Trusty: A Sociological Analysis of an Inmate Elite. Unpublished Doctoral Dissertation, Southern Illinois University, 1972.

Mangrum, C. T.: Liability for correctional malpractice. *Youth Authority Quarterly, 30, 4 (Winter):* 8-16, 1977.

March, R. A.: *Alabama Bound*. University, U of Ala Pr, 1978.

Martinson, R.: What works? Questions and answers about prison reform. *The Public Interest, 35:* 22-54, 1974.

Mattick, H. W.: The prosaic sources of prison violence. In Guenther, A. (Ed.): *Criminal Behavior and Social Systems*, 2nd Ed. Chicago, Rand, 1976.

May, E.: Prison officials fear flat time is more time. *Corrections Magazine, 111, 3 (September):* 43-46, 1977.

Morris, N.: *The Future of Imprisonment*. Chicago, U of Chicago Pr, 1974.

Murton, T. O.: *Accomplices to the Crime*. New York: Grove, 1969.

Pallas, J. and Barber, B.: From riot to revolution. In Wright, E. O. (Ed.): *The Politics of Punishment*. New York, Torch. Har-Row, 1973.

Palmer, T.: Martinson revisited. *Journal of Research in Crime and Delinquency, 12, 2 (July):* 133-152, 1975.

Piliavin, I.: The reduction of custodian-professional conflict in correctional institutions. *Crime and Delinquency*, April, pp. 125-134, 1966.

President's Commission on Law Enforcement and the Administration of

Justice: *Task Force Report: Corrections.* Washington, U.S. Govt. Print. Office, 1967.

Robinson, J. and Smith, G.: The effectiveness of correctional programs. *Crime and Delinquency, 17, 1 (January):* 67-80, 1971.

Rothman, D.: *Discovery of the Asylum: Social Order and Disorder in the Republic.* Boston, Little, 1971.

Rusche, G. and Kirchheimen, O.: *Punishment and Social Structure.* New York, Russel, 1939.

Sherrill, M. S.: Determinate sentencing: History, theory and debate. *Corrections Magazine, 111, 3 (September):* 3-15, 1979.

———: Prison population rises again but at a slower rate. *Corrections Magazine, iv, 2 (June):* 20-24, 1978.

Singer, L. and Keating, M.: The courts and prisons: crises of confrontation. *Criminal Law Bulletin, 9:* 337-357, 1973.

Smith, R. R., Wood, L. F., and Milan, M. A.: Ex-offender employment policies: a survey of American Correctional Agencies. *Criminal Justice and Behavior, 1 (September):* 234-246, 1974.

Staudohar, P.: Prison guard labor relations in Ohio. *Industrial Relations, 15:* 177-190, 1976.

Sullivan, D. C. and Tifft, L. T.: Court intervention in correction: roots of resistance and problems of compliance. *Crime and Delinquency,* July, pp. 213-222, 1975.

Sutherland, E. and Cressey, D.: *Criminology,* 10th Ed. Philadelphia, Lippincott, 1978.

Sylvester, S., Reed, J., and Nelson, D.: *Prison Homicide.* New York, Spectrum Pub, 1977.

Sykes, G.: The corruption of authority and rehabilitation. *Social Forces, 34 (March):* 257-262, 1956.

Task Force, California Department of Corrections: Task force report on violence. In Carter, R., Glaser, D., and Wilkins, L. (Eds.): *Correctional Institutions,* 2nd Ed. Philadelphia, Lippincott, 1977.

Thomas, J. E. and Williams, T. A.: Change and conflict in the evolution of prison systems. *International Journal of Criminology and Penology, 5 (November):* 349-365, 1977.

Toch, H.: *Peacekeeping: Police, Prisons and Violence.* Lexington, Heath, 1976.

Travisano, A. P.: Overcrowding in prisons may hold seeds of future Atticas. *LEAA Newsletter, 10 (December):* 21, 11, 1978.

Van den Berghe, P.: *Race and Racism.* New York, Wiley, 1967.

Wiedrich, B.: Guards eye-view of life behind bars. *Chicago Tribune,* September 19, 1978a.

———: Riots show who runs the prison. *Chicago Tribune,* August 1, 1978b.

Williams, S. and Thomas, C.: Attitudinal correlates of professionalism and the correctional work. *Criminal Justice Review, 1, 2 (Fall):* 120-125, 1978.

Wilson, R.: U.S. prison population again hits new high. In Wilkman, P.

and Whitten, P. (Eds.): *Readings in Criminology.* Lexington, Heath, 1977.

Wright, E. O.: *The Politics of Punishment.* New York, Torch. Har-Row, 1973.

Wynne, J., Jr.: *Prison Employee Unionism: The Impact on Correctional Administration and Programs.* Washington, U.S. Govt. Print. Office, 1978.

PART II

BECOMING A GUARD

Since guards have the most direct and constant contact with prisoners, it follows that employees filling these front-line positions should be skillful managers of men. After all, not only are officers greatly outnumbered and unarmed, but they daily deal with men who are quite capable of violence. These conditions of prison work make the problems of guard recruitment and training especially important. The readings in Part II thus explore how men enter guard work and learn the job.

In the first reading, Gordon Hawkins examines how prisons select and train custody staff. He notes that selection criteria are both too rigid and too lax. Criteria are too rigid because many persons, otherwise able to do the job, do not qualify because they are, for example, small in stature or ex-offenders. At the same time, selection criteria are too lax because they neither screen out unfit persons nor adequately identify the best recruits. In considering formal training, Hawkins points out that while the general qualities needed for prison work can be readily identified, training men to reflect the necessary, but often diffuse, skills is difficult indeed. Low pay and too lax screening methods make training even more difficult. Hawkins reviews several alternatives for improving the selection and training of prison officers.

Although prison recruitment efforts and formal training procedures often produce poor results, men nevertheless do enter prison work and somehow become more or less successful employees. This suggests that other, less formal or official factors may actually determine who takes a guard job and how those persons behave on the job. Such is the argument presented in the second paper by Crouch and Marquart. These writers suggest that entry into prison work is quite often acci-

47

dental and discuss typical circumstances that lead men into prison work. Crouch and Marquart are primarily concerned, however, with the informal means by which recruits become knowledgeable officers. Drawing on several types of data, they explore first what guards must learn through informal interaction with both the inmate population and the guard subculture. They then consider the question of how men change after exposure to the demands of the job.

Chapter 2

CORRECTIONAL OFFICER SELECTION
AND TRAINING

GORDON HAWKINS

SELECTION

VERY little has been published about the recruitment and selection of prison officers. This is probably in
part due to the fact that manpower, recruitment, and retention
problems have long been widespread in the correctional field. It
is impossible to be highly selective in a situation where there is
a shortage of guards, a high turnover rate, and not infrequently
political interference, that is, patronage; and as a consequence
selection procedures for the most part remain at a rudimentary
stage of development. Ironically, however, it is probably in part
due to failure to consider the question of selection objectively
that the shortage exists.

The truth is that selection procedures and recruitment standards are commonly both too rigid and not restrictive enough.
Thus the task of a custodial officer calls for, and always has
called for, a great deal more than the minimum height, weight,
vision, and hearing requirements and high school diploma
demanded at Attica and in the majority of penal institutions in
America. At the same time it also calls for a good deal less.
Indeed a great many of the restrictions currently imposed in
personnel recruitment are not only irrational and unnecessary
but also prejudicial to the effective functioning of the prison
system.

One thing which is quite certain is that the almost universal
insistence on certain physical standards which restrict the selec-

From Gordon Hawkins, *The Prison: Policy and Practice*, 1976. Courtesy of University
of Chicago Press, Chicago, Illinois.

tion of potentially qualified employees is a mistake. The fact that a man weighs 145 pounds (the Attica requirement) is no index of character or ability or indeed of anything except the extent to which he can tip the scales. In fact the emphasis on such nonmerit factors must have frequently excluded otherwise well-qualified candidates. A good case can be made not only for the abolition of such rigid exclusionary rules but also for the recruitment of physically handicapped persons. The Joint Commission on Correctional Manpower and Training put this very well: "In the present labor market, as well as in the interest of full utilization of the nation's manpower resources, there should be an understanding of the contribution the physically handicapped can make in correctional institutions. . . . A positive point can be made for their employment with a realization that in the personal adjustment of many who are physically handicapped, they carry a message through to others in visual contact and in compassionate understanding that often characterizes a very effective relationship with other people" (1970, p. 124.)

The racial disparity mentioned above between the guards and inmates at Attica is common throughout the American prison system. As the National Advisory Commission on Criminal Justice Standards and Goals put it: "For too long, minority groups have been overrepresented as offenders and underrepresented as staff" (1973, p. 599). The Commission found that of the total number of correctional employees (110,000) only 8 percent were blacks, 4 percent Chicanos, and less than 1 percent American Indians, Puerto Ricans, or Orientals. All institution administrators in the adult correctional system were white. Although racial discrimination is prohibited in most civil service jurisdictions, the Joint Commission on Correctional Manpower and Training acknowledged: "Undoubtedly discrimination in some forms still persists" (1970, p. 125). At a time when racial strife is a major problem in many correctional institutions a policy of active recruitment of such minority groups as blacks, Puerto Ricans, and other Spanish-speaking Americans, rather than discrimination against them, is necessary.

In most states laws or civil service policies or practices prohibit the hiring of ex-offenders, although a number of experi-

mental correctional programs have employed them. It is clear
that this is a large, underutilized manpower resource pool
(Joint Commission on Correctional Manpower and Training,
1968). There are two powerful reasons why ex-offenders should
be recruited as prison guards. The first is that it is reasonable to
assume that some ex-offenders will have a better understanding
of other offenders than staff members who have never themselves been involved in serious crime or delinquency. The other
is that correctional institutions and other government agencies
have a responsibility to set an example of less discriminatory
employment practices in relation to ex-offenders.

Other restrictions on staff selection which are both unnecessary and unreasonable relate to age and residence. It is very
common for those under twenty-one and over forty-five to be
excluded from employment as prison officers as well as for a
mandatory retirement age of sixty-two to be fixed. The Joint
Commission found in fact that only 26 percent of all correctional employees are under thirty-four years of age (1969, p. 13)
which is a curious situation in view of the fact that crime itself
is so largely a function of age. In the year 1965 persons under
the age of twenty-five constituted 68 percent of the arrests for
robbery, 77 percent of the arrests for burglary, 72 percent of the
arrests for larceny, and 88 percent of the arrests for motor vehicle theft. (The President's Commission on Law Enforcement
and Administration of Justice 1967, p. 56). If the "generation
gap" does constitute a problem it is likely to be exacerbated if
more attempts are not made to recruit younger personnel, and
one of the best ways to do this would be to recruit young
persons from eighteen to twenty-one. The upper age limit for
recruitment should be at least fifty-five and the mandatory retirement age should be at least sixty-five. And residence requirements ought to be abandoned: "Residence of the state as a
requirement of selection on condition of continuing employment imposes a limitation on the public service that no private
employer has to contend with. Such a requirement is obviously
a non-merit factor in excluding a candidate. It is based primarily on political considerations" (Joint Commission 1970, p.
123).

But if some selection criteria are arbitrary and unnecessary it is equally true that some are not merely desirable but essential. Back in 1961, Clarence Schrag, who has had considerable practical experience in correctional institutions, pointed out that the idea that the custodial officer is able to control inmates because he has unlimited authority and that his orders carry the full sanction of the prison's administration is an illusion. In fact, he says, "The officer's control over an inmate depends primarily on his skills of persuasion and leadership." Schrag sees "skill in interpersonal relations" and the ability to win voluntary cooperation as being the crucial factors in securing and maintaining control (1961, p. 340).

There is no doubt that Schrag is right, but a high school diploma is no guarantee of the possession of such skills, and, in the absence of a training program designed to teach them, the fact that a number of officers are recruited with the necessary ability must be almost entirely fortuitous. There is no reason, however, why this situation should be regarded as unalterable. Personnel selection is not an arcane mystery open only to those possessed of special gifts of insight. If it was possible for the New York State Special Commission on Attica to discover, *after* the Attica uprising, by means of interviews, that many of the Attica officers had negative attitudes towards criminals and blacks, it would have been possible for others to have done the same *before* those officers were recruited. It is true that, to take racism as an example, many people would deny on questioning that they felt any racial prejudice, but skillful interrogation can, as the Attica Commission discovered, undercover underlying prejudice and reveal racist feelings of which individuals may not themselves be consciously aware. Of course more positive qualities than an absence of racial prejudice and of negative attitudes to criminals are necessary for the performance of the custodial officer's task.

Over a quarter of a century ago D. E. Lundberg wrote: "Methods of selection of the Prison Guard are generally loose and have had little experimental study of validity. Of some 13,000 guards in this country, it is safe to say that over three-fourths have been selected by unscientific methods" (1947, p. 38). A decade later Richard Downey and E. I. Signori asserted: "[S]o far as one can discover, there are no reported attempts to investigate the problem of prison guard selection in terms of interest and personality objective testing procedures" (1958, p. 234). (They had in fact missed one reported attempt by the Federal Bureau of Prisons, described by A. A. Evans [1954, pp. 70-78].)

Downey and Signori report on a study of prison guard selection in which they administered four objective ability, interest, and personality tests: the Wesman Personnel Classification Test, the Kuder Preference Record-Vocational Test, the Minnesota Multiphasic Personality Inventory, and the Manson Evaluation. They found that fourteen out of an aggregate of thirty-eight measurement variables discriminated between "good" and "poor" job-performance-rated prison officers. Subsequently, William Perdue, in two papers (1964 and 1966), reported the successful use of the Johnson Temperament Analysis, devised by Roswell Johnson and published by the California Test Bureau, in screening applicants for custodial work. As Perdue wrote, "The Johnson Temperament Analysis is certainly not the sole answer to the many and complex problems that arise in personnel work in a prison, but it might be a step toward the direction wherein the real answers might lie" (1964, p. 19). It may be that such tests are better as "eliminators" than as "selectors," but even if that is true the need for "eliminators" is clearly considerable. And there is no reason why temperament and aptitude tests should not be devised to be used in the selection of custodial officers.

More recently, in fact, Don Hardesty described an attempt to develop selection standards in order to obtain better qualified and more effective correctional officers. Hardesty found that it was possible to identify reliably good correctional officers and poor correctional officers prior to appointment and that there were measurable differences between these groups which could be used, in the process of selection, to identify more accurately potentially good correctional officers (1969, 1970). While it is true that Hardesty's proposed correction-officer testing selection battery and procedure were developed on the basis of a particular set of measures of correctional-officer performance (both objective and supervisory appraisal measures), which might not be generally regarded as acceptable, the essential point is that he demonstrates that effective and objective selection procedures for correction officers are feasible.

TRAINING

No less important than personnel selection is the training of personnel. Two of the foremost prison administrators of this century were James V. Bennett of the U.S. Bureau of Prisons and Alexander Paterson of the British Prison Commission. They both wrote on the subject of prison staff selection and training. Although they were both convinced of the supreme importance of training, when it came to the content of a proper training program for what Paterson called "subordinate officers" they were both afflicted by a lack of precision.

Paterson speaks of "the grave responsibilities" of prison officers. Bennett tells us that correctional work is "a highly complex activity." Paterson offers: "Candidates for the prison service ought to familiarize themselves with the history of prisons, the rules which govern them, and the principles which have dictated the choice of those rules" (1951, p. 105). Bennett echoes that the new correctional employee should be taught "the background and development of modern penology, and the history, present organization, philosophy, and goals of the employing agency" (1964, p. 266). Paterson says: "So far as this exceedingly subtle art can be learnt they must learn to be leaders." Bennett says that the period of basic training should "be a time for molding desirable employee attitudes." Phrases like "breadth of vision," "sense of perspective," "well integrated," "force of character," "self-reliance" recur in both papers.

There is nothing much wrong with what they say, but to anyone with experience in prisons they sometimes seem removed from the reality of the actual prison world. Paterson asserts that we must "select and train masters who will control men by force of personality and leadership, who will by example and influence train them in decent habits of self-control and industry" (1951, p. 102). Bennett writes: "[T]he task of supervising and guiding prisoners is no job for amateurs. . . . It is necessary to look for skills, talents, and unusual capabilities in persons recruited for this work. This means not only the necessary skill and capacity for doing a particular job, but also the ability to instill the same skill and capacity in untrained and frequently hostile inmates. . . . There is no substitute for personality, genuine interest, judgment, and understanding in personal relationships between workers and inmates" (1964, pp. 262-263).

If it were possible to recruit such professional paragons as prison guards the problem of training might prove a relatively simple one. But in real life such persons are rare in any trade or calling. Moreover, although it is easy to talk, as Paterson does, about the necessity for "a rigorous course of training" or, as Bennett does, about "the progressive development of skills and knowledge essential for the rehabilitation of prisoners," it is, as no doubt they discovered, extremely difficult to go much further than that. For when we ask what body of knowledge exists, what discipline, what field of study do we look to, to provide the content of the "rigorous course of training" which will enable men to function in the required manner, we find no answer at all forthcoming from either Paterson or Bennett or indeed anyone else.

Indeed even if we retreat from the illusory pursuit of men with "special gifts of personality and character" capable of achieving the moral transformation of their fellow men merely by the exercise of "personal influence," there still remain problems. Thus the Joint Commission on Correctional Manpower and Training provides a much more modest definition of the custodial officer's role. "Line Personnel," they say, "are charged by management with maintaining the security of institutional property and assuring peace and equity among offenders." But they go on to say that even in relation to this role the officers receive little guidance. "Too often they receive little useful direction from management or professionally trained staff, and they find themselves in something of a sink-or-swim situation."

Why is this? Why are there no members of "management or professionally trained staff" prepared to teach them to swim or at least to throw them a life preserver? It is because "unfortunately, there is little scientific knowledge about handling offender populations, few principles for consistent practice, and almost no provision for assessing the value of particular measures in various situations. Custodial staff generally operate on the basis of lore which has made for continued improvements in practice in other fields and occupations. Very little has been written on group management practices with confined offenders. What there is has come mainly from social scientists and has little relevance for the line practitioner."

In the circumstances perhaps it is not surprising that the Joint Commission was unable to provide much more on the subject of training than the somewhat jejune statement that "considerable thought and attention will be required by top experts in various fields of endeavor to devise ways of training correctional workers" (Joint Commission 1969, pp. 40-43). Nevertheless, it is possible to say something more about training even without the benefit of top expert advice. Thus in a situation where, as the 1967 President's Crime Commission put it, the majority of custodial officers are "undereducated, untrained and unversed in the goals of corrections," it is a simple truism that for all custodial officers an initial period of basic training is essential. As to the form and content of such training, the adoption throughout all states of the *Correction Officer's Training Guide* (1959), prepared by the American Correctional Association's Committee on Personal Standards and Training, would in itself constitute a significant advance.

But this provides little more than the basic essentials regarding the techniques and procedures of custodial care. And it is abundantly clear that while technical proficiency in this area is necessary and will in fact vastly improve the performance of officers, of much more fundamental importance is the officer's attitude toward inmates. This is because the officer's attitude toward inmates may be to a greater or lesser degree a factor in determining the inmates' attitude not merely toward the penal institution and the experience of imprisonment but also toward society and social values generally. This has long been recognized in some European countries, and the syllabi of such establishments as the Central School of the Danish Prison Administration in Copenhagen, the Dutch Central Training School in The Hague, and the Norwegian Training School for Prison Staff in Oslo reflect this fact.

Thus the three-month course for candidates for positions as prison officers provided at the Danish school, which is designed, among other things, *"to develop the proper attitude of mind,"* includes courses of lectures not only in criminology and in penology but also in psychiatry and in "knowledge of human nature" (Council of Europe 1963, p. 37; my italics). Advanced courses are also provided for more experienced prison officers after six to eight years of service. At the Dutch Training School the aim of the course is not merely imparting of technical knowledge and functional skill but also *"bringing about a change in attitude"* (my italics). Attempts are made to achieve this by "confronting the students with situations and problems identical with those of everyday practice, in this case through single and multiple role-playing, group discussions, case-study and group experiments." It is interesting to note that in the Netherlands the retraining of more experienced prison staff is also regarded as a function of the training school. Norwegian candidates for the prison service, who are required to take a six-month course of practical training, which is followed by another six-month course of theoretical training, are given instruction in nineteen subjects including criminology, psychiatry, psychology, sociology, and even moral philosophy (ibid., pp. 64-67).

The most sophisticated prison-officer training program in the U.S. is that conducted by the U.S. Bureau of Prisons at its two regional staff training centers (Atlanta, Georgia, and Dallas, Texas) and by institutional training coordinators at each of the major institutions operated by the Bureau. Thus the syllabus includes, in addition to the conventional training in, amongst other areas, disciplinary procedures, report writing, and "correctional techniques," a forty-hour introduction to interpersonal communication as well as twelve hours on improving staff relations and communication, for all employees.

One of the most interesting studies of correctional-officer training is David Duffee's. Duffee took the view that the conventional training programs, in which the courses principally "tend to be taught in the style of a several-period lecture on the freshman level in a university," were inadequate even where the goal of the educator was merely to impart information. Where attitudinal and behavioral change was required, he argued, the usual educational techniques would be unlikely to be at all effective. Accordingly, he devised an experimental in-service training project in which he employed a combination of Floyd Mann's survey feedback technique, which has been used in upper management training (Mann, 1961), and participant-observer group research. A small group of correctional officers was brought together at a minimum-security prison in 1971 and given three charges. These were: first, to study the goals of the institution and the role of the officer in achieving them; second, to study the organizational structure and operations to ascertain if there were any problems in day-to-day operations; and, finally, to study the activity of two other projects in prison, team classification groups and inmate discussion groups.

Duffee's conclusion is that, evaluated in terms of criteria formulated prior to the beginning of the project, such as the admission of inmates into the group, the program was successful. He sums up by saying that the group proved: an effective method of achieving a new, more open perception of inmates by officers; an effective method of improving officers' problem-solving skills; and a potentially sound device, if expanded, for freeing top institutional managers for policy decisions and more interaction with other agencies (Duffee, 1972). Of course it is not possible on the basis of one small experimental project to make general recommendations. But what Duffee's work does is to point in the direction in which officer-training programming should be oriented.

Another method that may be used to increase the officer's understanding of inmates is the case-study method, which is used in mental hospitals. The use of this method with prison officers is well described by Dr. Hector Cavallin. The method used by Dr. Cavallin was that of small-group discussions (each group consisting of eight correctional officers, a senior correctional supervisor, and a clinical person who was either a psychiatrist or a psychologist) in which the teaching material used consisted of a psychiatric report and an autobiography prepared by the prisoner. He reports that because of the fact the cases were known to the officers "very soon they were able to make a comparison between the way they had looked at this particular prisoner in the past and the new insights that the clinical evaluation had given them. This was manifested for instance in their becoming very much involved... in discussing the dynamics of the prisoner's personality development and attempting to make sense of the longitudinal study of the prisoner as a whole" (1967, p. 15). Dr. Cavallin was concerned with turning prison officers into "therapists"; but the case-study method can be equally well employed with the more realistic aim of enabling officers to view inmates' behavior more objectively and with more insight and understanding.

One of the best general discussions of the problems involved in prison-officer training was written by Dr. J. E. Thomas, who has had experience in both prison administration and prison staff training. He maintains that a crucial prerequisite to successful training is a clear answer to the question: What is this training intended to achieve? A good deal of confusion has been generated in the past, he argues, because prisons have been set "entirely unrealistic reformative goals." He advances a case for a training program which in addition to providing education in essential practical and vocational material also deals with the other constituent of the prison officer's role, which is concerned with how he deals with prisoners. This part of the officer's role involves treating prisoners "with sympathy, with dignity, and with respect." He advocates the inclusion in the syllabus of what he calls "a liberal component" aimed at helping officers "to be more tolerant, more capable of accepting difference, and generally more sympathetic (in the best sense) to the prisoner's position." He also gives a salutary warning about expecting training to achieve too much: "Much disappointment and misunderstanding can be avoided if it is emphasized that training is no substitute for the remedying of organizational defects such as inferior staff, low salary scales, or weak communication systems" (1972, pp. 200-205).

CONCLUSION

In 1945, Joseph F. Fishman published an article dealing with the life of the prison guard. It is a superficial article which does little more than stimulate momentary interest by the use of lurid detail. But the author had a good idea for a title. He called his article "The Meanest Job in the World." Over a quarter of a century later the title remains apposite.

One of the most curious features of the whole history of modern imprisonment is the way in which the custodial officer, the key figure in the penal equation, the man on whom the whole edifice of the penitentiary system depends, has with astonishing consistency either been ignored or traduced or idealized but almost never considered seriously. Thus Tannenbaum, in 1922, thought that "the keynote to understanding the psychology of the prison keeper" was "the exercise of authority and the resulting enjoyment of brutality" (p. 29). In 1943 Barnes and Teeters saw prison guards as suffering from "lock psychosis" as a result of a routine make up of "numbering, counting, checking and locking." Their personalities were warped by "the unnatural life they lead" (pp. 428-429).

More recent sociologists of the prison have seen the guards, when they have seen them at all, variously as involved in corrupt "alliances" with inmates, as ignorant and prejudiced functionaries of a corrupt system, or as featureless robots performing purely mechanical functions. By contrast many penal reformers and reformist administrators have endowed them with qualities of mind and character that recall the days of chivalry of those morally improving tales which used to form the staple content of Sunday School instruction. Thus Alexander Paterson opposed any time being allocated to the study of psychology for prison officers on the ground that "It is much better to leave them to their own natural good will and common sense than to stuff their ears and memories with a few scraps of scientific jargon" (1951, p. 104).

Today we have the advantage of being able to see that an ingenuous reliance on the assumed benevolence and soundness of the unreflective opinions and attitudes of ordinary men, characteristic of both nineteenth- and twentieth-century penal reformers and administrators, had led us to a crisis in penal affairs that makes the problems which those reformers faced appear relatively diminutive both in scale and significance.

Moreover there is no reason at all why instruction in elementary psychology should not be given in terms of functional skills rather than theoretical abstractions. The stress should be placed, to use the words of the U.S. Bureau of Prisons training syllabus, "on easily used and understood techniques for resolving day-to-day problems."

The truth, as it emerges from the few studies which pay attention to prison guards and view them objectively, is simply that these guards were and are for the most part ordinary human beings with ordinary human failings and virtues. They have in the past been asked to perform impossible tasks without being properly trained to perform even possible ones. It is an extraordinary feature of the history of prisons that it was not until the 1930s that the first formally organized training programs for prison guards and custodial officers appeared in America. Many institutions still provide no full-time preparatory training for them before they start work. At the same time, they are the lowest paid of all correctional employees. We shall achieve nothing — worse, we are likely to do active harm — in prisons until we carefully select, train as thoroughly as we know how, and properly recompense the prison officer of the basic grade.

REFERENCES

Barnes, Harry E. and Teeters, Negley K.: *New Horizons in Criminology.* New York, P-H, 1943.

Cavallin, Hector: The case study: a clinical approach to the training of the correctional officer. *American Journal of Correction, 29:* 14-18, 1967.

Council of Europe: *The Status, Selection and Training of Prison Staff: First Report of Subcommittee of the European Committee on Crime Problems.* Strasbourg, 1963.

Downey, Richard N. and Signori, E. I.: The selection of prison guards. *Journal of Criminal Law, Criminology and Police Science, 49 (September-October):* 234-236, 1958.

Duffee, David: *Using Correctional Officers in Planned Change.* Washington D.C., National Institute of Law Enforcement, National Technical Information Service, 1972.

Evans, A. A.: Correctional institution personnel: amateurs or professionals? *Annals of the American Academy of Political and Social Science, 293:* 70-78, 1954.

Hardesty, Don: *A One Year Personnel Study of the Correctional Officer and His Work in the Kansas Penal System.* Topeka, Consulting for Business, Industry and Government, 1969.

———: *Kansas Correctional Officer Selection Study: Final Report.* Topeka, Consulting for Business, Industry and Government, 1970.

Joint Commission on Correctional Manpower and Training: *Offenders as a Correctional Manpower Resource.* Washington, Joint Commission on Correctional Manpower and Training, 1968.

———: *Perspectives on Correctional Manpower and Training.* Staff Report. Washington, Joint Commission on Correctional Manpower and Training, 1970.

———: *A Time to Act.* Washington, Joint Commission on Correctional Manpower and Training, 1969.

Lundberg, D. E.: Methods of selecting prison personnel. *Journal of Criminal Law, and Criminology, 38:* 14-39, 1947.

Mann, Floyd: Studying and Creating Change. In Bennis, et al. (Eds.): *The Planning of Change.* New York, HR&W, 1961.

National Advisory Commission on Criminal Justice Standards and Goals: *Task Force Report on Corrections.* Washington, U.S. Govt. Print. Office, 1973.

Paterson, Sir Alexander: Recruitment and training in prison staff. In Rusk, S. K. (Ed.): *Paterson on Prisons: Being the collected papers of Sir Alexander Paterson.* London, Frederick Muller Ltd, 1951.

Perdue, William C.: Screening of applicants for custodial work by means of a temperament test. *American Journal of Corrections, 26:* 14-19, 1964.

———: The temperaments of custodial workers. *American Journal of Corrections, 28 (2):* 16-19, 1966.

President's Commission on Law Enforcement and Administration of Justice: *Task Force Report: Corrections.* Washington, U.S. Govt. Print. Office, 1967.

Schrag, Clarence: Some foundations for a theory of correction. In Cressey, D. (Ed.): *The Prison: Studies in Institutional Organization and Change.* New York, HR&W, 1961.

Tannenbaum, Frank: Wall Shadows: A Study in American Prisons. New York, Putnam, 1922.

Thomas, J. E.: *The English Prison Officer Since 1850: A Study in Conflict.* London and Boston: Routledge & Kegan, 1972.

Chapter 3

ON BECOMING A PRISON GUARD

BEN M. CROUCH AND JAMES W. MARQUART

LIKE police (Van Maanen, 1975), physicians (Becker, 1961), prostitutes (Heyl, 1977) or any other occupation with an organized work setting, the prison guard learns appropriate work behavior and attitudes through a process known as "occupational socialization" (Moore, 1969; Pavalko, 1971). For the prison guard, occupational socialization means becoming a part of the world behind the walls where he shapes the behavior of others and where that experience, in turn, shapes him (Jacobs and Retsky, 1975). To become an effective part of this unique world, the new man must perceive and incorporate into his occupational self a wide range of job requirements. While some of these requirements can be found in his employee's manual, some of the most important cannot. He must learn these unwritten, but very important, requirements regarding how he should think, talk, and act on the job through interaction with inmates and especially with other officers who reflect the prevailing guard subculture (Duffee, 1974; Esselstyn, 1966). With time, the recruit becomes a part of this subculture, for he cannot remain on the job without accommodating to it in some way. However, despite the fact that it shapes individual careers and maintains the character of the informal guard subculture, this socialization process has been consistently overlooked as an important prison phenomenon.

In this chapter, therefore, we present an analytic description of the guard socialization process. It is important to note, however, that this description is not based upon data from a single study. Instead, it represents the authors' efforts to distill from a variety of sources an account of how men become prison officers. We must, therefore, review the several types and sources of data on which we base our analysis.

First, we examined all relevant prison literature. Although

very few published studies dealing with guard socialization exist, several studies, which we draw upon throughout, did provide indirect evidence on the process. We blended this evidence from published material with data from the second source, participant observation. Specifically, both authors worked as uniformed officers in large (over 1500 inmates) maximum security prison facilities located in separate states. The first author spent a period of one and a half months in a facility, which we will call Trinity in this chapter, located within an extensive southwest prison system. The second author spent a period of three months employed as a uniformed officer in a Midwest prison, which we will call Midwest in this chapter.[1] The field notes generated during these two projects provide important insights and illustrations, which we will employ throughout. Finally, in addition to the insights derived from actually experiencing guard socialization, we also draw upon extensive formal and informal interviews with guards outside the participant-observer role. Specifically, the second author conducted in-depth interviews with twenty-five officers in two Midwest prisons. Conducted both in the prison and in the homes of respondents, these interviews focussed on selection of and adjustment to guard work (Marquart, 1978). The first author gained additional information in less formal interviews with guards in Louisiana, Mississippi, Oklahoma, Arkansas, California, and Nebraska (Crouch, 1977). Although not designed to investigate guard socialization, these interviews with custody personnel at all levels in several different state prison systems provided important comparative insights that augment data from other sources.

Our strategy in this chapter is to examine in chronological order the stages and experiences a man[2] goes through in be-

---

[1]For methodological details of these two participant observation studies see Ben M. Crouch, "The book vs. the boot: Two styles of guarding in a southern prison," reproduced in this volume, and James W. Marquart, "Career contingencies of correctional officers," Unpublished M.S. thesis, Kansas State University, 1978.

[2]Despite the fact that women play important roles in corrections, including working as officers along side male staff in prisons such as San Quentin, there is simply too little information on their experiences to consider women in our account. For some insight into female prison officers see Giallombardo (1966), Heffernan (1972), Kassenbaum et al. (1962), Becker (1975).

coming a prison officer. Specifically, we begin with how officers enter prison work in the first place. Next we consider formal training. Our discussion of this initial stage is perfunctory simply because we contend that while socialization may begin with the receiving of a uniform and attending academy classes, the most important experiences come on the job. We thus spend much of the chapter examining how and what the recruit learns informally. Finally, we focus on the changes men may undergo as they experience job demands and then consider several different career outcomes for prison guards. In short, our objective is to depict the world the recruit enters and the impact that entry has on him.

ENTRY AND FORMAL TRAINING

Turning to Guard Work

Children often state that when they grow up they would like to be a doctor, policeman, nurse, etc. However, they seldom express a desire to become a correctional officer. Jacobs and Restky (1975) describe a study by Lou Harris in which only 1 percent of the teenagers surveyed indicated they had considered corrections as a potential career. The decision to become a guard thus occurs later in life and in fact often appears to be somewhat accidental, a rather unplanned response to a fortuitous opportunity or a need for immediate employment.

People appear to apply for a job as a guard when they have reached a turning point in their lives. Lofland (1966; Strauss, 1969, p. 100) describes a turning point as a "moment when old lines of action were complete, had failed, or had been or were about to be disrupted, and when (persons) were faced with the opportunity or necessity for doing something with their lives." The significance of turning points lies in their having produced an increased awareness of a desire to take some action, combined with a new opportunity to do so.

While there may be numerous life changes or turning points conducive to entering guard work, several seem to predominate.

These include leaving or retiring from the military; being dissatisfied with prior jobs; being laid off; needing correctional experience.[3]

Even if a man retires from military service after twenty years of service, he is likely to be under fifty years old. Despite being middle aged, the military retiree still has many productive work years remaining. Consequently, these men may seek employment in the criminal justice system, especially if they had experience in the military police or in military corrections. As one officer put it:

> "When I was in the Army they shipped me out to Korea and before long I was in charge of a prisoner of war camp. After I retired, I signed on ——— Department of Corrections."

Military experience, whether involving corrections or not, is good preparation for the paramilitary regimes characterizing most police and correctional organizations. However, being middle aged at retirement precludes these individuals from most police work and federal corrections. Since the age factor blocks other careers, state corrections offers an opportunity to remain active while supplementing a military pension. Although the percentage of men who enter prison work after military service is uncertain, some estimates suggest 20 to 25 percent (Marquart, 1978; Davidson, 1974, p. 30).

The next turning point concerns dissatisfactions with previous jobs. In some cases, previous jobs do not provide enough hours for work, or there are conflicts with supervisors. The available evidence indicated that this type of turning point may lead a large percentage of men into guard work (Marquart, 1978; Davidson, 1974, p. 30). The following quote illustrates how one guard turned to corrections:

> "I have held down lots of jobs, but when I became a bartender I really liked it. I met lots of people and made good money. They (owners) cut back my hours and since I was just divorced, I had to pay off some debts. So I became a nightwatchman. It was mentally lonely and the pay wasn't good

---

[3]The following discussion of turning points, including quotes and illustrations, stems from focussed interviews conducted by the second author with twenty-two guards in two midwestern prisons (Marquart, 1978). For an excellent analysis of turning points in police careers see Cross (1977).

($2.00 per hour), so I went to the prison and got hired. Least
ways I knew there would be a check every month."

Odd hours and low pay, plus proximity to a Midwest prison
(when this man applied he lived two blocks from the prison)
led him to seek employment in state corrections. Another
guard, indicating how prior job dissatisfaction prompted his
entry into prison work stated:

"I worked on a bread route and I really liked it because I had
a chance to meet people but I quit because we never got a
vacation."

This man, born and raised close to a Midwest prison, knew
correctional officers obtained vacation time. When he saw a
newspaper advertisement calling for persons to be guards, he
applied and was hired.

A final example illustrates both how job dissatisfactions
prompt a man to consider correctional work and also how
social relations with people associated with the prison help
finalize the entry decision. In this example, the officer, in his
previous position as a shift supervisor in a factory, had
an argument with his superior over the way he managed his
shift. His boss criticized and accused him of being a "rate
buster."

"The only reason they didn't like me was because the people I
supervised liked me and we accomplished more on my shift
than the other shifts."

After the argument, this individual left his job. He tried several
other jobs but quit them and went on unemployment. His
friends who worked at a midwest prison convinced him to work
there also. When he told his father about his decision to apply
for a job at the prison, his father replied he would be proud to
have a son who was a correctional officer. For this individual,
entering guard work involved first starting then quitting several jobs, living close to the prison, and having friends who
were guards. The confluence of these situational factors describes how many men apparently turn to correctional agencies
for employment.

The third turning point concerns those individuals who were
forced out of their previous occupations either by being laid off
or by their own business folding. One individual stated that he

had worked in a door company for twenty years when the company went broke and laid him off. His age, fifty, limited other job opportunities and made "total retirement" impossible because of financial reasons. He observed simply:

> "I live only five minutes from the prison and my friends (who worked at a Midwest prison) told me the place would hire me."

Again, we see how a turning point (being laid off), social relationships, and close proximity to the prison resulted in this individual's applying to become a guard.

In another case, a guard stated he had a long "career" of being laid off from jobs.

> "When I graduated from high school I worked as a welder and I liked it because it was a trade. They laid me off. So I joined the Navy and when I got out I did construction (built basements) until I was laid off. I went back to the welding shop and worked as an assistant pressman until I was laid off."

When applying for a guard job at a Midwest prison, he perceived correctional work as providing security without lay-offs.

Another officer revealed that he too had an on and off work record (military service, carpentry, trade school, and hospital work) that ended when he hurt his back working at an automobile plant. While recuperating from the injury, his uncle, an officer at a Midwest prison, convinced him to fill out an application to work there in 1970. In five years, he worked his way up the prison hierarchy to a lieutenantship. By 1975, however, when the lieutenant accumulated enough capital to start a service station, he quit the penitentiary. He had no intentions of going back to the prison "now that he was his own boss." Things did not work out as well financially as he had anticipated, and the service station folded in 1977. Here is another clear indication of a turning point. In fact, his decision in 1977 to go back to the prison was similar to that of when he first applied in 1970.

> "I didn't have any other place to go for work and I've got a wife and four kids to feed. Besides I was a good officer, made lieutenant in five years. Since I came back it took me only a year to be lieutenant anyways."

For this individual, lay-offs, his uncle's influence, and proximity to the prison prompted him to seek employment at the prison.

Although these interviewees had experienced lay-offs, layoffs by themselves were not enough to lead them into applying for correctional work. It took the simultaneous effects of the turning point, age, proximity, and social relationships (friends and relatives who were officers) to lead the individual into applying to become a correctional officer.

The fourth turning point concerns those individuals who become guards to gain experience and then apply for more lucrative jobs within corrections. For these individuals, guard work is a stepping stone, not a permanent occupation. For example, one person became an officer at a midwest prison intending to gain the three years of state correctional experience required to become a more financially rewarded officer on the federal level. Although raised near a Midwest state prison, the chief reason this man went into corrections was his father, a counselor at the federal institution. Not only was his father a counselor, he was also one of the few persons who interviewed job applicants. Proximity to the prison and his father's influence provided the necessary impetus leading this man into making corrections a career.

Another guard stated his previous job as a painter was seasonal, and he needed full-time employment to support his family. This man was also raised near a Midwest prison and knew the prison involved year round work. He applied at the prison with the intention of being an officer for one year to obtain experience in working with inmates and then take the necessary tests to become a counselor. Thus, we find some individuals who actively seek guard work experience to open doors leading to better positions in corrections.

The evidence reviewed here suggests that turning to correctional work is quite opportunistic and sometimes accidental. Typically, people do not have lifelong aspirations to become a prison guard. Rather, getting into correctional work seems typically to be a reaction to unanticipated job changes, the need for full-time employment, supplemental income, or other life circumstances marking the job histories of many working class males. Under such circumstances men tend to select prison work when the prison is near at hand offering a secure pay check and when a friend or relative has already paved the way.

Before leaving the question of what prompts men to turn to correctional work we should briefly consider the possibility that some turn to this work not accidently, but rather consciously seek it out. The motivation of such persons may be of two types. First, some men may view a guard job as a unique vantage point from which to help the poor inmate. Motivated by such social-work concerns, such men will likely experience considerable frustration when they find job realities preclude an overt treatment orientation. As we shall indicate in a later section, these officers will either have to drastically alter their orientation and definition of the job or leave. A second type of man might seek out prison work because it offers an opportunity to be in a position of power and authority.

Whether a desire to dominate prompts a significant percentage of men to enter guard work, however, is unclear. That is, research done by Motivans (1963) indicates that applicants for custody positions are not psychologically unique, while Perdue (1966) finds them quite aggressive. Certainly, aggressive men do enter corrections just as they might be found in police work, in fire departments, and on construction crews. Davidson (1974, p. 30) notes, for example, that a few guards at San Quentin are "out-and-out sadists." However, it is not likely that guard forces anywhere contain a significant proportion of officers who sought out the job for the power over inmates it offers. When such men do begin to interact with inmates, they will likely find that opportunities to exercise unfettered dominance are few and the probability of some sort of reprisal from inmates for taking such an opportunity is high. Guards are locked up much like inmates and, being very outnumbered, never have anything near total power over inmates (Sykes, 1958).

Getting Hired

Except for those men with military or police experience, few potential officers have the technical skills needed for the job.

However, this seldom presents a problem, for job requirements are few and the screening process limited. Generally, eligible applicants must satisfy a few legal requirements for the job. These include being at least eighteen years old, being a high school graduate or possessing a G.E.D., and being free from felony convictions.

Once these requirements are met, actually being hired may be informal and simple or quite complicated, depending upon where one applies.[4] Gottfredson and his associates (1978, p. 209) report, in a survey of forty-six state correctional agencies, that in most state prisons, hiring involves only a cursory screening of applicants for fitness, an employment application, and a personal interview. Few state prisons base their hiring decisions on more than these few selection devices. For example, only eight states required an additional background check, six states a screening committee interview, and two states a trial period of service. In addition, not one state of those surveyed employed all of these devices to screen their applicants. Essentially then, filling out an application plus an interview are the main criteria for getting hired.

Formal Training

Once hired, the recruit begins formal training, the initial step in becoming a prison guard. That is, rookies begin to learn various skills preparing them for actual work experience. In some states, formal training consists of classroom instruction in which training officers cover topics such as map reading or first aid. In this instance, training is fast paced and multifaceted, resembling a high school. Formal training programs vary from state to state, with some involving only a few days while others require as much as six weeks of classroom work.

Essentially, formal training emphasizes the learning of practical or mechanical skills. In other words, training officers lecture on such topics as riot control procedures, first aid, disciplinary report writing, shakedown tactics, shackling of

---

[4]For a comparison with police requirements, see Drummond (1976) and Skolnick and Gray (1975).

inmates, legal rights of officers, and weapons maintenance. Training officers also demonstrate (usually by touring the recruit class through the prison) how to operate locks and keys, two-way radios, and counting procedures. In addition, formal training instructs new officers regarding their duties in such prison areas as gun towers, cellhouses, the hospital, and dining hall. Despite the emphasis upon practical skills, the trainees are constantly reminded of their position of authority. At every opportunity, training officers remind the trainees to avoid doing favors for and/or associating with inmates. Yet, the trainees do not understand the full implications for the potential of corruption of authority until they begin working on their own.

In summation, formal training attempts to give the trainees a small dose of the realities of prison work. This is apparent from the emphasis upon learning practical skills. Yet, learning to become an officer does not depend solely upon formal training. It is through the informal socialization process that rookies really "learn the ropes."

ON THE JOB

During formal training recruits learn about the prison world second hand. Wearing a uniform, attending classes, touring the prison facilities and going to the firing range allow the recruit to anticipate some of what it is like to be a guard. But until actually on the job, he cannot really know what will occur and how he will react. In this section we examine the two experiences that significantly influence recruit socialization: (1) encountering inmates, and (2) entering the guard subculture.

Encountering Inmates

Since the average recruit has little prior experience with prison, his first days actually on the job expose him to a world for which he is not really prepared. Consequently, he will experience some degree of "reality shock" (Cross, 1973; Marquart, 1978; Neiderhoffer, 1967). The ghettolike atmosphere of a maximum-security prison is quite overpowering to the uninitiated. Perhaps as many as 2000 men live, eat, work, urinate, sleep, and recreate in a very limited concrete and steel building. This concentration of life presents the new guard with an unfamiliar and at the very least distracting sensory experience as simultaneously he hears doors clanging, inmates talking or shouting, radios and televisions playing, and food trays banging; he smells an institutional blend of food, urine, paint, disinfectant, and sweat. And what he sees is a vast array of inmate personalities portrayed by evident behavior styles. Some, he notes, move easily, joking with both inmates and guards. Some glare and seem to be animated by a barely controlled rage, while others seem quietly resigned to their status. Finally, he sees inmates segregating themselves by race at every opportunity. And if he is a white recruit, the typically disproportionate percentage of black inmates (40 to 80% is not uncommon in many states) may be unnerving. For example, a new man at Midwest Prison found himself in the yard supervising inmates on his first day of regular assignment. Because almost all of the inmates in his charge were black and numbered well over 200, the officer, drawing on his own stereotypes plus the advice given him in formal training about black inmates, became quite concerned for his safety. At the end of his shift, he went straight to the captain and quit.

Another kind of shock in store for the new recruit involves the sexual behavior of inmates. The unisex world of prison both thwarts sexual desires and offers aberrant sexual alternatives. Generally the most acceptable sexual release is masturbation. An inmate may be heard to say, "Tonight is 'Jack' night, baby!" (quoted in Griswold et al., 1970, p. 163). Or inmates may gain sexual release in a Pringles® potato chip can filled with petroleum jelly or even in warm loaves of bread if they happen to work in the bakery (Griswold et al., 1970). But the more visible inmate homosexuality may provide the greatest reality shock for the new guard. During formal training the recruit heard about this important aspect of prison life, so intellectually he knows about "pitching and catching," "queens," "punks," "wolves," "jockers," and "gal-boys." But encountering it first hand may create at the very least some unease. In prisons that allow little or no individuality in dress among inmates, overt homosexuals must be identified either by reputation or by their feminine walk or "swish" and gestures. But where wide latitude in dress exists, "flaming" may be more visible and more shocking to the prison novice. The recruit, for example, may have to deal with (and even "pat down") inmates who act and relate to other inmates like a female. Such effeminate inmates may avoid all physical labor to reduce musculature, pluck their eyebrows, shave their body hair, wear bright-colored briefs and tight shorts customized to look like hot pants. To the typically working-class recruit with a fairly clear notion as to appropriate masculine behavior, such inmates may be a source of confusion and even anger, and any negative attitudes that the recruit initially has will likely be reinforced by his co-workers.

Being "the Man"

In addition to physical exposure to the inmate population, the recruit may also experience tension from realizing that he is an institutional policeman. To the inmate population, all guards, recruits and veterans alike are the "the Man" or the "heat." Since prison is by definition a coercive organization (Etzioni, 1961) holding inmates against their wills, there exists a constant hostility between the keepers and the kept. The terms inmates use for guards such as "bulls," "hacks," and "screws" reflect the hostile attitudes inmates hold toward their keepers. Disdain is also reflected in the nicknames inmates apply to individual guards such as "Pecker neck," "Squeaky," "Tomato face," and "Pussy foot." These negative attitudes and names indicate that inmates are keenly aware of their relationship to guards is an adversary one, and guards represent the state's intent to curtail or squelch the wide range of illicit goods and services inmates deem necessary for their survival.

When the recruit comes on the job, he wears the most graphic symbol of the state's authority, a uniform. According to Roucek (1935, p. 147) and Jacobs and Retsky (1975), authority is not a function of the officer's uniform. Instead, the sole function of the uniform, in their views, is to distinguish the officers from the inmates. These researchers are correct when they assert the uniform functions to identify the officers, but they have missed a very important point. That is, an officer's uniform (Banton, 1964, p. 168; Rubenstein, 1975, p. 70) symbolizes the laws of the state, much in the same way the soldier's uniform symbolizes the power of the state (Gerth and Mills, 1953, p. 284). The prison guard's uniform serves to legitimize his position with certain rights and privileges such as power to enforce prison rules and freedom to move within the prison. Thus, if the officers did not have a uniform then their position, power, and authority would have to be negotiated everytime they had an encounter with the inmates. Moreover, the officer's uniform is a visible symbol to the inmates that their behavior is continually being scrutinized.

The recruit's uniform as well as his notebook for recording inmate rule violations identify him as an adversary to be manipulated and/or avoided, regardless of what the officer's inclinations toward inmates might be. As the Man, the recruit must become used to being watched out of the corners of eyes at all times. He must realize that just being there as part of the guard force makes him subject to being viewed with suspicion. When he enters a cellblock for whatever reasons, he might hear an inmate shout, "Jigger on the run," to warn others that the Man is about. Even at his station, the new man realizes that the mirrors in disembodied arms protruding through cell bars are reflecting his image. Or worse, the recruit may experience degrading villification by inmates he does not even know. The following observations, which appear in a diary kept by an Illinois prison guard, illustrate the point:

> "I was inside West Cellhouse segregation unit today. It smells and sounds like the monkey house at Brookfield Zoo. The yells and screeches and stench lend an almost unreal aura to the place. The throwing of urine and excrement at the officers is a common occurrence, the men assigned to this duty will surely go to heaven. They have already spent their time in hell" (Weidrich, 1978a).

Testing

Even though guards wear the same uniform and envoke the

official power of the state, inmates know that vast differences exist across guards in terms of their reactions to similar situations. Since daily inmate activity depends in large measure on their ability to discern these differences, inmates regularly check reactions, especially among new guards. This strategy, which involves placing guards in stressful situations, is essentially a testing process. Although not unique to prisons, testing new authority figures is particularly important in this closed and coercive environment.

Designed to measure the new guard, tests contrived by inmates range from minor transgressions, which can quickly be defined as mistakes or lapses by inmates, to more serious confrontations. The first author's early experiences in the inmate dining hall at Trinity illustrate fairly minor tests. Working in the dining hall for the first time, this new guard was told by his captain that his job was to keep inmates from "running their heads" (officially they are supposed to eat without any unnecessary conversation), skipping seats (inmates are to take the first available seat instead of sitting where they please), and wasting food ("destruction of state property"). In addition to constantly glancing sideways to see where the "Man" was, many inmates proceded to talk, skip seats, and waste food. Knowing a new guard was on duty, inmates wanted to see if the officer, alone in the dining hall with as many as 200 inmates, would try to "go by the book" or realize that some transgressions must be allowed.

Less subtle but specifically intended to test a new man is a ploy used from the anonymity of the cellblock at Trinity. When a new officer closes the steel cell doors on a cellhouse tier or run, the doors move slowly but with great weight. As the doors clang shut, the rookie may hear an inmate scream in mock pain and terror, "My hand! You got my hand!" If the officer rapidly reopens the doors in fear, he will have been played the fool. Another example of a very direct test that occurred at Midwest involved a small-statured new officer. As this man walked down an aisle in the dining hall, a large, muscular inmate suddenly jumped in front of the officer. The new officer laughed and continued on his way. He had been tested in front of many inmates but refused to react in a startled way. If he had jumped back, the inmates would have taken this as a sign of fear. Or, finally, inmates may stage a fight in a cellhouse or the yard to observe a new man's reactions. If he calls for help and then breaks up the fight, inmates learn that he is resourceful. Some officers are frightened when they see a fight and look the other way. From the inmate's point of view, ignoring an inmate fight is again a sign that the officer is weak and fearful.

Most recruits are very aware they are being measured by inmates. An Illinois guard at Pontiac prison recorded his sensitivity to testing in the following manner:

> "Today, we started on our assignment as regular officers . . . I was assigned to the north cellhouse today. The process of intimidation began almost immediately. An inmate told me that if anything goes down, the guard will be the first target. He didn't have to tell me; I figured that out all by myself. The best attitude seems to be one of impassivity. Most of the inmates are just testing the new officer, trying to get a reaction" (Wiedrich, 1978b).

If the officer's reactions convey indecisiveness, weakness or fear, then this man will not only continue to be tested but he may eventually lose all his authority over inmates.

Corruption of Authority

An erosion of the recruit's authority over inmates has other sources beyond failing direct testing and losing inmate respect. Sykes (1958) and McKorkle (1970), under the rubric "corruption of authority," describe three types of involvements with inmates that undermine a guard's capacity to control. First, authority may be lost because guards become too friendly with inmates. With no personal hesitancy to be friendly with inmates, the recruit may be especially vulnerable to the smooth and very solicitous inmates. Although an offer of help from an inmate may be a contrived test of the recruit's openness and potential for subsequent exploitation, it might also be genuine. Feeling that he is closer physically and organizationally to inmates than to his superiors, the recruit may gradually become quite close to several inmates. The danger is that these relationships will place the officer in a very uncomfortable position should he catch one of his "friends" in a serious transgression of prison rules.

A second means by which recruit authority may be corrupted is through reciprocity. Under pressure to "handle" inmates, the new man may discover order can be maintained via a series of trade-offs. That is, in exchange for a willingness on the part of selected inmates to keep the cellhouse quiet and clean, the guard tacitly agrees either to overlook or make sure he will not discover transgressions committed by those select prisoners. Traditional illustrations of these trade-offs include special privileges (choice of cell partner; keeping commodities that are not regularly allowed in a cell) to inmates capable of aiding authorities by stopping fights, informally disciplining other inmates or passing along information. Although a guard may maintain order by allowing these privileges and by overlooking minor transgressions, he may find it difficult to be assertive with those inmates involved in the informal trade-offs. To that extent, authority is lost.

The third process by which the recruit's authority may be weakened is the gradual yielding of many guard tasks to inmates. Where willing and able inmates perform counting, filing, mail delivery, and other house keeping duties, the guard may become dependent on them and, to that degree, find his authority over them whittled away. Thus through friendship, reciprocity, and default, guards and especially the more naive recruit may lose authority. Once dissipated, authority is extremely difficult to reclaim.

A final way a recruit might lose his capacity to exert authority over inmates involves inmate knowledge of guard transgressions. Inmates watch officers as closely as officers watch them. Moreover, inmates know the rules governing guard duties as well as those related to inmate behavior. Thus, when the recruit studies or sleeps on the job inmates learn about it. This knowledge can serve as the basis for subsequent blackmail of the recruit. Fearing that the inmate will relay the information to his superiors, the guard feels compelled to allow the inmate special favors.

Entering the Guard Subculture

The recruit learns how to be a guard most directly by observing, listening to and imitating the veterans with whom he works.[5] Those veteran guards constitute an important reference group, physically backing him up, offering advice, reinforcing him, and judging him. Through interaction with them over time, the new man picks up the values of the officer subculture and what other officers expect of him. Specifically, the recruit learns (1) how to perceive inmates, (2) how to anticipate trouble, and (3) how to manage inmates.

Perceiving Inmates

In the most general terms, guards perceive inmates as volitional actors who chose crime from among other, presumably equally available, life-styles. Guards tend to view prisoners as men who, on the streets, were lazy and adverse to work, and who turned to crime as a more expedient life-style. Guards are also probably inclined to judge inmates in terms of their own lives. In this connection, an officer at Trinity remarked to the first author: "I'm twenty-four years old and *I* was able to stay out of trouble." Guards feel that because inmates opt for crime it is justifiable to classify inmates as lesser beings and to treat them as objects. Indeed, a traditional term used by guards at Trinity to refer to inmates is "ol' thang."

One way veterans convey to recruits the perception that inmates are fundamentally different is through atrocity stories. Told both during formal training, passed along on the job, and focussing only on inmate behavior, these stories serve to heighten officer solidarity by pointing out that "we," the guards, have got to stick together against "them," the usually unpredictable and sometimes dangerous inmates (Etzioni, 1966, pp. 172-173). An example of an atrocity story shared at Midwest involves an inmate who tried to procure sexual favors from this cellmate. Despite his cellmate's pleas the aggressor tortured him by sticking a pencil under his fingernails. Still refusing to give in, or even cry out, the attacker poked both his eyes out

---

[5]For example, by listening to veteran officers converse, rookies soon learn the prevailing prison argot, an important dimension of the prison world. For accounts of prison language see Kuethe (1935), Hargan (1935), Clemmer (1958), and Guenther (1978).

with the pencil. The tortured inmate still refused to submit. In desperation, the aggressor placed the pencil in his victim's nose ramming it into his brain and killing him. Once his victim was dead, the torturer sodomized the body. Other stories, usually related with humor by veteran officers, involve accounts of inmate self-mutilation. For instance, the recruit may hear about an inmate who inserted a nine-inch section of a broom handle into his rectum and "lost it." Or the rookie may learn about a "queen" (male prostitute) who had received five hemorrhoid operations within two years.

Such stories about the sexual and violent behavior of inmates are important to the learning process of rookie guards. According to Dingwall these stores are a "depiction of the performance requirements of the work and obstacles which lie in their path. They also perform a peculiarly dramatic part of the oral culture of the occupation" (1977, p. 394). These accounts point up the danger of inmates to each other and to themselves and characterize inmates as being morally degenerate.

Beyond the designation of inmates as different and inferior, the recruit soon becomes aware of more specific categorizations of inmates held by the custody staff. These informal categorizations somewhat parallel those used by police to classify the citizens they encounter on the streets. Van Maanen (1978), for example, reports that police sort citizens into *suspicious characters* who may have committed serious crimes but who are cool and deferential to police; *know nothings* who know little about crime or police and usually require little attention; and *assholes* who regularly refuse to accept police definitions of the situation. In prison, the prisoner smart enough to avoid drawing undue attention to himself through confrontations with officers parallels the suspicious character on the streets. This type of inmate usually remains deferential, even solicitous, while guards strongly suspect he is behind various disturbances and exploitations. Veteran guards will typically point these inmates out to the rookie, noting that as gang leaders or big time thieves in the free world, they will always prompt their followers into the overt action that comes to the attention of authorities while they themselves remain uncompromised.

Corresponding to the citizen police sometimes characterized

as an asshole, the inmate troublemaker soon comes to the new guard's attention. If the rookie has not directly encountered regular troublemakers in some sort of test, he will hear about the asshole behind the wall from other officers. Sitting with other men in the officers lounge, the recruit may hear specific inmates in this category discussed. On one occasion, for example, the first author learned the name of a troublemaker as one officer related a recent confrontation with him. At the mere mention of his name, experienced officers nodded and grimaced knowingly. It seems this inmate was always ready to dispute an order, exploit other inmates, and generally be, according to one officer, a "bona fide son of a bitch." Because this particular inmate regularly refused to define situations as guards did, a Lieutenant observed: "The best treatment for (this particular inmate) would be a .38 slug between the eyes." This type of designation communicates to the recruit the need, indeed the requirement, to keep an eye on particular inmates. Officers regularly pass such information about inmates through the informal grapevine as Guenther and Guenther note:

> In Atlanta it is standard procedure to keep a "Hot Book" (referred to the inmates as a "Hunting List") of selected records of those inmates whose potential for trouble is felt to merit special attention of employees. Theoretically, staff members consult the volume from time to time, but in practice most officers find out who is "hot" through hearsay (1974, p. 50).

A third type of inmate defined for the recruit in the course of daily interaction with prisoners and other guards is the "good" inmate. The good inmate does not exactly parallel naive or "know nothing" citizens in police encounter, because the good inmate is certainly knowledgeable, especially about the prison and its routines. However, this type of inmate causes little or no trouble for other inmates or for officials. A good inmate is dependably willing to recognize the authority of guards and thereby not threaten the internal order of the prison. Of this type of prisoner veteran officers at Trinity, for example, may say approvingly he has "learned to do it right," or that he has learned how to "make it."

Sorting inmates into these informal categories requires guards to become familiar with the behavior of given inmates either directly or through hearsay. However, another means of sorting inmates, namely by race and ethnicity, requires only that the recruit see the inmate. By hearing other officers attach significance to race and ethnicity, the recruit becomes conditioned to respond to black and Chicano inmates in certain ways. First, the recruit learns that in the absence of all other information, black inmates should be watched more closely than other inmates. At Midwest, for example, an entire training class of guards heard the instructor comment that "most of your trouble will come from niggers." The instructor also commented offhandedly that "if you kill a nigger attacking an officer from a gun tower, you will be awarded a raise by the warden." Veterans continue to reveal such sentiments on the job either to the recruit directly or in his presence. Such sentiments sensitize recruits to the special stigma and potential aggressiveness, defiance, and even danger of black inmates.

Besides black inmates, the new guard will likely learn that Chicano inmates merit special attention, especially if their numbers are at all significant within the prison. Guards, with some justification, see Chicano inmates as reflecting a kind of inscrutable clannishness not found among other groups of inmates. This feature is due in large part to the use of the Spanish language. In prison, as well as in the streets and barrios, Spanish-speaking persons appear somehow more foreign and different. Because society perceives them in this way, Chicanos in both worlds generally turn to and rely only on other Chicanos. This clannishness is emphasized by the fact that, even where large numbers of Chicanos are incarcerated, few officials speak Spanish. Where Chicano inmates are both numerous and powerful, as in San Quentin, rookie guards learn to view them as having the same potential for danger and threat to security guards reserve for black inmates elsewhere (Davidson, 1974).

In contrast to San Quentin, Trinity guards generally do not view Chicanos in terms of a threat to order. Indeed, at Trinity, with a Chicano population constituting nearly 20 percent of the total, the new guard may even hear veteran guards speak of Chicano inmates, somewhat approvingly, as generally "good" inmates. Guards there view Chicano inmates as hard workers and relate to new guards how Chicanos control and discipline those of their kind who lag behind in work details. This trait, plus the frequently noted tendency of Chicanos to take official punishment rather than snitch on their own kind, is the basis for a grudging respect which guards hold for Chicanos.

The prejudicial attitudes toward minority group members in the larger society becomes heightened within prison. In the eyes of most guards, these prisoners are not only suspect due their minority status, but they are clearly inferior for having chosen crime instead of legitimate work. And since guards are predominantly white and typically come from rural, working-class backgrounds, they are the more likely to be prejudiced in their attitudes toward minority inmates (Carroll, 1974, p 126). Consequently, the recruit will regularly hear other guards refer to inmates as "spicks," "Meskins," "niggers," "black freaks," and even expect the new officer to use them. While such epithets may reinforce guard's sentiments about certain groups of inmates, the use of them before those inmates would clearly cause trouble (Goffman, 1956). Thus, guards typically avoid such terms in interaction with inmates.

Anticipating Trouble

Most of the time prisons function quite smoothly with inmates and staff carrying out daily routines with little apparent friction. However, the possibility of *trouble* always exists. Trouble refers to such occurrences as escapes and escape attempts, hostage situations, riots, collective vendettas, consuming homemade intoxicants, or any other event which violates rules and undermines order. Since guards are primarily responsible for maintaining order, they must be able to anticipate trouble. But anticipating trouble is not simple for veterans and next to impossible for the newcomer. Unlike more experienced guards, new men cannot "feel the tension" or "sense something coming down." Veterans feel it takes months for a guard to learn to recognize trouble in its early stages because the ability is, as one Trinity officer put it, "90 percent in the guts." Only through experience in dealing with inmates and interaction with other officers can the recruit learn the shadow organization and behavior patterns invisible to the uninitiated but which serve as a barometer for trouble to experienced eyes. In short, to detect trouble, guards must know the normal to place significance on the abnormal.

Several examples illustrate the types of cues recruits learn to anticipate trouble. First, behavior of individual inmates can be an important cue. The sudden sullenness of an inmate known to be extroverted can make an observant guard curious. Also some type of trouble may be at hand when an inmate with a good job and an acceptable work record suddenly comes to an official and wants to quit that job, even if it means taking a poorer one. That man may be under pressure or may perhaps know something is about to happen and simply wants to be elsewhere when it occurs. In both cases, the reason for the changed behavior may be personal, involving only one or two inmates, but it may have wider implications.

Changes in the behavior of many of the inmates is a more significant cue to trouble, however. When the number of men who normally go to the cafeteria drops significantly while the volume of goods sold in the commissary increases, men may be trying to avoid involvement in a major disturbance. Because the cafeteria is an open area where many men congregate at one time, it is a good place for a collective disturbance. Knowing through the prison grapevine about the possibility of a disturbance, many inmates may opt to purchase foodstuffs to consume in their cells rather than go to a potentially dangerous cafeteria. Another clue, especially to impending racial trouble, is the increased clustering of inmates by race. Of course, this naturally occurs, so the officer must learn to discern an unusual tendency to band together in the halls and in the cafeteria. Perhaps the most obvious cue to an abnormal situation is noise. Inmates' conversations and shouts produce a rather constant noise level varying with time of day and week. Should that level perceptibly and suddenly drop, then something is wrong. Quiet communicates preparation or anticipation of something by inmates, a condition experienced guards know to heed.

The recruit must do more than learn to recognize the signals of trouble, however. Knowing the prison is "ripe" for trouble produces a great deal of uncertainty unless guards can determine the source of the tension and judge its potential for real trouble. Such a determination requires information on the intentions and frustrations of individuals or groups of inmates. One source of such information is the inmate "snitch." Without the snitch to tell authorities what inmates intend or feel, the prison would be much more unpredictable for guards. However, motivations for snitching vary (Johnson, 1961), and guards must be sensitive to these variations to assess the information the inmate relates. On the one hand, the inmate may be known to snitch regularly in an effort to elevate himself in the eyes of the officials. Guards, like inmates, tend to hold this type of inmate in very low esteem. On the other hand, some inmates provide information about trouble for their own protection. In this instance, the inmate may know where a weapon or some other form of contraband is located in his cellblock; by relating this fact to an officer, he might avoid injury or involvement in the impending trouble.

Now for an inmate, especially one bringing information surreptitiously for his own protection, to come to an officer the inmate must know the officer will react in an acceptable manner. That is, the guard should not react so as to expose the informing inmate to ostracism, (if he is not already a known "rat"), or worse, injury and perhaps even death in retaliation for snitching. Thus, the inmate with information will contact an officer he believes to understand how to receive information and protect its source. The inmate, for example, may send a note to an officer asking to be called out of the cellblock under some pretext. In this way, the guard seems to contact the prisoner instead of vice versa. After coming out into a hall, the inmate shares his information and depends on the officer to follow through with the charade. This means that the officer will simply send the inmate back in to the cellblock perhaps with the command: "Now, get yer ass back to your house (cell)." Such a command suggests to any nearby inmates that the purpose of the discussion was informal discipline and not snitching. By sending the snitch gruffly back to his cell and by waiting several hours or even a day before searching the implicated inmates and cells, the guard may both defuse trouble and augment his reputation as a guard with "savvy," one who can perhaps be trusted.

Managing Inmates

The most fundamental message received by the new officer during his formal training and continually from veterans on the job is that he must always dominate inmates by his words and behavior. Although outnumbered by inmates and without weapons, veterans may employ several informal strategies to dominate inmates and maintain order. Recruits gradually, even unconsciously, absorb these strategies through observation and imitation. One strategy is maintaining social distance from inmates. From the very beginning veterans stress: "Don't trust or take the word of an inmate." This admonition means that guards should avoid any interaction and involvement with inmates beyond what maintaining security requires. By staying away from involvements with overly solicitous inmates, new men can avoid the erosion of "corruption" of authority, which we discussed. The advice that guards not trust or become involved with inmates is never absolutely followed by guards. Some men do get to know and like certain "good" inmates. An example of how experienced guards do get involved with such inmates comes from the first author's field notes at Trinity. One evening this writer, while working with a young officer with about a year's prison experience, returned from a minor duty to find the officer enjoying a steaming bowl of chili and franks, crackers, and a glass of iced orange juice. When asked about it he said he had won a bet with a popular and privileged inmate (the "major's boy") and the spread (food) was the pay off. The guard added that he would not trust just any inmate, but this food was as safe as from his mother's table. The special relationship with an inmate illustrated here did not appear to undermine this guard's authority. Other examples of informal (though not illegal) relations at Trinity involved officers calling to and kidding with inmates. Similarly, at Midwest, a veteran introduced the second author to two black inmates he called "Sambo" and "Cheetah," two men with whom he was obviously on good terms, since both inmates took the nicknames in apparent good humor. Such contacts indicate that in practice officers do get close to inmates. Nonetheless, as the new man can easily observe, such relations are typically superficial and are tolerated only so long as the dominance of the guard is not questioned.

Another strategy for establishing dominance, which the recruit may pick up from the veterans, involves the use of profanity and "bluster." Quite evident at Trinity was the assumption that in order to make inmates understand the significance and the substance of a directive, that directive must be delivered loudly and profanely. A co-worker advised the first author early in his tour of duty as a guard that an inmate cannot simply be asked to do something. Instead, he suggested in tutorial fashion, something like the following would be better: "Listen, motherfucker, get over there and (mop the floor) or I'm gonna do somethin' bad to you' god damn ass." It is important to note that guards do not regularly give orders in this way, for to do so would be clearly counterproductive. Nonetheless, the guard gave the rather extreme advice to convey the importance of not appearing weak before inmates. The same objective can be achieved nonverbally through "bluster." Invoked during adverse encounters with inmates and regularly accompanying profanity, bluster involves glowering stares, headshaking in disgust and aggressive posturing.

While heated confrontations do occur, they are a much less frequent part of prison interaction than the myriad requests and questions inmates present to their keepers. Learning how to handle such inmate interrogatives is an important lesson for new men. The inmate, for example, may tell the officer that he is ill and needs to go to the infirmary or that when the cell doors opened for a meal, he was on the toilet and could not get out before the doors closed. Is the inmate just trying to leave the cellblock by feigning illness or trying to go through the cafeteria line again? These questions suggest the uncertainty line officers face. To allow an inmate to leave the cellblock upon such a request when in fact the inmate is lying constitutes a victory for the inmate and makes the guard appear malleable or "easy." Since guards view such a reputation as unsavory, they admonish new men not to trust or believe inmates. In those situations where the new man is uncertain about an inmate's query, veterans typically advise rookies to "always say no." At Trinity the new officer learns to "just send 'em back to their house (cell)."

A final means of maintaining dominance is to keep inmates off balance, to manipulate the interaction so as to remind inmates of their subordinate position. Since there are many techniques of keeping inmates off balance, the following examples merely illustrate the variety and subtlety of the strategy. At Trinity, this strategy of keeping inmates off balance is more likely referred to as *messin' with their minds*. Partly as a means of handling uncertainty in the face of inmate questions, co-workers told the first author to "act crazy" or confuse inmates in such situations. Acting crazy means the guard responds to the inmate in ways quite unrelated to the inmate's question or problem; in this way the inmate is put off and becomes uncertain himself. Or the officer may place the inmate very much on the defensive. The following dialogue, recorded by the first author at Trinity, illustrates this tactic for underscoring official dominance. The inmate has come to the cellblock bars to ask the officer if he can visit the infirmary.

Officer: "What the hell do you want?"
Inmate: "Boss, I got a terrible headache. Can I go to the hospital?"
Officer: (Loudly) "How the hell do I know you've got a headache?"
Inmate: "Well . . . " (inmate returns to his cell).

Two final illustrations of how guards can keep inmates off balance involve guards actively structuring the situation to place inmates at a disadvantage. The first involves confronting an unsuspecting inmate with feigned seriousness and asking about something which may make the inmate uncomfortable. For example, at Trinity an officer asked an inmate if he was the one who *slumbered* in bed. The inmate paused, looked at the officer, his feet, the first author, then replied: "I don't know uh-I-maybe-uh-you mean do I sno'?" The officer asked about slumbering again and got a similar reply. The inmate admitted he did not know what slumber meant and by not knowing appeared inferior to all present and to himself since everyone but him clearly knew the term. A more aggressive tactic for keeping inmates off balance observed at Midwest by the second author involves prolonged staring at selected inmates. After a time, the inmate will notice the stare and become increasingly nervous and uncertain. Although the staring is not necessarily prompted by official suspicion and any wrong doing, the inmate does not know this and thus worries about what he has done or what the guard really knows.

Fundamental Tenets of Guard Work

The recruit's encounters with inmates and his fellow officers' advice and reinterpretation of these encounters gradually reveal to him the essential elements of the guard role. With time, the new man becomes aware of the several tenets of subcultural wisdom which define acceptable guard behavior.

The first of these tenets is that security and control are paramount. Custodial officers become keenly attuned to inmate behavior in an effort to avoid any threat to security. Inmate transgressions not only threaten prison order, but the personal safety of the guards themselves. So, like police sensitivity to the possibility of danger, what Skolnick (1966) calls the *symbolic assailant*, guards are also ever mindful of the potential for personal injury (Marquart, 1978; Jacobs, 1978). These concerns for maintaining prison order and personal safety prompt both the periodic "shakedowns" of inmate living areas as well as the random personal "pat downs" of inmates.

Being charged with and constantly concerned about security and control, guards tend to view suspiciously any intrusions which upset the custodial routines. For example, the presence of treatment programs and personnel sometimes produce concern among the security staff. The problem from the guard's point of view is that free world treatment personnel, e.g. teachers, psychologists, etc., know very little about inmates and fail to appreciate the importance of establishing security measures. Thus through ignorance, oversight, or exploitation, treatment personnel may jeopardize security. An officer at Trinity, expressing the sentiments of many, stated: "Things would be a

lot better around here if they'd just wall up that schoolhouse"
(education facility at one end of the building). Other activities,
such as visits from evangelists complete with large choirs, volunteers, and sports stars or movies that run over the time routinely allotted, all upset schedules and cause guards to question
their utility.

A second important tenet of guard work that the recruit
encounters involves maintaining social distance from inmates.
As we noted above, inmates should not be trusted because even
those the guard thinks he knows can "burn" or take advantage
of him if the opportunity is right. The experience of one officer
at Trinity illustrates how officers learn not to trust their
charges. This particular young officer lived in the bachelor
officer's quarters located on the prison grounds and had gotten
to know well the trusty assigned to clean the building. The
guard bought the inmate soft drinks and candy and talked with
him often. One afternoon, however, the trusty stole the sleeping
guard's car keys from his drawer, took his car, and escaped.
Although the young guard got his car back reasonably un-
scathed, he yielded, as a result of the incident, all hope that any
inmate could be trusted. Officials use stories such as this to
document the wisdom of maintaining considerable interpersonal distance from inmates.

The third tenent, which gradually becomes clear to the new
man, is that guards must be tough, knowledgeable, and able to
"handle" inmates. These role expectations emanate from both
inmates and other officers. In large maximum security prisons,
including Trinity and Midwest, inmates who expect guards to
evince "toughness" are sensitive to shortcomings in this regard.
Knowing this to be an important basis for inmate respect,
guards may specifically urge the recruit to address inmates in
an authoritative manner, perhaps even stressing the use of profanity as we noted earlier.

A rather striking illustration of how guards' beliefs about
inmate expectations shape their behavior occurred in a cotton
field at Trinity. Learning that the first author was a researcher
instead of simply an extra mounted field boss, an officer in
charge of one of the inmate work squads rode over to discuss
the possibility of getting into college teaching. He held a Mas-

ter's degree in criminal justice and came not from the surrounding rural area but from one of the largest cities in the state. His speech involved a vocabulary and pronounciation commensurate with an advanced education. However, during the conversation he saw his squad needed some prodding and direction so he excused himself and turned to them. These directions were frought with profanity, swallowed and truncated words and delivered in a loud, rural twang. The contrast between these two styles of speech was remarkable even to the officer himself since he commented spontaneously: "You just have to talk to them that way or they won't pay any attention to you."

Beyond toughness, the new guard learns inmates, and officers alike, expect him to be or become *knowledgeable*. By knowledgeable we mean the guard must be (1) informed as to the informal rules and organization guiding daily prison interaction and (2) able to avoid being duped by inmates. A guard who is not easily manipulated can, from the authorities' point of view, better maintain order and, from the inmates' point of view, better protect inmate from inmate.

BECOMING A GUARD

To this point we have reviewed the substance of the prison world encountered by the new guard and we have identified the key elements of the guard role. We can now consider the impact of role demands We focus first on the process of accommodating to those demands and then examine several career outcomes.

The Guard Socialization Process

The central question is the following: how do recruits' attitudes and behaviors change as they encounter inmates and enter the guard subculture? Although very limited, evidence suggests several types of changes during guard socialization. One of these involves role conflict and a related attitude, cynicism. Some recruits enter the maximum-security prison with fairly well-developed intentions to help or "work with" inmates toward rehabilitation. Such intentions are consistent with the term "correctional" officer and employment in a department called "corrections." However, recruits find that inmates tend to interpret an initial helping orientation as a sign of weakness and veteran officers may condemn it. Moreover, being low in the paramilitary guard hierarchy may limit a recruit's freedom to engage and interact with inmates towards a remedial end. One study (Crouch, 1976) reveals that a specific concern for helping inmates can produce role conflict among prison officers charged with exclusively custodial tasks. Particularly relevant to the process of becoming a guard is the finding in this study that role conflict is not random. Generally, role conflict was inversely related to time in prison work; as tenure increased, role conflict became less of a problem. These results suggest that, with time, men who remain in guard work reassess their own aspirations in relation to the day-to-day exigencies of guard work and, as a consequence, gradually give up their more naive treatment aspirations.

Another attitude that may emerge in the course of guard work is cynicism. Closed behind the walls like inmates, the recruit comes to realize the public knows little of or appreciates his work situation. This feeling of limited support from the public and perhaps even from superiors, plus the difficulty of actually maintaining control over increasing numbers of inmates can foster cynicism toward correctional work, an attitude that grows with time on the job (Sommers, 1976, p. 72). Such a hypothesis would be consistent with Neiderhoffer's (1967) findings on police officers. He reported that cynicism among police rookies is very low, rises steadily through midcareer and then drops markedly toward career end. Unfortunately, we are aware of no similar cross-time study on prison guards. A study by Farmer (1977), however, does provide some evidence on the conditions under which cynicism may be more likely. Using an adaptation of Neiderhoffer's cynicism scale, Farmer examined the responses of guards in treatment- and custody-oriented prisons. Results reveal cynicism to be highest among guards in the treatment-oriented setting. Farmer did not examine the distribution of cynicism over time so we still know very little about how this attitude might change. However, the study indirectly underscores our argument that traditional expectations requiring guards to guard, and do nothing else, is strong, even in so-called treatment-oriented facilities.

Besides experiencing changes in role conflict and cynicism, guards may also become more "authoritarian" in disposition. Persons with authoritarian attitudes are typically rigid in thinking, hold to a simple version of right and wrong and are intolerant and even aggressive toward unconventional persons and behavior (Adorno et al., 1964). Moreover, they may seek out and feel most comfortable in highly structured environments that reinforce these attitudes. Several aspects of guard work would seem to foster authoritarianism. These aspects include operating under a mandate to control society's rejects, having access to a variety of weapons and at least some training in their use, and being uniformed and employed in a paramilitary hierarchy. Media portrayals, especially in movies, demonstrate how easy it is to translate these aspects of guard work into an image of guards as insensitive and brutal, unconcerned about inmates. But do guards really become increasingly authoritarian, rigid and aggressive with time on the job? The evidence on this question is limited and mixed. Perhaps the most famous piece of relevant research was conducted at Stanford University by Zimbardo and his associates (Haney, Banks, and Zimbardo, 1973, pp. 69-77; Zimbardo, 1972, pp. 4-8). These researchers created a mock prison, randomly assigning as either guards or prisoners young men who were clinically normal and similar. Designed to last six weeks, the experiment to study guard and inmate behavior had to be stopped after only two weeks because "inmates" became alarmingly submissive and alienated while "guards" became almost pathologically intoxicated with power. The researchers write:

> The use of power was self-aggrandizing and self-perpetuating. . . . The most hostile guards on each shift moved spontaneously into leadership roles of giving orders and deciding on punishment. They became role models whose behavior was emulated by members of the shift. . . . Not to be tough and arrogant was to be seen as a sign of weakness by the guards, and even those good guards who did not get as drawn into the power syndrome as the

others respected the implicit norm of *never* contradicting or even interfering with an action of a more hostile guard on their shift (1977, pp. 88-89).

Though quite dramatic, the finding that guards become increasingly oppressive and unfeeling is open to the serious objection that the subjects and the situation were artificial and the findings thus suspect. A study reported by Kercher and Martin (1975), however, avoids this objection and offers data on how actual prison guards might respond to inmates over time. In this study, guards with varying lengths of service responded to a series of inmate transgression scenarios presented on a questionnaire. Guards selected from among several responses varying in severity the one they felt they would make if faced with that particular inmate transgression. Kercher and Martin found that very new men, perhaps because they are inexperienced and relied extensively on prison rules, chose fairly severe responses. Somewhat more experienced guards (seven months to one year), however, appeared to feel more flexibile in dealing with inmates since their severity scores dropped markedly. But, for men with more than one year and especially two or more years on the job, the severity scores rose again very rapidly. These data indicate, according to Kercher and Martin that:

> ... officers ... may come to recognize that promotion is based primarily upon how well the officer's job performance conforms to the expectations of his superiors. Some of these officers may change their behavior in the direction of these expectations ... and thereby improve their chances of promotion (1975, pp. 6-7; see also Guenther and Guenther, 1974, p. 47).

The implication here is that men adopt the attitudinal and behavior trappings of guarding in a rather conscious, even calculating, manner.

The most immediate conclusion from these studies is that with time guards become more aggressive and punitive. Such a conclusion, however, may oversimplify a very complex process of social psychological change that guards undergo. It may be that with experience guards become both more stern and more understanding. Research by Hogan (1971), for example, suggests such an attitudinal change over time. Using the F-scale

(Facism) developed by Adorno et al. (1950) to measure authoritarian tendencies, Hogan examined the scores of a sample of guards in terms of length of employment. He found that guards with three or more years in uniform scored somewhat higher, i.e. more intolerant, than those with less than three years on the job. However, using a more specific measure of punitiveness (Attitude toward the Punishment of Criminals Scale), Hogan found an inverse relationship; with experience, guards become less punitive.

Although these studies are limited and vary in quality, it seems useful to attempt at least a tentative integration of them with our field observations. The result is a conceptualization of the guard's working personality (Skolnick, 1966). This concept connotes both a product and a process. The product is a patterned configuration of attitudes and behavior styles that results from learning the elements of the guard role we reviewed earlier, such as social distance from inmates and toughness. But, especially early in a guard's career, the working personality is also an emergent process as the guard moves more or less steadily toward an ideal of the *good* officer. The studies just reviewed suggest some conclusions about this process. For example, giving up early aspirations of "helping" individual inmates and becoming more stern in dealing with inmates both reflect practical and, we think, generalizable adjustments to prison realities. With time, both through their own experience and the advice of veterans, once naive men become convinced that there are indeed some "bad actors" in prison who can only be dealt with in a direct and even stern way. Having experienced the testing by inmates and the potential dangers of guard work, the guard may truly become more intolerant, apparently more authoritarian, in dealing with his charges. It does not follow, however, that the guard becomes increasingly punitive, indiscriminately aggressive, or given to physical abuse of inmates as the Stanford prison experiment suggests. If he becomes more severe, less likely to "cut inmates slack" in given situations as Kercher and Martin (1975) reported, it is, we believe, more reflective of learned subcultural values and pragmatic decisions than a growing pathology of power. Indeed, Hogan (1971) indicates that guards tend toward lesser, not greater, punitiveness as they gain experience. Apparently, then, guards do come to feel, after exposure to prisoners, that society and prison should be strict in terms of control and discipline. This attitude, however, is part of a learned role fostered by the demands of the job. With age, skill in anticipating trouble and discerning inmate types, and with the establishment of a reputation of being a nonmanipulable, feared and/or respected officer, men may mellow. Earlier, more punitive, attitudes toward prisoners may wane.

The emergence of the working personality, the acquisition of an acceptable style of doing guard work, is in some respects a conscious process. To some degree, men change, temper, or give up inappropriate attitudes. However, the process of taking on the guard role can also be so gradual as to go unnoticed by the man himself. Like the slow accretion of barnacles to a ship, the superficial trappings of the guard role gradually become a part of the self and may remain as long as reinforcement continues in the prison work setting.

Outcomes

In a recent study, Jacobs and Kraft (1978) examined differences in attitudes between black and white prison guards at Illinois' Stateville facility. They concluded that black guards, thought by many to be more effective in light of large black inmate populations, differed little in terms of attitudes from their white counterparts. The researchers found black guards to be no more sensitive to or supportive of inmates than white guards; neither were they more treatment oriented. A major implication of this study is that exposure to the demands of guard work produces a kind of attitudinal homogeneity. That is, regardless of the individual backgrounds of men who remain in correctional work, the outcome or result of the guard experience is a marked similarity among working personalities. But this conclusion, though generally correct, masks more specific outcomes of the prison guard socialization process. In the following paragraphs we identify several of these career outcomes and how they relate to our discussions of major elements of the guard role.

Before considering the various outcomes, however, we must first specify our basis for differentiation. Whereas a good "pinch" defines success for police, there is no such clear criterion for defining guards' success. Indeed, often the most quantifiable index of a guard's success is absenteeism. But there is a more diffuse definition of a successful guard, a definition as important as it is difficult to quantify. We refer to a guards' ability to project and maintain a certain image before inmates and other guards. Successfully projecting this image — what Goffman (1959) calls *impression management* — is functional for a guard's career in two fundamental respects. First, when a guard learns to deport himself in the approved manner he is better able to maintain internal order. A very important means for handling any sort of trouble with or between inmates is to keep it from starting in the first place. Having established a reputation for being fair, tough, knowledgeable, and not manipulable by inmates, guards can better forestall trouble. Inmates will either wait to initiate trouble on another shift or one or more inmates will come to the respected officer and pass along crucial information. Second, reflecting appropriate behavior to others within the guard subculture indicates the recruit is or can become "a pretty damn good officer." Acceptable role performance then means the officer can become mobile within the prison organization.

As the recruit learns and meets the informal expectations of all others in the prison setting he begins to move both *radially* and, perhaps, upward within the guard hierarchy. Radial movement describes a recruit's shift from the organizational and subcultural periphery as a trainee toward acquisition and acceptance of the secrets, shared meanings, and ideologies that define guard work among veteran role models (Schein, 1968; Van Maanen, 1975). Upward movement, of course, refers to elevation in rank and responsibility. These two types of movement are clearly variables and, though generally correlated, they may vary separately. The following discussion examines outcomes in terms of success and failure as indicated by both radial and upward mobility.

The Abject and Limited Failure

Abject or complete failure occurs when the recruit leaves

prison work quite early in his career. In many cases, the recruit brings to the job aspirations or outlooks that are incompatible with the pecularities of guard work. For example, a young man just out of college desires to help offenders, so he becomes a prison guard. When he finds these treatment aspirations are quite difficult to mobilize and he cannot adjust those aspirations, he quits (Davidson, 1974, p. 30). Others may leave due to fear or perceived racial discrimination (Jacobs and Grear, 1978). Some men, however, may desire to move toward becoming a successful officer, show up for work regularly, and try, yet they cannot project the approved guard image. Such an officer is thus a "limited" failure. One reason for such failure may be physical. That is, an officer may be obese or slow and consequently have great difficulty commanding respect from either inmates or other officers. For instance, one portly officer at Trinity worked cellblocks for nearly a year and absorbed verbal abuse from inmates (e.g. "Bubbles," because of his size and demeanor). His unimpressed superiors finally moved him to a security car to prowl the prison perimeter out of inmate contact. A limited failure may also simply lack "common sense" (Becker and Karper, 1956). One officer at Midwest, for example, frantically called his captain one night claiming he heard an airplane nearby that was trying to land in the prison yard. This event and the reporting guard became especially questionable when no other tower officer saw the plane or feared a landing. Given the high turnover rate among prison guards, such men will be used, but their responsibility and contact with inmates may be limited. Clearly, they will remain on the subcultural periphery (little radial movement) and upward mobility will be unlikely.

The Ritualist[6]

Some men enter and remain in guard work because it is just a secure job, and it means a predictable paycheck. Personal ambitions are quite limited. These men learn the requirements

---

[6]Merton uses this term to describe bureaucrats concerned primarily with "playing it safe," and having little commitment to the general goals of the organization that employs him (1968, pp. 203-207).

of the job and the essentials of how inmates should be handled and thus reflect at least some radial movement. However, their job performance involves meeting minimal expectations. So, although they take on the general knowledge and skills communicated through the guard subculture, they prefer to maintain a low profile and shun responsibility. Typically, they have little to do with other guards on or off the job. Because of this type of orientation to the job, the ritualists prefer and are allowed to work in situations where duties are routine and that require few control decisions. Assignment to a cellblock, for example, allows these men to go through the motions of the job (counting, opening, and closing doors, handing out mail) in a highly structured immediate work environment. Often enclosed in a cage or "picket," they can simply call superiors in the event of any trouble. Much the same may be said for assignment to tower duty. This is not to say such men do not perform their tasks well; they may be dependably employed for years. But, although they play the guard role better perhaps than the limited failures, their low ambition and lack of commitment means they will experience little upward mobility within the guard hierarchy.

The ritualist's outcome is perhaps the most frequently encountered among line officers. As we noted in an earlier section, many men enter this field almost accidentally. Either because they have tried many other jobs or because they need an extra income to supplement their nearby small business or farm, the security of prison work is attractive. For them, the process of socialization primarily involves learning enough to reach and hold the first plateau at which danger, inconvenience, and personal discomfort can be reliably minimized.

The Successful Officer

Success as a guard means that a man is worthy of respect from other officers, and, perhaps grudgingly, from inmates as well. The basis of that respect stems from a demonstrated ability to play the approved guard role we have characterized above. Clearly, then, this outcome connotes a capturing of the major subcultural norms, a radial movement toward the center of the guard world. This ability to handle oneself and inmates can, of course, lead to upward mobility. At Trinity, for example, all men begin in the cellblocks. With experience and a practical demonstration of security skills, men may move from the highly structured cellblocks to regular duty in the hall. Becoming a hall boss means more responsibility since the traffic in the central hallway is constant and involves men from all cellblocks.

It is important to note that success judged in terms of one's capacity to handle a variety of inmates and problems does not imply that successful guards necessarily reflect clonelike role performances. Instead the manifest demeanor of men considered good officers may be quite different. A comparison of two sergeants at Trinity illustrates the point. One man quite capable of loud, profane reprimands relates to inmates in a blustery, even aggressive, manner. The other man seems much less intense, smiling regularly in interaction with inmates as well as officers. On the face of it, the behavior of the second man seems out of character with the tough, competent image we have insisted on as basic to guard work in maximum-security prisons. The inconsistency, however, disappears with further knowledge of the second officer's legendary temper, infrequently roused, but terrible; inmates warn new arrivals that this quiet soft-spoken man should not be crossed or "tried." Thus, though they have different styles, both men carry a well-earned reputation. The respect from inmates, however, stems not entirely or even primarily from fear. While these and other successful officers can project the expected guard persona, they also employ discretion judiciously and avoid capriciousness in their dealing with inmates.

Successful role performance may depend to a considerable degree on factors that cannot be taught in formal training or summarily conveyed on the job. Certain kinds of prior job experience such as military prison work, for example, may foster subsequent success. It may be that age and the maturity it brings (Sandhu, 1972) are important attributes of the good officer.

The Insider

We have noted that radial movement in the socialization process is generally correlated with upward mobility in the guard hierarchy. However, most line officers would cynically contend that doing a good job is no guarantee of promotion. Upward mobility, low ranking men argue, requires "pull," "juice," or "connections" with a superior, or better, the warden. In Jacobs' (1978) survey of Illinois guards, for example, 68 percent replied that politics determines whether one gets promoted or not. This widely held belief regarding promotion among line officers is probably true in a fundamental sense. Some men do move up more rapidly than other equally (or more) successful officers. In some cases, inordinate mobility is due to blatent nepotism. More often, however, it can be better understood in terms of the prevailing conception of personal and official guard behavior favored by wardens and other high officials. Prisons and prison managers are conservative, given to maintaining what they believe works best. Thus they may recognize and subsequently reward those men they deem most capable of maintaining traditional, often informal, policies; in this way the *status quo* can be maintained. Following this reasoning then, those men whose personal attitudes and political leanings seem best suited to this end are most apt to have the "inside track" for promotions. We do not mean to contend, of course, that men who are so favored merely wait to be tapped by superiors who have secretly admired their style to that point. More likely, men with ambition and high commitment to the prison organization or to the field of corrections seek out relationships with influential superiors.

CONCLUSION

This analysis argues that, instead of being a simple matter of putting on a uniform and learning about schedules, becoming and being a prison officer is a complex process. Behind the walls, through constant interaction that is typically informal and subtle, yet sometimes frighteningly bold and sudden, the recruit learns the contours of the prison world and his place in it. Our account emphasizes the significance of this dynamic process for the recruit. However, guard socialization and outcomes are also important to prison administrators and reformers.

For prison administrators, the problem most obviously affected by the socialization process is custody staff turnover. In state prisons today, the annual guard turnover rate is often as high as 50 or 60 percent (May, 1976). And a recent study of the Texas Department of Corrections revealed that 44 percent of the new officers leave prison work within the first month after training (Texas Research League, 1978). Clearly, some of this loss in manpower is due to low pay and working conditions that are not easily altered by administrative decree. Yet, some of the turnover likely stems from the recruit's reaction to what he encounters on the job. How he accommodates to informal job requirements communicated by inmates and veteran officers will determine his satisfaction and ultimately whether or not he remains in prison work. The significance of this argument for administrators is that men may sometimes, and perhaps often, leave because they were not adequately trained or prepared for guard work. That is, the formal training may be too little related to the realities of the job. A greater sensitivity on the part of prison managers to these on-the-job realities and their consequences for new men could reduce the inefficiency caused by security staff turnover.

The influence of the informal guard subculture on recruits should also be of interest to reformers interested in prison change. The custody staff works at the operational level of prison policy. Organizationally positioned between administration and outsiders on the one hand and inmates on the other, guards can significantly shape the fate of prison programs and policies. It follows then that efforts to change prison institutions in ways veteran guards deem unwanted can be seriously undermined (McCleery, 1957). Veteran guards abide by shared subcultural values; they also communicate those values to new recruits while using those same values to judge the men they supervise. Since this communication process may have a significant impact on how new men define guard work generally and changes in policy specifically, an opposition to change can be perpetuated. In short, because guard subcultures are powerful and essentially conservative, prison reformers desiring to actually reach the daily life of the keepers and the kept should recognize that understanding the guard world is crucial to effecting change.

Implied in these points about the relevance of the subcultural context and guard learning process to administrators and reformers is a call for much closer study of these phenomena. Although our account is in many respects tentative, it represents a first step by defining the issues and problems that subsequent investigations of prison guard socialization should consider.

REFERENCES

Adorno, T. W., et al.: *The Authoritarian Personality.* New York, Harper, 1950.

Banton, Michael: *The Police in the Community.* New York, Basic, 1964.

Becker, Arlene M.: Women in corrections. *Resolution,* Summer, pp. 19-21, 1975.

Becker, Howard S., et al.: *Boys in White.* Chicago, U of Chicago Pr, 1961.

Becker, Howard S. and Karper, James: The development of identification with an occupation. *Am J Sociol, 61 (January):* 253-263, 1956.

Carroll, Leo: *Hacks, Blacks and Cons.* Lexington, Lexington, 1974.

Clemmer, Donald: *The Prison Community.* New York, IIR&W, 1958.

Cross, Stan: *Social Relationships and the Rookie Policeman.* Unpublished Ph.D. dissertation, Department of Sociology, University of Illinois, 1973.

———: Turning points: an alternative view of becoming a policeman. *Journal of Police Science and Administration, 5:* 155-164, 1977.

Crouch, Ben M.: *Role Conflict and the Correctional Officer.* Presented before the Midwest Sociological Association. St. Louis, 1976.

Davidson, R. Theodore: *Chicano Prisoners.* The Key to San Quentin. New York, HR&W, 1974.

Dingwall, Robert: Atrocity stories and professional relationships. *Sociology of Work and Occupations, 4:* 371-395, 1977.

Drummond, Douglas S.: *Police Culture.* Beverly Hills, Sage, 1976.

Duffee, David: The correctional officer subculture and organizational change. *Journal of Research in Crime and Delinquency, 11 (July):* 155-172, 1974.

Esselstyn, T. C.: The social system of correctional workers. *Crime and Delinquency,* April, pp. 117-124, 1966.

Etzioni, Amati: *A Comparative Analysis of Complex Organizations.* New York, Free Pr, 1961.

Farmer, Richard E.: Cynicism: A factor in corrections work. *Journal of Criminal Justice, 5, 3 (Fall):* 237-246, 1977.

Gerth, Hans and Mills, C. Wright: *Character and Social Structure.* New York, HarBrace World, 1953.

Giallombardo, Rose: *Society of Women: A Study of a Women's Prison.* New York, Wiley, 1966.

Goffman, Erving: The nature of deference and demeanor. *American Anthropologist, 58:* 473-501, 1956.

————: *The Presentation of Self in Everyday Life.* Garden City, Anch. Doubleday, 1959.

Gottfredson, Michael, et al.: *Sourcebook of Criminal Justice Statistics.* U.S. Department of Justice. Law Enforcement Assistance Administration, U.S. Govt. Print. Office, 1978.

Griswold, Jack, et al.: *An Eye For An Eye.* New York, HR&W, 1970.

Guenther, Anthony and Guenther, Mary: Screws vs. thugs. *Society, 11 (July-August):* 42-50, 1974.

Guenther, Anthony: The language of prison life. In Johnston, N. and Savitz, L. (Eds): *Justice and Corrections.* New York, Wiley, 1978.

Haney, C., Banks, C., and Zimbardo, P.: Interpersonal dynamics in a simulated prison. *International Journal of Criminology, 1:* 69-97, 1973.

Hargan, James: The psychology of prison language. *Journal of Abnormal and Social Psychology, (30):* 359-365, 1935.

Heffernan, E.: *Making it in Prison: The Square, the Cool and the Life.* New York, Wiley, 1972.

Heyl, Barbara: The madam as teacher. *Social Problems, 24:* 545-555, 1977.

Hogan, H. W.: *A study of Authoritarianism, Job Satisfaction, and Personal and Social Characteristics of Prison Guards and Guard Applicants in Tennessee."* Unpublished Master's Thesis, Department of Sociology, University of Tennessee, 1971.

Jacobs, James B. and Grear, Mary: Drop-outs and rejects: An analysis of the prison guard's revolving door. *Criminal Justice Review, 2 (2):* 57-70, 1977.

Jacobs, James B. and Kraft, Lawrence J.: Integrating the keepers: a comparison of black and white prison guards in Illinois. *Social Problems, 25:* 304-318, 1978.

Jacobs, James and Retsky, Harold: Prison guard. *Urban Life, 4:* 5-29, 1975.

Jacobs, James B.: What prison guards think: a profile of the Illinois Force. *Crime and Delinquency, 24 (2):* 185-196, 1978.

Johnson, E. H.: Sociology of confinement: Assimilation and the prison 'rat.' *Journal of Criminal Law, Criminology and Police Science, 51, 5:* 528-533, 1961.

Kassebaum, Gene, et al.: Job related differences in staff attitudes toward treatment in a women's prison. *Pacific Sociological Review,* Fall, pp. 83-88, 1962.

Kercher, Glen A. and Martin, Steve: *Severity of Correctional Officer Behavior in the Prison Environment.* Presented before Texas Academy of Science, Huntsville, Texas, 1975.

Kuethe, J. Louis: Prison parlance. *American Speech, 9-10:* 25-28, 1935.

Lofland, John: *Doomsday Cult.* Englewood Cliffs, P-H, 1966.

Marquart, James W.: *Career Contingencies of the Correctional Officer.* Unpublished Master's Thesis, Department of Sociology, Kansas State University, 1978.

May, Edgar: Prison guards in America: the inside story. *Corrections Magazine, 11, 6 (December):* 3-12, 36-44, 44-48, 1976.

McCleery, R.: *Policy Change in Prison Management.* East Lansing, Mich St U Pr, 1957.

McKorkle, L. W.: Guard-inmate relationships. In Johnson, N. et al. (Eds.): *The Sociology of Punishment and Corrections.* New York, Wiley, 1970.

Merton, Robert K.: *Social Theory and Social Structure.* New York, Free Pr, 1968.

Moore, Wilbert: Occupational socialization. In Goslin, D. (Ed.): *Handbook of Socialization Theory and Research.* Chicago, Rand, 1969.

Motivans, Joseph: *Occupational Socialization and Personality: A Study of the Prison Guard.* Proceedings American Correctional Association, 186-196, 1963.

Neiderhoffer, A.: *Behind the Shield.* New York, Doubleday, 1967.

Pavalko, Ronald M.: *Sociology of Occupations and Professions.* Itasca, F. E. Peacock, Inc.

Perdue, William C.: The temperaments of custodial workers. *American Journal of Correction,* March-April, pp. 16-19, 1966.

Roucek, Joseph: Sociology of the prison guard. *Sociology and Social Research, 20:* 145-151, 1935.

Rubenstein, Jonathan: Cops rules. In Skolnick, J. and Gray, T. (Eds.): *Police in America.* Boston, Little, 1975.

Sandhu, Harjit: Perceptions of prison guards: a cross-national study of India and Canada. *International Reviews of Modern Sociology,* March, pp. 26-32, 1972.

Schein, Edgar H.: Organizational socialization and the profession of management. *International Management Review, 9:* 1-16, 1967-1968.

Skolnick, Jerome: *Justice Without Trial: Law Enforcement in a Democratic Society.* New York, Wiley, 1966.

Skolnick, Jerome H. and Gray, Thomas C.: *Police in America.* Boston, Little, 1975.

Sommers, Robert: *The End of Imprisonment.* New York, Oxford U Pr., 1976.

Strauss, Anselm: *Mirrors and Masks: The Search for Identity.* San Francisco, Sociology Pr, 1969.

Sykes, Gresham: *The Society of Captives.* Princeton, Princeton U Pr, 1958.

Texas Research League: *Staffing and Managing the Texas Department of Corrections.* Texas Department of Corrections, Huntsville, 1978.

Van Maanen, John: Police socialization. *Administrative Science Quarterly,*
    32: 404-417, 1975.
———: The asshole. In Manning, P. and Van Maanen, J. (Eds.): *Policing a*
    View from The Street. Santa Monica, Goodyear, 1978.
Weidrich, Bob: A guard's diary of prison inferno. *Chicago Tribune,* August 9,
    1978a.
———: Guard's-eye view of life behind bars. *Chicago Tribune,* September 19,
    (3): 4, 1978b.
Zimbardo, Phillip: Pathology of imprisonment. *Society,* March, pp. 4-8, 1972.

PART III

DOING GUARD WORK

The popular stereotype of guards reflects a strange mixture of images. People think of guards, on the one hand, as simply head counters and door lockers and, on the other, as all-powerful figures whose words prisoners always heed. Yet another image, implied by prison organizational charts and official descriptions of prison operations, is that guards follow administrative rules regularly and well. These images of what guard work involves are essentially fictitious. A much more accurate imagery would depict the job as very problematic, one in which informal negotiations with inmates are more likely than bald imperatives. The purpose of Part III is to present the best available accounts of the dynamics and difficulties of contemporary guard work and thus dispel misconceptions about the guard role.

In the first selection, Edgar May provides a unique overview of guard work today. Drawing on interviews in several state prisons, May presents a view of prison work largely in the guards' own words. He considers questions such as what makes a good officer, the current state of employee loyalty and involvement with unions, and the degree of guard brutality. The next chapter, also by May, offers a picture of one man's day on the job. In this account, the reader can glimpse at some of the pressures and compromises that officers experience everyday.

The selection by Webb and Morris further describes how guards view their world by presenting guard conceptions of (1) themselves, (2) social services personnel, (3) administrators, and (4) inmates. At Mid-State prison, guards see themselves as constantly having to accommodate to or bend prison rules. Guards also feel considerable distance from treatment personnel and even administrators. Attitudes toward treatment reflect the tra-

ditional conflict between custody and noncustody staff while
coolness toward prison administrators stems from the fact that
guards frequently view administrators as outsiders. Finally,
Webb and Morris point out that although guards get close to
some inmates, fear and uncertainty color their conceptions of
inmates.

In the next reading, the Guenthers take up the problem of
uncertainty in greater detail. Specifically, these writers examine
four sources of unpredictability: (1) malfunctions of plant or
equipment; (2) problems among employees; (3) problems
created by inmates; and (4) difficulties produced by the free
community. Since inmates constitute the greatest source of uncertainty, the Guenthers examine several means prison officials
employ to maximize control and thus reduce uncertainty.
These include the shakedown, the count, information obtained
from "rats," the "siphon," and contingency planning.

The next two chapters argue that the physical and social
conditions under which guards work are important determi-
nants of their attitudes and behavior. In the first of these
papers, Jacobs and Retsky discuss how several aspects of the
guard role both shape behavior and create frustration among
line officers. Not only do guards receive conflicting role demands (custody vs. treatment), they also receive low pay and
little community respect. These writers further observe how
differing job assignments within the prison can shape officer
relations with inmates. Finally, because of the hierarchal, paramilitary organization of guard work, rank significantly influences how guards interact with other officers as well as inmates.

Although the chapter by Crouch reports on a prison very
different from Stateville, his conclusions on guard work parallel those of Jacobs and Retsky. In a participant observation
study of a "plantation prison," Crouch records two styles of
guarding. One style dominates the prison compound and reflects a rather bureaucratic concern for adherence to official
rules for both officers and inmates. The other style emerges in
the fields where a large portion of the inmate population works
each day. This latter style reveals greater personal dominance
by guards and less interest in formal procedures. Crouch shows
how these two work settings, the building and the field, pro-

duce, or perhaps allow, two divergent styles of guard work.

The last two chapters of Part III consider the quality of guard-inmate relations in maximum-security prisons. Both demonstrate that, contrary to popular images, guards do not have total power over convicts. Gresham Sykes notes that inmates often fail to recognize official authority as legitimate. Moreover, since inmates are already quite deprived, there is little officials can do to force inmate compliance. But perhaps the most important limitation on guard power according to Sykes is that guards themselves are often reluctant to employ what power they do possess. This reluctance to use authority, whether because of a desire to be a "good joe" or an inadvertant indebtedness to or an overdependency on particular inmates, means that guards sometimes lose their authority altogether. Thus, in practice, guards actually have less power than their positions and uniforms signify.

Morris and Morris further explore the compromise and constant negotiation that marks relations between guards and inmates. Their work not only provides important insights into an English prison, Pentonville, but also indicates considerable similarity between English and American institutions regarding staff attitudes toward inmates and the potential for violence. Moreover, English officers, like their American counterparts, abide by unwritten guides concerning how to treat inmates and when to bend or freely interpret official regulations. Finally, Morris and Morris reexamine Sykes' analysis of guard power in light of their own observations at Pentonville.

Chapter 4

PRISON GUARDS IN AMERICA — THE INSIDE STORY

Edgar May

THE motion picture camera pans down the seemingly endless tier of cells. The lens zooms in on inmate hands banging tin cups. Above the din there are gravel-voiced shouts of authority.

The camera lens shifts to the perspiring face of a menacing guard with a shotgun. A well-chewed cigar is clenched between his teeth and an ample portion of belly flops over his belt. At his side, a black polished billy club dangles from a leather holster.

In a few minutes, the camera will flit to another scene . . . elsewhere in the prison . . . in a prosecutor's office . . . or a police station. There it will focus on the tough-talking star — someone like James Cagney, Edmund O'Brien or Humphrey Bogart.

It is vintage Hollywood. And it is a stereotype, a cliché-ridden portrait of the prison and its guardians. It is current because frequently millions of Americans can find variations of these scenes on the Late Late Show of their local television stations.

For the contemporary correctional officer, who may well be enrolled in the criminal justice program of a community college, the TV image has a strange reality. He is convinced that this is how outsiders see him in his job.

"The average person, the only connection they have with prisons," says Conneticut's maximum-security officer Raymond A. Zapor, "is what they've seen in the movies . . . 1938, James Cagney, you know. The officers walk around with clubs

From Edgar May, Prison Guards in America — The Inside Story, *Corrections Magazine*, pp. 4-5, 12, 36-40, 44-48, December, 1976. Courtesy of Criminal Justice Publications, Inc.

111

and they do nothing but beat on these people or look to get 'em into trouble. When you say prison, prison guard, even to my neighbors, the only thing that comes to mind is the movies."

The celluloid stereotype haunts correctional officers throughout the nation. Convinced that the image is firmly in the public's mind, they see themselves on the lowest rung of the law enforcement pecking order. And they have this standing confirmed by small irritants that are like pebbles in a shoe.

In Illinois, for example, the Department of Corrections staff doesn't get new state cars for official business. Guards transport inmates in hand-me-down State Police cruisers that have too much mileage to be considered suitable for troopers.

When off duty at a social gathering, where no other correctional personnel are present, many officers resist volunteering where they work.

"I just avoid mentioning the the fact that I'm just . . . you know . . . just a correctional officer," says another Connecticut officer. "It would be: 'Oh, you're a guard, oh!' and then they sort of would look down on you. 'Not really,' I would say, 'I'm a correctional officer.' Now, see if I use that word it would sort of soften the situation a little bit, just a little. If I would say that I was striving to be a treatment officer, that would even bring me up another level. But the idea that I'm just a guard embarrasses me because I know what the connotation is."

This embarrassment, rooted in lack of public acceptance and lack of understanding of what the job is, ranks high on the national problem list of those charged with guarding a record quarter of a million adult inmates in state prisons throughout America.

With more men and women in prison than ever before, the correctional officer is in a growth industry. Including the prisons and the nation's jails, there are now an estimated 100,000 men and women in custody jobs alone. A *Corrections Magazine* national survey shows that of the total, 42,324 are in state-operated institutions, and their numbers are increasing.

But even during recent difficult economic times, when national unemployment statistics hit new post-Depression peaks, some prison jobs have gone begging. Correctional officer turnover in some places continues at such a rate that some adminstrators say it is almost impossible to run their institutions with any kind of consistent policy. Officers aren't there long enough to understand the policies. In Louisiana, the annual turnover of correctional officers is 74 percent; in New Mexico it's 65 percent. In states with far lower system-wide turnover percentages, the maximum-security institutions report that it's not unusual for them to lose at least half of their new officers in the first year.

But there are exceptions and a few are spectacular. Illinois' Vienna Correctional Center — a tranquil, college-like minimum-security institution — has file cabinets bulging with job requests. Last October it had 1,428 applications on file for the security force alone.

For most shift supervisors and personnel directors, however, the manpower dilemma is not surplus, but shortage. "Supervisors think more in terms of bodies rather than quality — are the job stations going to be filled is the overriding question," says Massachusetts' Frank Gunter, who until recently was superintendent of the maximum-security prison at Walpole.

Because of the almost constant problem of empty slots on various shifts, the burden of filling them falls on officers who stay. At San Quentin in California, some members of the custody force complain about being ordered to work on their days off. They grumble about the inability to schedule vacations. At Walpole, staff shortages this summer resulted in a mandatory sixth work day for every officer.

THE GUARDS: A NATIONAL PORTRAIT

Why are the men who watch the men in America's prisons so often their turnstile guardians?

How do those who stay, year after year, see themselves and their work?

How valid is the often held public perception that guards rule by force, with a club and blackjack that foreshadow implied or real head-cracking violence?

There are no simple answers. To study the correctional officer, *Corrections Magazine* spent several hundred hours tape recording the thoughts, concerns and the hopes of guards in six states — California, Connecticut, Massachusetts, Illinois, Rhode Island and Arkansas. Questionnaires were sent to and returned by all fifty states and the District of Columbia.

Unlike the picture of the Hollywood formula guard, his real life counterpart does not lend himself to a capsule portrait. There is no national model. There is none even within a single state or, for that matter, within different prisons under the jurisdiction of the same department.

The inability to generalize about the contemporary correctional officer even is apparent inside one single institution. Attitudes, behavior, enforcement of regulations differ markedly from shift to shift. It is a common observation made by both custody officers and inmates in maximum-security prisons.

> "There are two completely different prisons here," says Supervising Correctional Officer Leo Bissonnette at Massachusetts' Walpole facility. "It changes the minute the night shift comes on. The tensions on that three to eleven shift . . . you can cut them with a knife. I was on the three to eleven for thirteen years, and I never left a cup of coffee where an inmate could get at it. The three to eleven . . . they have rules that don't bend. It's weird. You could research this for the rest of your life and you'd never get an answer."

Nationally, America's correctional force is marked by disparity . . . disparity in everything from training to paychecks, from guard-inmate ratios to uniforms and equipment. Even the dangers connected with the job fluctuate widely among different prisons.

In Maine, the officer injury rate is so low that the department doesn't bother to keep statistics. In California, in 1975, there were 414 injuries among a state-wide custody staff of 2,888. Even there some officers suggest that sometimes the public perception of the dangers of the job is exaggerated. In Rhode Island, a maximum-security officer suggests that "if you think you're going to go twenty years in an institution without getting a rap in the mouth, you're kidding yourself. That's part of the job. That's part of what you're getting paid for."

The number of inmates a guard is responsible for varies dramatically among maximum-security prisons. Some may have fewer inmates than other institutions, yet have three and four times the number of guards. New Jersey's state prison at Trenton has a custody staff of 330 and an inmate population of 870. In Arkansas' Cummins unit there are 1,505 inmates. The total security force number 97.

In many prisons, officers grumble about the public image of guards carrying clubs and mace. In the Arizona State prison, however, officers still carry nightsticks on virtually every post. Some sergeants are armed with small cannisters of mace. But in other institutions there are no clubs and even traditional uniforms have been discarded.

At the Vienna Correctional facility — reported to be the largest minimum-security institution in the nation — correctional officers wore civilian clothes during a two-year test period. Now, with a population pushing toward the 550 capacity mark, the security force has gone back to uniforms. They wear smartly tailored forest green blazers that do not have the aura of the more traditional law enforcement garb.

Salaries, too, range across a broad spectrum (See Table 4-I). In some urban states a few correctional officers working double shifts have parlayed their overtime and regular salary earnings into $30,000 annual incomes. In rural states, many of which don't pay any overtime, take-home pay for a new officer sometimes is around $100 a week.

Arkansas is near the bottom nationally in starting salaries — $6,942 a year. Ray Mathew, a young officer who began work there last February, took home $96.50 every week for his first six months. In New Jersey, his counterpart at the state prison two years ago received almost that much money in overtime pay alone. Although overtime has been cut back at the Trenton State Prison, it still totals about $1.3 million a year, or nearly $4,000 per man.

In Rhode Island, where some officers work double shifts at the state's maximum-security prison, a union spokesman said that their yearly earnings would be just around $25,000.

The beginning salary leaders in the continental United States are California, $13,164; New York, $11,410; and Michigan, with $10,795. Alaska, with very high salaries in all fields, leads all the individual states with beginner's pay at $15,744. The lowest starting pay is in Maine — $6,240.

Table 4-I

National Survey of State Correctional Officers

State	Number of state correction officers as of 7/1/76	Annual turnover rate for correction officers	Starting Salary	Do correction officers receive overtime pay?	Minimum entrance requirements for correction officers**	Percentage of racial minorities among officers	How many violent deaths among correction officers from 1/1/74 to 7/1/76
Alabama	482	25%	$ 7,111	No	21, H.S.*	22%	2
Alaska	105	-	15,744	Yes	H.S, 4 yrs. work exp.	-	0
Arizona	651	25%	9,771	Comp. Time	none, personal evaluation	17%	1
Arkansas	315	30%	6,942	No	18, H.S.	33%	0
California	2,888	10%	13,164	Yes	Equiv. H.S., 2 yrs. work exp.	28%	1
Colorado	157	9-12%	10,368	Yes	None	-	0
Connecticut	819	4%	9,383	Yes	None	30%	0
Delaware	187	25%	7,218	Yes	H.S.	28%	0
Florida	2,620	29%	7,976	Yes	18, H.S.	-	-
Georgia	1,161	-	7,278	No	H.S.	13%	-
Hawaii	253	32%	10,476	Yes	Equiv. H.S.	-	0
Idaho	142	20%	8,940	Comp. Time	2 yrs. work	3%	3
Illinois	1,162	32%	9,912	Yes	Equiv. H.S.	17%	0
Indiana	980	17%	8,918	Yes	H.S. or GED†	13%	-
Iowa	482	40%	8,476	Yes	H.S. or GED	4%	0
Kansas	439	-	8,016	Yes	21, H.S. or GED	9%	0
Kentucky	500	30%	7,914	Yes	H.S.	12%	0
Louisiana	1,206	74%	6,348	Yes	18, exam	20%	0
Maine	244	20%	6,240	Yes	H.S.	0%	0
Maryland	1,233	7%	9,300	Yes	H.S. or GED, 3 yrs. work	29%	0
Massachusetts	1,198	12%	10,228	Yes	19, H.S. or equiv.	6%	0

State							
Minnesota	675	40%	10,476	Yes	21, H.S.	14%	0
Mississippi	390	54%	7,716	No	None, oral exam	7%	0
Missouri	485	27%	7,536	Yes	21, H.S. or GED, 1 Yr. wk.	48%	0
Montana	92	60%	9,022	Yes	H.S., 2 yrs. work	8%	1
Nebraska	294	34%	7,956	Comp. Time	H.S.	4%	0
Nevada	210	24%	8,801	Yes	H.S. or equiv.	6%	0
New Hampshire	100	20%	7,098	Yes	H.S., 2 yrs. work	7%	0
New Jersey	1,351	20%	9,813	Yes	20, H.S. or GED	-	0
New Mexico	107	65%	7,476	Yes	18	28%	0
New York	5,209	4%	11,410	Yes	H.S. or GED	78%	0
North Carolina	1,723	-	8,016	Yes	20, H.S.	18%	-
North Dakota	64	20%	8,364	Yes	20, H.S. or GED	27%	0
Ohio	1,603	14%	8,819	Yes	4th grade	3%	0
Oklahoma	662	29%	7,680	Comp. Time	H.S. or GED	6%	-
Oregon	262	36%	10,152	Yes	H.S. or GED	11%	0
Pennsylvania	1,318	7%	9,869	Yes	H.S. or GED	10%	0
Rhode Island	250	-	9,386	Yes	H.S. or equiv.	9%	0
South Carolina	835	31%	7,355	No	H.S.	-	0
South Dakota	80	2.5%	8,322	Yes	H.S. & certificate	43%	0
Tennessee	1,200	40%	5,852	No	18, H.S. or GED	4%	0
Texas	2,123	36%	8,640	No	18, H.S.	30%	0
Utah	135	30%	9,252	Yes	18, H.S. or GED	24%	0
Vermont	74	63%	7,072	Yes	21, H.S. 4 yrs. work	5%	0
Virginia	1,819	30%	7,680	Yes	H.S. & 2 yrs. work	0%	0
Washington	611	25%	9,512	Yes	H.S. or 8th grade with exp.	23%	1
W. Virginia	378	-	7,296	Comp. Time	H.S. or GED	20%	0
Wisconsin	624	-	9,506	Yes	10 yrs. ed. & work exp.	2%	0
Wyoming	57	30%	8,796	Yes	18 or H.S.	3%	1
Washington DC	1,220	18%	9,546	Yes	College grad., or 3 1/2 yrs. counseling, supervising.	57%	0

*High School
†High School Equivalency
**Some states may not have
listed all requirements

But if there are disparities within and among individual corrections systems, there are similarities that transcend departments in large and small states alike. They are the similarities of attitudes, worries and, often, frustrations. Superimposed on them all are the similarities shared by both guards and inmates.

"Look, we live with these guys," is a common refrain from officers. The cellblock for the officer's eight-hour shift is no different than the block for the inmate who does a twenty-four-hour shift. The food served officers and inmates, whether good or poor, is the same. The language of the prison, a shorthand idiom flavored with heaping portions of four-letter Anglo-Saxon words, is spoken by both the guards and the guarded. In Walpole, a cell is "a room" for both prisoner and officer. In Arkansas, someone can "short hair you" (lie to you) whatever side of the bars he's on. For the inmates in the nation's prisons, those who watch them are "cops, hacks and screws." In their own conversations, guards who may prefer to be called "officers" sometimes refer to each other as cops, hacks and screws.

The similarities shared by officers in one prison may belong to inmates in another. In Massachusetts, the guards' chino khaki summer pants and shirt are the same color and material as the mandatory clothing worn by inmates in neighboring Connecticut. At New York's Attica, an armed tower guard does an eight-hour shift surveying the yard and earns about $200 a week for his watchfulness. At the maximum-security Cummins unit in Arkansas, the unarmed men surveying the yard from all but two guard towers work twelve-hour shifts. They are unpaid. They are inmates.

THE JOB

What is the job of a correctional officer?

For most officers, the technical language of their job description can be found in the rule book, or in the advertisements for new recruits. But the realities of their task remain blurred. "Never mind what the rule book says," one guard remarked, "the fact is that you've got to work it out for yourself." The lack of clarity and, particularly, consistency regarding what is expected of them is a frustration that links officers from one part of the nation to the other.

"The idea of what a prison should be like," says Albert (Bud) Gardner, a maximum-security officer and acting president of Rhode Island's Brotherhood of Correctional Officers, "has swung from one end of the pendulum to the other. No one really knows what the answer is. A lot of people think they do. One day this is o.k. and the next day it's not o.k. And the next day . . . well, maybe it's o.k. There are no rules, no regulations for the correctional officer himself . . . there is no direction and he more or less fends for himself.

"One thing that I remember, a couple of years back we had a small confrontation in the gym area. I called one of my superior officers and asked, 'What do you want done?' and he says, well, you've been here longer than I have, do what you think is right. I kind of laughed. Everything worked out all right, but I wonder how many times this has been told to other people. . . .

"You're expected to think for yourself in certain situations. If it turns out fine, all's well and good. If you make a decision they expect of you and it doesn't turn out right . . . even if it might not have been the wrong decision but it just didn't work out right . . . then you're an asshole. After a while, if you're called an asshole enough by the inmates, and you're called an asshole enough by the brass and, from what you read in the newspapers, [by] the vocal minority [those fighting for prison reform] . . . well, after a while you begin to feel like one. Who's the asshole? Me for staying, or the guy who left?"

Often at the nub of officer confusion and uncertainty is department policy governing relationships with inmates. Most prison staff handbooks have attempted to spell it out. The language is there, but the words are subjective and open to individual interpretation; meanings differ from one officer to another.

In California, it's Departmental Rule 3400: "Familiarity. Employees must not engage in undue familiarity with inmates . . . . Whenever there is reason for an employee to have personal contact or discussions with an inmate . . . the employee must maintain a helpful but professional attitude and demeanor."

"It's hard to draw a line between fraternization and being friendly," says Anthony P. Travisono, executive director of the

8,000-member American Correctional Association. "That line still is a large, monumental dilemma for the correctional officer."

Sometimes the uncertainty over where that line is creates friction among the officers themselves. Frederick Forté, who has been a correctional officer at San Quentin since July, 1973, says he was criticized because he was "too friendly with the inmates."

"That kind of bugged me. It was just because I stopped and took time to listen to a guy, I didn't see that as being overly friendly. . . . At first, I was concerned about what they were saying about me. But as time went on when I knew I was doing the job right — I wasn't breaking any institutional rules — and I felt I was right. . . . I have to live with myself. I don't have to live with those people. I'm not going to change myself so they'll say 'Forté's a good guy.' I won't do that for staff or inmates or anybody. . . ."

The different views of what rules mean to both administrators and officers have made the guards' job more complex. As short a time as ten years ago, most officers say they were not troubled with making such interpretive decisions. Most prisons had a clear policy and tradition that discouraged anything more than minimum verbal contact with inmates.

"In the old days," a more than twenty-year veteran on a New England prison staff said, "we watched them, we locked 'em in and we counted 'em. That's all there was to it."

In Illinois' Vienna facility, Sergeant Hartley Hilton concurs, recalling his assignment in the maximum-security prison at Pontiac in the mid-sixties. "If you stopped and talked to a convict for more than one or two minutes, you were being watched. And someone would write you a pinky." (A reprimand that meant days off without pay.)

While there may be confusion sometimes about what administration policies really mean in officer and inmate relationships, there is near unanimity in the essential standards that America's correctional officers set for themselves. In corrections departments large and small, distant or adjacent, the same words keep cropping up. They, too, are subjective, open to individual interpretation: "firm," "fair," "down the middle."

Officers at opposite ends of the country use them to respond to the question: What is a good officer?

Ronald J. Englund, a nine-year veteran at San Quentin, answers by pinpointing the two extremes of the job.

> "If you come in here and feel a man is worthless because he's a killer . . . or if you start feeling sorry for these guys, you've lost all your perspective . . . you won't last six months. Convicts will run him off the yard if he tries to be a hard-nose . . . I've seen it happen. You can't come in here and be one extreme or another. You've got to walk right down the middle of the road.
>
> "I think a lot of people come in here with the concept that this is a place full of hardened criminals and they're going to have to show them that they're going to be a lot tougher. It doesn't work that way.
>
> "I treat every guy as a human being. Now, if he wants to carry that a little bit further and treat me with a lot of disrespect, . . . I'm going to give that right back to him, except I may give it back to him just a little bit heavier. I don't want him to come up to me and say 'yes sir,' 'please, sir,' no. I just want him to treat me with the respect I have coming, and I'll treat him with the respect he has coming."

In Rhode Island, a similar assessment is made by Bud Gardner:

> "The hardnose, thick-headed, bull correctional officer of the movies in the Jimmy Cagney era doesn't exist. And if he comes in here, he doesn't last very long. Your first goal ought to be to gain the respect of an inmate.
>
> "You can't gain respect from an inmate from being an easy mark. They don't respect easy marks. You don't gain respect through bully tactics, then everyday he comes into the joint it's going to just wear him down a little bit more. Things just don't work that way anymore.
>
> "You gain respect by attempting to treat everyone the same . . . equally . . . no matter what they're in for. As a matter of fact, myself, I try not to find out what a man's in here for. It might change me a little bit . . . I might not feel that it showed, but it shows. Now, someone will ask me to do something, send a request out to the visiting desk or something like that . . . his request might sit in my pocket where someone else's request would be expedited right off the bat

because of maybe what he did on the street . . . so I try not to
even know what he's here for. . . . "

If there is agreement on what the officer's standard should be,
there often is agreement, too, that sometimes, with high turnover, inadequate training, low salaries and that ever-pervasive
public image of the guard, the standard may not be met. Officer
Donato DeRobertis, with thirteen years in Connecticut's
maximum-security prison, acknowledges the gap that sometimes exists between what a guard is and what he should be.

"There are some who think their word is law and they feel
this sense of power maybe because they couldn't have power
anywhere else. I think that's part of it. They go home and
they tell the wife 'get me a glass of water, and she says 'get
your own glass of water.' Now he's all frustrated because
during the day he can have a 350-pound muscleman to whom
he says 'do this' and the man jumps. He goes home and his
little wife says 'go to hell.'

"An officer may try to live up to a certain image, that he's
the authority. The minute he does that and an inmate questions his authority . . . now there's an image to attack and
he's got to come on strong. Now if you're just yourself, I
don't care if you're a bastard, if that's the way you are, hey,
these inmates don't mind. As long as you're constant. They'll
know what to do. They'll leave you alone. This idea of
smiling today and stabbing them in the back tomorrow . . . because your eggs were burned you come in with a
grudge, this don't go."

The words "consistent" and "respect" are not only focal
points for officers describing the qualities of their job, but they
also are used frequently by inmates when questioned about
what they expect from their guards.

"I act respectable and they give me respect. That's what I
want," says an inmate in an Arkansas maximum-security cellblock. "I want an officer that has understanding . . . knows
how to talk to inmates . . . help the inmate as much as he
can . . . an officer who does his job."

For an inmate, is there a "good" guard?

While many grouse about the quality of guards as a group,
most inmates will point to an individual officer whom they
consider fair, who has helped clear bureaucratic hurdles, en-

couraged them to apply for school ... who has made a difference in their personal lives.

"Yeah. There's a fair guard," says the Arkansas inmate. "There's officers that would try to help you ... quite a few of them. There's a fair guard just like on the street there's a fair cop."

COMPLAINTS ABOUT LOYALTY

Older officers in maximum-security prisons today, however, talk of more than "respect" and "fairness" when you ask them to define the qualities required of their job. They talk of loyalty to the institution and to the other officers who work with them. They grumble about its decline. "The new guys here," one veteran said, "they come here for the money. Just the money. That's all."

Like older workers in other fields far beyond the prisons, they complain about shrinking loyalties to the job, the decline of authority, the indifference to excellence. Their criticisms are parcelled out to inmates and their younger colleagues alike. In Massachusetts, a veteran officer complains about the slovenly dress of the younger officers, the hair styles that run over shirt collars. At San Quentin, older officers complain about the lack of dress requirement for inmates. . . . "Now, he can wear the dirty old clothes he's been working in all day to dinner," fifty-four year-old Lieutenant William Faust observes. "I think with this freedom of expression thing he's infringing on the freedom of the other guys."

In both Massachusetts and California, the older officers quarrel with the decline of authority, a quarrel they have not only had within the prison, but also outside of it as well.

"Today, a man would question an order ... if I was given an order when I first come to work here, I did it," says Captain Norman Carver, a twenty-three-year man in Massachusetts' prison system. "If there was any question in my mind, then I might have said 'how come I had to do that?' Today, when you give a man an order he asks: 'how come I have to do that?' ... before he carries it out.

"If you go to work for a company, and this includes the Commonwealth of Massachusetts, I don't think you should steal from them. I think you should put your time in, do your job, just as you would if you were sitting on a production line making automobiles. . . . You take automobiles today. How many automobiles have you heard about where the rear end drops off because there's a loose screw somewhere or something else happens to it. A brand new car. You've paid four thousand dollars! They don't do their jobs, those fellows on the production line. Well, it's the same type of thing in this institution."

In California, Bill Faust is in charge of a special security squad which covers the gunrails, does searches, and is on standby for emergency situations. He is one of 390 custody officers, sergeants, and lieutenants at San Quentin. He, too, talks about the decline of authority, about permissiveness, and the changes since he started as a guard for $231 a month twenty-six years ago.

"When I was a sergeant of that yard out there, we'd blow a whistle at 4:25 and they'd know it was time to lock up. They'd line up in four lines, for (each) cellblock and file in. But now, everything seems to be a mass movement. This is an expression of 'move yourself.' We're just seeing the same things that are happening outside filtering in here," he says.

Some of the older convicts, those who have served lengthy prison terms spanning both the old, more rigid and the new expanded rights regimes, sometimes also look back with some of the same nostalgia.

"The old screws were hard and fair," says a forty-one-year-old Walpole lifer who has spent most of his years in prison. "I'd like to have the old screws back. If a guy is doing a lot of time, he's got to know where he stands. There was no ———— game playing. With them (it was), 'This is the way I want it' and 'this is the way it's going to be.' You knew where you stood."

But if there is nostalgia, it is selective and does not enshrine all the old ways. Most veterans interviewed by *Correction Magazine* said that longing for the past was more a longing for the simplicity of discipline for both the guarded and the guards, rather than for the arbitrary, lock-step prisons of the past.

"Hey, years ago an inmate would come in and say 'the officer lied.' The deputy superintendent would say: 'My officers don't lie.' Hey, I know some officers lie," said Albert B. Carr, associate deputy superintendent at Walpole.

In Connecticut, Ray Zapor, who complains of the James Cagney film stereotype of guards, has one more year before he qualifies for his twenty-year retirement. He is regarded by his fellow officers as a model of the old school correctional officer.

"The only thing I liked about the old school is I think we had more control. I think we had more respect from the inmate. They wouldn't dare talk in front of the officers the way they do today.

"We had the silent system, you know, when the inmates weren't allowed to talk. It was just in the mess hall. I don't see where that helped anything. When an inmate goes to eat, it's a big time of his day. It's socializing. It's an event in their day to break up the monotony. So I think that the talk back and forth is good for them. If they have something that's bothering them, they can talk it over with their buddy. I think it takes a lot of pressure off the inmate so I'm not in favor of the silent system. Never was.

"We carried clubs when I started. And they were of no value to us. You ran the risk of having it taken away from you and having it used on you. If you went and broke up a fight and there were two inmates fighting and you went to use the club, you had two hundred inmates fighting ... the first thing we'd do is throw the clubs over the wall. They only got in our way.

"If [you] saw a man walking back and forth wearing a club, you know every time you saw that club ... I have no doubt that these people have been hit sometime in their life by a cop ... even the badge ... they look at the badge. All their life they've had trouble with the police officer. They go to prison, the correctional center as you call them, and they see the badge and, hey, what do they see? The cop they had trouble with all their life. They don't see a correctional officer, just another cop ... it all depends on what you want to do. Do you want to help the inmate? And that's really a tough thing to do, to help somebody who doesn't really want to be helped. But I don't think you're going to do it with badges on.

"Like I say, I'm considered about the hardest ... what is the word for the most hard-nosed person who is in here? Hard Rock. Yeah, this type of thing. Perhaps the jacket [reputation] that I carry is, you know, a little heavier than I deserve.

"I've talked to inmates who come in and figure the guards are going to make them toe the line . . . and they're really disappointed . . . it's like they're looking for their masculinity. Their conception of a man is tough, physically tough. My conception of a man is a guy who pays the mortgage every month. That's tough."

IS THERE BRUTALITY TODAY?

Veteran correctional officers acknowledge that the "old school" had more ramifications than just tougher discipline. Prisons were tougher physically. While clubs may not have been used in day to day institutional security chores, they were used selectively, in a segregation wing, in the privacy of an inmate's cell. "The ultimate method of control was a rap in the head," says a veteran maximum-security guard who was, by his own admission, part of what he called "the head knocker period."

How much is violence part of the arsenal that maintains contemporary prison order today?

The answers are elusive. They are often limited. Rarely are they made for attribution to a particular officer, inmate or administrator. After a serious prison disturbance and the investigations that follow, they sometimes crop up in testimony of witnesses.

Some inmates and ex-offenders interviewed by *Corrections Magazine* had individual vignettes of what they considered guard violence. An unruly inmate hurled — unnecessarily, they said — down a stairway . . . beatings in an elevator stopped between floors — "they called it the bucket of blood" — force used against an inmate when they believed force was unnecessary.

One ex-convict who had been held in a number of maximum-security prisons within the last five years said that in one of them, beatings were considered routine. In others, physical attacks by officers were more muted and less frequent.

"There is a correlation between how unstable an institution is and how much head-cracking goes on," says the commissioner of an eastern state. "When it's unstable then everybody's frustrated and heads get beaten."

It still happens today?

"Yes," in a few places.

"None of my colleagues would admit to me that they look the other way. But I know a couple do. When I started in this business fourteen years ago, captains and lieutenants clearly said to you the way they maintained control was to crack a head or two now and then. Now, at least, they don't talk about it anymore."

Physical attacks by guards on inmates, he said, have been sharply reduced because prisons everywhere are far more open to outsiders than ever before "Probably the most important factor has been the legal movement into the prison. Systematic beating to maintain control just isn't there anymore."

The few officers who would discuss their own part in the head-knocker era concur with the commissioner's assessment. Some, too, suggest that they have changed their minds about the usefulness of beatings as a method of prison control.

> "If you have to thump a guy's head and you have to do it again in two months, and again two months later, you're not doing any good," says a supervisor who for five years has been in the segregation unit of a major midwestern maximum-security prison. He allowed that the club was used regularly as a persuader, sometimes landing on the inmates regardless of their guilt or innocence.
>
> "I thought it helped at the time. I thought it helped even after I left. In fact, if you had told me up there that it wouldn't do any good to beat a guy's head, I would have probably escorted you right out of there. I would have told the warden you was crazy and he would have believed me."

Among America's professional prison monitors, the ombudsmen for corrections, cases of overt guard violence are reported infrequently. Minnesota's Theartrice Williams, the nation's senior prison ombudsman, and James T. Bookwalter, his counterpart in Connecticut, believe that unprovoked beatings don't occur in their state prisons.

"I don't believe that in Connecticut people are taken out of their cells and worked over anymore. It happened in the past, but it doesn't happen anymore," says Bookwalter.

"What does happen when there is a physical conflict between an inmate and an officer and force is required to bring an inmate under control, the inmates believe that the guard gets in a few extra licks."

In three years as Connecticut's ombudsman, Bookwalter has received 1,062 different complaints from the state's maximum-security prison at Somers. Between ten and fifteen of these, he said, involved charges of guard violence. He has been unable to document any of them. "There are certainly incidents where an inmate has been injured while physically resisting an officer, but it's impossible to document if an officer used necessary or excessive force, but no inmate ever has said to me that he has been slugged without any reason."

"I would be very close to that," says Minnesota's Williams, who in four years has pursued about 4,500 inmate complaints. Fewer than half of dozen, he says, have involved charges of officer violence.

"We've had accusations made in the maximum-security prison that officers have attacked inmates, but when we began to check it out, it began to fall apart. I know we don't have a documented case of so-called brutality. What we have had is a case where the question was how much force is enough force."

Williams recalls an incident where an inmate filled a cup with urine and threw it at a passing guard. The officer happened to be carrying a pot of coffee and the inmate got the coffee. "Now if he had done that three days later, making sure that the coffee was good and hot, I would have considered that brutality," he said.

"The officer — at least in the Minnesota system — who provokes a situation where he is the aggressor, he'll be in trouble on two counts: The inmates wouldn't tolerate it, and the administration would want to deal with it quickly because that's a situation that leads to a riot."

THE QUESTION OF JOB COMPETENCE

While opinions about current violence may vary among inmates, there is near unanimity on another question: the inmates claim that many correctional officers are not prepared for their jobs. They tick off a litany of complaints that, in less-harsh language, often parallels the complaints of officers and prison administrators as well: There isn't any real screening to weed out the psychologically unfit . . . officers sometimes bring their personal "hang ups" into the prison . . . rural guards from the small towns where prisons generally are located do not understand the inmate who generally comes from the city . . . and, most often heard, they are untrained.

Entry requirements for correctional officer jobs are minimal and vary from state to state. Many now demand a high school diploma. In Ohio, however, the minimum is a fourth grade education or its equivalent. In some states an applicant must be twenty-one, in others only eighteen. Many now give standard state civil service tests, others have no tests at all. Some give physical examinations, some don't.

In 1974, a study of the Commission on Correctional Facilities and Services of the American Bar Association found that only seven of forty-six states that participated in the survey made background checks on applicants. Few states have detailed psychological fitness standards, the survey said. A dozen states acknowledged that the screening methods for emotional and psychological fitness they did have were "not very effective."

"Since correctional agencies commonly administer a battery of tests to aid in classifying inmates, which result in rather specific indications of strengths and weaknesses," the ABA report said, "the primitive 'state of the art' as regards staff selection was not fully anticipated."

Once an applicant is accepted, training, too, differs from state to state. Sometimes an individual department will curtail a training program in mid-year because educational funds are running low or are needed elsewhere. With increased availability of federal Law Enforcement Assistance Administration (LEAA) training funds, more states have organized at least some formal programs. These range from pre-service, full-time academies, to a smattering of basic courses sandwiched between or ahead of work shifts.

In New York State, a new man goes to an academy for thirteen weeks before he is assigned his first prison post. In other states, however, the recruit still learns most of his trade by doing it — on-the-job training, labeled by one officer as a euphemism for "flying by the seat of your pants."

"I've worked in places," says former Massachusetts penitentiary superintendent Frank Gunter, "where the inmates showed the new man how to use the key."

In Arkansas, Arthur L. Lockhart, superintendent of the maximum-security Cummins unit, tells a similar story of his early days as a correctional officer in the Texas system. "I had OJT (on-the-job training) from a convict. He showed me how to shake down and do the count."

The Arkansas Department of Corrections, in many ways, is among the newest in the nation. It has virtually no veteran correctional officers. Until 1971, custody at the maximum-security Cummins unit was in the hands of trusty inmates. Six years ago, Cummins contained about 900 inmates. The total staff, from secretary to the superintendent, was 28. The custody staff alone is now close to 100.

With the help of an $80,000 LEAA grant, the department is now beginning to develop a series of in-service training courses. A formal, pre-service academy program is about two years away, said Lockhart.

Ray Mathew is a soft-spoken twenty-year-old who will complete his first year as a correctional officer at Cummins in February. Before he came to the maximum-security unit, he was unemployed for three months after he lost his job as a cafeteria worker in Little Rock. He said that he had never seen a prison before.

> "My idea was that they all would be locked up. When I saw 'em all walking around it made me scared at first. During the first two days, I walked down the barracks and there was about 100 inmates. I thought 'there I was alone and any one of 'em could jump me.' But then I realized they could just as easy get out the door.
>
> "The employment office sent me over. I talked to the personnel manager at Cummins on a Monday. He looked over the application and at the end he said there was no reason why I couldn't start Wednesday night.
>
> "I got here Wednesday night and they told me they didn't need me,... that. I should come back the next day at 2:30 ... We all met in the officers' mess. We had our (shift)

briefing and they told me to work the hospital door. I had to ask another officer where the hospital door was.

"There were two of us at the door. The other officer explained to me what we were supposed to do. He showed me how to shake down. During the first two weeks, sometimes, I took it over alone. Some weeks — on Tuesdays and Thursdays — they had me come in at 1:30 PM instead of 2:30. They'd choose a certain assignment and they explained what you were supposed to do."

Minimal or virtually no training is not unique to Arkansas. Dr. John E. Grenfell, professor of rehabilitation at Southern Illinois University at Carbondale, has been training officers and their training supervisors for more than ten years. He has produced training handbooks for LEAA. He says that some training programs in the Midwest and South still are rudimentary and offer only a few basics. "Some years ago I interviewed guards in Tennessee who were on the wall with guns they didn't know how to use," he says.

In a survey of midwestern correctional officers conducted by Grenfell ten years ago to find out what kind of training the guards wanted, they listed a combination of academic courses and instruction in security techniques. "What they wanted most was a course in human relations . . . how to predict inmate behavior . . . when somebody was going to blow his top and how to prevent it. . . . " Professor Grenfell believes that those training priorities still are wanted today. They were mentioned frequently by young officers interviewed by *Corrections Magazine*.

In departments throughout the nation, some officers are obtaining these courses on their own. They are enrolled in psychology and sociology classes in four-year colleges as well as in community colleges.

In Rhode Island, Bud Gardner obtained his degree in criminal justice by going to college after his day shift ended at the maximum-security prison. He found the psychology and sociology courses particularly helpful.

"I grew up in a suburban community. I went to suburban schools. Up until I went into the service, I had very little contact with people from other backgrounds. The education taught me a little about what it's like for other people. I find myself not bothered as much . . . somebody directs a remark to you, a hostile remark, and you start to take it personal. But I began to realize that it's not Bud Gardner they're talking to, they're talking to the uniform, the symbol that's standing in that spot . . . they're venting their frustrations there because there's no other place to vent them. . . . "

EMPLOYEE ORGANIZATIONS

Those who administer today's prisons have more woes than coping with untrained manpower. Beyond the often high correctional staff turnover, those who stay are making stronger employee demands in many states. Unions and their drive for collective bargaining agreements are on the rise.

Only a handful of states now have no employee organizations representing their correctional officers. The groups vary from in-state associations to international trade unions that range from the American Federation of State, County and Municipal Employees (AFL-CIO), to the Teamsters. In Ohio in 1974, the Director of Rehabilitation and Corrections signed agreements with forty separate collective bargaining units representing five different employee groups.

A study of management-employee relations in corrections now being conducted by the American Justice Institute, of Sacramento, California, shows not only unionism in prisons on the increase, but also an upswing in demands for collective bargaining. Preliminary information collected in 1975 indicated that fourteen states had collective bargaining agreements.

Some state corrections departments reported breakdowns in negotiations that led to strikes and organized sick outs. The Ohio Department of Rehabilitation and Correction has had ten strikes in the past five years. In Pennsylvania, correctional officers have boycotted their prisons thirteen times via waves of sick calls.

A veteran corrections administrator with experience in labor relations believes most prison administrators are not equipped to deal with union-management negotiations. "They are babes in the woods," he said, adding:

"Management in many of these states have had very little experience with collective bargaining and have gotten themselves into some incredible messes. They've been giving them things they didn't have to give them because they didn't know how to negotiate."

Many urban state prison administrators are caught sometimes between increasingly militant union demands and cumbersome civil service systems that can delay routine decisions for months. The Massachusetts Corrections Department recently waited more than half a year to obtain the scores of Civil Service exams. A written test was given in November, 1975, and the oral component was held last March. By the end of this summer, the results had not been reported to the prison. At Walpole, twelve of eighteen supervisors held provisional appointment because the scores from supervisory examinations had not been furnished by the state system.

While these administrative headaches are mounting for shift supervisors in many prisons, the immediate overriding concern often is absenteeism. It is so pervasive in some institutions that job assignments are juggled daily and last-minute calls are sent out for men to give up their days off to replace an absent coworker.

At San Quentin last May, the work force of 451 employees of the Security Division — including secretaries, counselors, sergeants and lieutenants — compiled 4,464 hours of sick leave. It averaged nearly ten hours per employee for the month. At Walpole, the sick leave totals during the same month averaged three hours for members of the custody force. In New Jersey's maximum-security prison at Trenton, the average member of the custody force took three weeks of sick time per year, just about the allowed maximum.

In institutions with less stress, the "illness" frequency is dramatically reduced. In the minimum-security facility at Vienna, Ill., the sick leave totals were half of those at San Quentin for the same month. The custody force of 171 averaged five hours per man.

"Sick leave has turned into a right rather than a privilege," says ACA director Anthony Travisono, the former head of the Rhode Island prison system. "When they gave that away, we lost a helluva lot. The job is so rotten, they look for any way to get out of the prison even if it means fudging it."

Job dissatisfaction increases where turnover and absenteeism are higher, frequently in the overcrowded maximum-security institutions. Both older and younger correctional officers acknowledge that often they accepted their jobs in the first place largely because of the security it offered, the steady work, the retirement plan. "This place is just not about to pack up and move some place else," one of the officers said.

But many correctional officers emphasize that they want and look for more than a steady paycheck. Officers with less than a year of service and those with more than two decades behind them share common job-goal frustrations. Many resent what they believe is their too limited role as jailors of America's convicts as well as the lack of encouragement from administration to work more actively with inmates. There is also resentment over what they see as the gap between themselves and the treatment staff.

"You've got to show that he (the officer) is needed," one of them says. "You've got to show that we're doing something that's worthwhile . . . but how in the world can you feel worthwhile if you're just opening and closing doors?"

Everywhere *Corrections Magazine* interviewed officers, they defined the "worthwhile" aspects of their jobs in highly personal anecdotes of inmates they believe they may have helped: Unscrambling administrative snarls for an inmate who may not have received what was due him . . . the isolated success stories of those who "made it on the street," job assignments they urged for a man who later used the newly learned skill "on the outside."

In Arkansas, a young black sergeant in a segregation unit talks about being the link between the inmate and the world beyond the fence. He points to examples that would be trivial outside of prison — some writing paper, a phone call. "I try to get things for the inmate that he's supposed to have. If I can do that, that makes me feel good."

In Connecticut, a lieutenant talks about an inmate in the maximum-security prison who recently took his college entrance exams:

"He came in first in the state of Connecticut . . . twenty-eighth in the United States. Things like that make you feel good... We get judged on our failures. Corrections always gets judged on its failures ... we do ... never on the positive things that happen. When something like that happens it really makes you feel good if you're really into what you're doing... I couldn't get over that. The guy came in No. 1 in the State of Connecticut."

In Rhode Island, Bud Gardner talks of satisfactions. "... seeing them a year or so later on the street and having them go out of their way to say hello to you. You'll be in a store somewhere and not even notice that they were there and they would spot you and cross the store to say hello and sit down and have a cup of coffee together.... This helps on the other end of the scale for some of the things that go on in the institution."

In California, San Quentin's Fred Forté suggests "there's a lot more to this than just locking a guy up and unlocking him. You get into a lot of heavy personal things that you wouldn't think a guard would be concerned about. The majority of the officers I've seen do take some concern in where a guy is, what his problems are. I would like to think that most consider it at least a part of the job."

Some officers believe that they and their colleagues often have been an unused resource within the prisons. They insist that they should have had a part in staffing the raft of new programs that have been brought into institutions in recent years.

Ronald W. Phillips is a lieutenant on the custody dayshift of Connecticut's maximum-security prison. A former president of the correctional officer's union, he was one of the "Young Turks" who fought not only for greater benefits, but also for increased professionalism among guards. Five years ago, at age thirty-eight, he was promoted to lieutenant, one of the youngest men to make that rank in the Connecticut system. Phillips today is concerned about what he fears is a retrenchment of prison programs because of a belief that they don't work.

"I think if they had gone to the people that they already had in their system and put them in to run those programs, they would have made them work. Everyone who came from outside had to learn what this was all about first. They had expertise here that they didn't use.

"If they had made it graceful for those men (older correctional officers) to throw away the stereotype . . . you know you just can't blast people . . . there's an amount of personal pride in everyone, whether they're wrong or they're right. If they would have allowed them to put down that stereotype that they had armored themselves with, then these programs they're now complaining are not working would have worked. The people they brought in are very intelligent people, well educated people, good people, o.k.? But it took them so long really to grasp the situation about the types of people that we work with . . . why didn't they make a little effort to give them (the guards) the academics that were needed and work it that way instead of bringing in new people?

"Now what you have are two groups of people who are disillusioned. You have those who you brought in. They're saying 'shit, you know, it's not working.' And you still have the people we've been talking about, the officer who feels, 'I can't move myself, I can't do anything for myself in this business. I've got a lot to give and they're going outside to get people to give it.' He's still disillusioned."

Lieutenant Phillips has allies for his views among some prison administrators. Dr. David Fogel, formerly the commissioner of the Minnesota Department of Corrections and frequently an outspoken critic of prison policies, also suggests that the guard had been overlooked in the nation's prisons. Now executive director of the Illinois Law Enforcement Commission, he wants officers to be at the center of an institution's treatment system. "The talent is there," he says, "or it can be developed if we bite off manageable pieces."

The officers can deliver treatment, he insists. "They can either embarrass the best effort, they can sabotage it or they can outright do it. What's the use of sending an inmate for an hour to the pressurized cabin of a treatment situation with a psychotherapist and then have him return to a concentration camp atmosphere where he's spending virtually all of his time.

"It's not hard to figure out that these guys would like to be involved. Why can't the guard be in the helping profession and still make sure that nobody runs away?

"Stop the rhetoric and send me your tired and your sick. Stop the rhetoric that we can cure them. Just start talking about fairness. The guards know that. They know it because they've been treated just like the inmates, often unfairly."

In Connecticut, Ray Zapor, and others like him who are nearing retirement, doesn't think he will see those changes. When he quits within a year, he says he will take with him "very little satisfaction" from the job he did for twenty years.

"My whole family is in construction. They're masons. They take me to show me a building they finished. They're proud of it. They come home at night and they get a feeling of accomplishment. You can show it to somebody.

"But you come out of a prison . . . and what can you show somebody?"

Chapter 5

A DAY ON THE JOB — IN PRISON

EDGAR MAY

THF. buzzer of the white clockradio drones through the bedroom. The hands of the luminous dial point to 5:20 A.M.

For Philip Martin Carvalho, the jarring sound is the same prelude to the morning ritual that millions of Americans call "going to work." But unlike most other job-bound early risers, his work place is different: it's behind eight steel and barred doors within the walls of the Massachusetts maximum-security prison at Walpole.

Phil Carvalho holds the rank of senior correctional officer. He has covered virtually every custody assignment in the eight years he has been in a prison that has been jarred by inmate riots and strikes by its personnel. Since last January, his post has been Ten Block, the segregation unit where Massachusetts houses up to sixty of its toughest and most incorrigible inmates.

It is a quantum jump from the bedroom of the modern brick and shingled Cape Cod house to the refuse-littered Ten Block twenty-seven miles away . . . from the oak trees on his lawn and the river view to the nine-by-six-foot cells where inmates build makeshift cardboard floor barricades to keep out mice and rats. On work days, Phil Carvalho doesn't use the handsome valet dressing stand in the corner. He slips into his khaki shirt and trousers, the same style uniform worn fifteen years ago by the bus drivers of the Massachusetts Street Railway Co. on the Boston to Providence run. After toast and coffee with his wife, Shirley, he grabs his brown bag lunch, a tall thermos with coffee and climbs into his van for the fifty-minute drive to the prison.

From Edgar May, A Day on the Job — In Prison, *Corrections Magazine*, pp. 6-11, December, 1976. Courtesy of Criminal Justice Publications, Inc.

Phil Carvalho is not necessarily the prototype of the American correctional officer. There probably is none. There is no mold that stamps out the "average" officer. But Carvalho, at thirty-four years of age, has biographical bench marks that are similar to his counterparts who guard America's quarter million adult prisoners. High school graduate . . . a couple of jobs in industry before he moved into the "steady work" offered by the state prison system . . . married . . . to the girl who lived four houses down from his own in the tight-knit Portuguese-American community in nearby Fall River . . . She was eighteen . . . he was nineteen.

For Phil Carvalho and thousands like him, reporting for the seven to three shift in America's maximum-security prisons, the work day begins with the small ironies that sometimes blur the distinctions between the guard and the guarded.

"All persons entering the lobby," the sign on the prison doorway says, "must have their packages, pocketbooks, etc. inspected. Failure to do so, the officer on duty will refuse entry to the lobby. *This applies to employees of the institution also.*"

Phil Carvalho punches the time clock, moves through the first of the electronically controlled steel doors, opens his lunch bag for inspection by another officer, empties his pockets of keys and small change, and removes his buckled belt before stepping through the archway of the metal detector. The unseen electronic eye doesn't flicker any alarm.

Door after door opens and closes. Click, bang, click, bang . . . some are operated by unseen hands secluded in the tower above the wall. The last two doors are at the end of the long corridor beyond the inside control room, with its barred, bullet-proof glass protective shield. Keys unlatch those last doors . . . click, bang, click, bang . . . and Carvalho is at his work place.

"They're not too many officers who beat a track to get down here," he says to a visitor who follows him through his work day.

Ten Block is a steel barred island within the walled continent of the prison . . . insulated and isolated for those who live there and those who work there. It is an island cut off from the institutional mainland by more than the click, bang of steel.

Because it confines or segregates those who have assaulted guards and inmates, it is often territory that is ostracized by other guards and inmates. "Nobody is going to be in a hurry to do anybody any favors down here," Carvalho says.

Ten Block also is an island marked by the paraphernalia of violence. Handcuffs dangling from a peg board . . . a trio of fire extinguishers within easy reach on the floor . . . a convex plexiglass riot shield resting in the corner. Its sixty cells are divided between two floors, fifteen to a corridor. Some of the cells on the first floor have solid steel doors, in front of the bars, that are clanged shut when an inmate does punitive isolation time.

When Carvalho arrives, nine young officers already are beginning to fill cardboard trays with muffins, cereal and paper cups of coffee from the kitchen wagon. Like Carvalho, all are volunteers for Ten Block.

"Yeah, you gotta be crazy to work here," one of them says, "but it's got good days off." Most of the officers have been spit at by some of their charges. Some have been hit by urine and excrement.

Before Carvalho has a chance to move through the door of the cubicle that serves as an office, one of the three phones inside rings.

"Ten, Carvalho."

The phone is sandwiched between the cheek and the shoulder of the 220-pound, six-foot, two-inch Carvalho. For the next eight hours, it will ring incessantly, with rare moments of silence. For Carvalho, the telephone is something more than an electronic instrument.

He growls at it, purrs into it, persuades, cajoles, allowing the cadence of his voice to vary with the purpose of his message. "Yeah, right. Hey, sweetheart, do me a favor. . . . "

Carvalho shares the responsibilities of running Ten Block with Arthur Latessa, the most recently promoted supervisor of the Walpole prison. Ten Block is the lowest rung of desirable supervisory assignments and the newest man usually is in the job. When Latessa is absent, Carvalho runs the block by himself.

For his efforts, Carvalho takes home $199 a week, some $17 more than the younger officers.

"Guard House, Guard House . . . " the inmate's voice comes from midway down the corridor. "Hey, Phil. . . . Phil . . . Phil Carvalho."

One of the other officers unlocks the corridor's steel entry gate. He never lets his eyes wander from Carvalho's back as he moves down the hallway.

Carvalho kicks aside an empty milk carton as he moves down the narrow aisle between the cells and the wall. The floor is littered with yellow paper food trays, used plastic forks and spoons, and the remnants of yesterday's evening meal.

The corridor is temporarily without an inmate porter. He lost his job after officers found a jug of home brew in his cell. The notice on the office bulletin boards says it's the responsibility of the 3 PM to 11 PM shift to sweep the corridor.

"Yeah, Charlie?"

"Listen, Phil, you gotta get that son-of-a-bitch out of here. . . . " The voice in the dimly lighted cell details a complaint against an officer on the 3 to 11 shift.

Other inmates shout their own litany of complaints. Hands holding mirrors protrude from the other fourteen cells in the section, giving their owners a glass-reflected picture of the officer and the visitor.

"The only thing I can tell you," Carvalho responds, "is that I've got to get McLaughlin down here."

Thomas McLaughlin is deputy superintendent at Walpole. He is one of the key reasons why Phil Carvalho volunteered for Ten Block. "He backs you up. And he's there when you need him. . . . All these guys," Carvalho says pointing to the young officers, "they're there when you need 'em."

"Who's that guy?" a voice queries from one of the cells.

"He's writing an article. . . . "

"Yeah, the mother f. . . . . looks at you like you was a f. . . . . lizard."

Back in his cubicle office, Carvalho's fingers dial the extension number

"Hey, Mac. . . . Phil. You gotta get down here. I need you. Yeah, fifteen minutes. No more. O.K.? Thanks."

The office in its clutter and congestion offers another reminder of the similarities between the guard and the guarded.

Like the cells, it, too, is cramped. It is only an hour into the shift and the half-empty coffee cups are beginning to accumulate. Cigarette butts are piling up in the ashtray, and some from days and weeks before are in the corners. A calendar with a picture of a nude girl dangles from a peg board holding twenty-one keys.

When McLaughlin arrives, Carvalho takes him through the corridor where the inmates are complaining about the officer. They move from cell to cell like army medics making rounds in a crowded hospital. The deputy superintendent is a listener. Occasionally, he asks a question, sometimes he nods, but his face shows neither a flicker of sympathetic agreement nor cynical disbelief. Later, he tells Carvalho there will be a meeting with the night officer at the end of the shift.

"Hey, Phil . . . Phil. . . . " Another voice from the cell in the corridor. Carvalho again moves into the narrow hallway.

"Hey, Phil, I need a legal visit. My case comes up on the fourteenth."

"O.K. I'll take care of it."

From a hall phone, Carvalho dials an extension. "Yeah, Phil Carvalho. I need a legal visit for. . . . "

The demands made on Carvalho are not phrased in convoluted euphemisms. They are direct. They deal with basic wants in the limited, cramped world of the segregation unit . . . an appointment for a visitor, a phone call to a relative . . . some writing paper. Sometimes the demands attempt to stretch the narrow boundaries of Ten Block. Either way, the answers are equally direct. Carvalho's booming voice, intoning, "I'll try," or "Yes," or "No," leaves little room for doubt.

The conversations are always on a first-name basis, sometimes flecked by touches of jail house humor that softens the harshness of where they take place. There is a subconscious line between Carvalho and the inmates that marks the perimeter between levity and insolence, between what is permitted and what is not. Since he arrived in Ten Block, Phil Carvalho never has been spit at or assaulted by anything more than a barrage of four letter words.

In the office, the phones are ringing again.

"Ten. Carvalho."

"Yeah, O.K. Sullivan's visit cancelled. O.K. Thanks."

"Ten. Carvalho."

"No. I can't do it. I don't have a place to put him. Look, sweetheart, he can have a legal aid visit. Yeah, but not today. I got visits at 11, at 11:30, 1:30 and a disciplinary board. Yeah, try tomorrow. Sorry. You're doing a great job . . . a great job."

Carvalho recalls that a few weeks earlier a lawyer had to interview his client in the elevator that is used to transport the food cart between the two floors of the block.

"It's confined, this block. It's too small a place. After a while, even the officers start arguing with themselves. It happens every day. Any old thing sets the officers off. Out in [the general prison] population at least you're walkin' around, you got space out there. Or you may have the yard duty or you go on transportation, or hospital detail or something. But down at Ten. Where you goin'? Upstairs, downstairs, that's it. We're bangin' into one another."

An officer comes into the cubicle with a handful of small brown envelopes. Carvalho counts them, records the total and the time in the dog-eared log book in front of him.

"Medication," he says. "O.K. give 'em out."

Ten Block distributes medication more frequently than meals. Four times a day, inmates may receive prescriptions that include sedatives, tranquilizers and sleeping pills. During the morning distribution, fourteen of twenty-eight inmates on the first floor receive pills. Five milligrams of Valium® four times a day plus a sleeping pill at night is not unusual.

"I can't understand it," says Carvalho. "These guys [when they're] on the street can't be gettin' that medication. Impossible. Some of 'em need it for their nerves. Being in this situation they need something to calm them down. But the pain pills they put out, the depressants . . . it's unbelievable. In the street, these guys don't go, 'Hey, wait a minute, I got to take my pill. I'll be right back to help you rob the bank or somethin'.' Everyday they've got to get their pills. Now they're dependent on it. They need it or they're goin' to crash."

"In a way, we're making pill addicts out of 'em. Yeah, and I've heard a medic say that, too."

Ring. Again, the phone.

"Ten. Carvalho."

"No, We can't take 'em. We haven't any room. Yeah. I'll call you back."

Carvalho slams the phone back and ticks off the names of inmates the administration wants to send to Ten Block. One prompts a groan from the officers in the room. All are known to them, but the last one is a particularly troublesome prisoner who shuttles back and forth from Ten Block and the state mental hospital at Bridgewater.

Carvalho dials again. He's thinking about making room for the newcomers, but he needs approval from a deputy superintendent before he can move any segregation block inmate to another unit or even to another corridor and cell within Ten Block.

"Hello, Mac. Suppose we move him up to forty-five? Yeah, we're playing checkers down here. You've got to talk to them and get some of these guys out of here."

Ten Block is nearly always at or pushing toward its sixty-cell capacity. Some have been in the unit for as much as two years. It is two years spent almost entirely in a nine-by-six-foot cell. Each man is let out for about a half-hour a day for a shower and some exercise in the narrow corridor. But there are never more than two men free in the corridor. On clear days, an inmate may be permitted as much as an hour in an outdoor exercise cage.

Within a half-hour, McLaughlin calls Carvalho to tell him that he has "front office" approval to move four inmates out of Ten Block. Carvalho instructs other officers to inform three of them that they will move out of the most restricted and confined cellblock in Walpole prison. Carvalho goes down a corridor to tell one of the inmates himself.

"Hey, Phil. I don't want to go. I got problems in Block three.

"Hey, this ain't the Holiday Inn. This is Walpole."

Back in the office other officers return shaking their heads. Carvalho reaches for the phone again.

"Hey, Mac. Nobody wants to go." He ticks off the names and adds, in an almost sorrowful monotone after each of them, "don't want to go."

"Oh, God! I've never seen anything like it. Guys refuse to move ... one big happy family...."

"Yeah, I know. Those guys on Top Right, they've got nothin'. No cans (canned snacks), no fans, no hot pots (to heat soup or coffee). These guys should be dying to get out of here. O.K. We'll talk to them again."

Carvalho shakes his head. "Ain't that a bitch when a guy doesn't want to move from Ten Block?" He explains that a forced move is pointless. The inmate will commit an infraction in his new block assignment and five minutes later will be returned to the segregation unit.

"They feel safer here. They'd rather be here than in that zoo at the max [maximum security] end. They get more attention here. They've got ten officers for sixty guys. Down there [in the general prison population] there's one officer for forty-five guys. It's filthy. Stuff all over the walls."

The conversation is interrupted by more phone calls. Visitors to be escorted. A three-man disciplinary board to be brought into the block. Appointment requests from social workers, medical personnel.

After each conversation, Carvalho makes notations in the log book or on a separate schedule he keeps for visits and appointments. Ring, Ring, Ring.

Carvalho laughs. "Yeah, my wife says: 'how come you never answer the phone when you're home.' "

An officer returns from the second floor and reports one man thinks he's willing to make the move to another block.

"Great, O.K., O.K. Get him out of here now before he changes his mind."

Moments later the inmate's replacement is led into the block, handcuffed and chained. He is searched before he is lead into his cell. An officer reaches into the prisoner's pocket and gingerly pulls out a broken half of razor blade.

"This guy shouldn't even be here," he says, shaking his head. "They should keep him in Bridgewater. He's just goin' to flip out again."

Carvalho is on the phone again.

"Good. We're not going to get him. Fine."

Carvalho reports to the junior officers that a second inmate scheduled for Ten Block just cut himself while he was in the hospital. "They've got blood all over the floor over there. They've got him in a hospital security room."

WHY THIS JOB?

The pressure is momentarily off. Carvalho lights another cigarette and tilts back in his chair.

Why did you become a correctional officer?, he is asked.

"One word, Security. That's what I was looking for. Not in two years, five years, but overall. In twenty years when you were ready to retire. The benefits are there. The job has its bad points and its good points."

What are those good points? What do you get out of this job besides security?

"Well, I try to accomplish something . . . personal satisfaction. If I've done somethin' to help 'em. Me, I can go home and use the phone, watch TV, go out to my neighbor's house, buy a drink if I want to . . . these guys can't. Their only line of communication is through me. So if they want to use the phone I'll say, 'I'll see what I can do.' "

"It's somethin' like that that makes you feel good — that would be the word for it. Especially when a guy is having trouble. His wife hasn't written him or come up to see him and you let him make a phone call and he goes back and he thanks you. Things are cooled down.

"You can't do it to them all because some of them don't even let you get near 'em. They're just cold. You don't make waves there either. You don't go out of your way to gaff this guy or stick him. Hey, you can't. It's impossible to go in there with that attitude. You're not going to last. I don't care if it's Ten Block or the rest of the institution. You're not going to last. Because one of 'em will definitely get you. A pipe, a knife or somethin' like that, but they'll definitely get you. Or if they don't do it that way, they'll make it miserable for you.

"Even though they're the toughest, hey, they're human beings, you know. I don't care what they did. Well, I shouldn't say that because we know what they did on the outside or what they did to other corrections officers, but when he comes into

Ten Block I'm not going to mess with a guy's meal or throw letters away. You've got to communicate. These guys are livin' with you. It's going to be an easy day or it's going to be a tough day.

The noon food wagon arrives and the officers dish out the meal onto the paper trays. After the inmates are served, the officers grab a tray and bring it into the office, a few at a time. Some have brought their lunch and eat it piecemeal between running upstairs or into the cell corridors. Elsewhere in the prison, most corrections officers eat in the staff mess hall. In Ten Block, there is no formal sit-down dining.

Carvalho, between bites, dials the phone again. "Yeah, Rus. . . . He's back in Block three. Yeah, he's back. My count is fifty-eight." The count of inmates is reported to control at the beginning of the shift, at noon or whenever any inmate leaves or returns to Ten Block.

The frequently interrupted lunch break conversation is devoted to shop talk. It is the small talk of infantry GI's dissecting the foibles of the higher echelons back at division headquarters.

"If the people out front who make up the rules had to come in here and enforce them, they'd never make them up. . . ."

". . . Yeah, they ought to have an officer out there with 'em when they make up those damn things. . . ."

"Yah, yah, yah, but then they'd pick some guy who never worked in population . . . you want to bet on it . . . that's what they'd do. . . ."

"If you run this institution by the book they give you you'd have a riot. You can't do it. It's impossible. Hey, they tell you a guy can't go to another tier to see another guy even if that guy's his brother."

A young officer comes in and hands Carvalho another packet of brown envelopes. Medication. Second distribution. Carvalho registers them in the log.

The log book is something of a barometer for the shift. It records the traffic like a counter at a busy intersection. And it offers some distinctions between the shifts.

The preceding 3 PM to 11 PM shift had seven entries for its entire eight-hour segment. The 11 PM to 7 AM shift showed three entries. By noon, Carvalho had written twenty-one separate items into his log.

"Hey, Phil," an officer says. "Listen, I can't get that canteen order. They say they just aren't going to fill it for him." The dispute is over how much credit an inmate has at the canteen. Carvalho's hands move back to the phone.

"Yeah, Phil Carvalho. Look, on that canteen order, . . . do me a favor . . . I know, I know. But I need it. Yeah, I do . . . do me a favor . . . I'll be down to get it . . . you're doin' a great job . . . a great job."

Carvalho tells one of the officers to unlock the double doors to Ten Block and let him out. He makes his way down through a series of corridors and cell blocks until he comes to the canteen. The officer in charge makes it clear he has no particular love for the inmate whose order hasn't been filled.

Carvalho's litany of praise begins again as he grabs a paper sack and starts filling the order himself. The inmate's canteen ticket is punched for the items and Carvalho reaches for four lollypops and throws them in the bag. "That's his change, right? Thanks, sweetheart, you're doing a great job . . . a great job."

"So I get the order myself. So? What the hell, it takes five minutes to get down there. You bring it back. You keep him happy and he thinks he beat you. Right? That's his job. To beat me. But I know better. He went into his room [cell] and he was happy. And it avoided a lot more b.s. Because with this guy, there would have been trouble. I know. I know him from the past."

The clock on the office wall ticks the shift slowly to an end.

Carvalho leaves a little early to attend the "front office" meeting with the administration and the officer of the incoming shift about whom the inmates complained. The decision: Keep him at his post.

Fifty minutes and twenty-seven traffic-congested miles later, Carvalho is back in his private world on the outer fringes of suburbia. He is greeted by his wife and his fourteen-year-old daughter, Cheryl. A miniature poodle and a tiny Yorkshire terrier come bounding across the lawn as the advance contingent of the welcome. Supper is on the table a half-hour later.

The small talk is about an afternoon shopping trip in search of parochial school uniforms for Cheryl. There is no small talk about Ten Block.

"He doesn't talk about the job," his wife, Shirley, says. "He tells his father about the job and his father tells his mother and she tells me some things. That's how I get information about the prison. If he comes home and he's in a good mood, I'll know he had a fine day. If he comes home a little bit aggravated, then I know he had a bad day and I'll just go about my business.

"But I worry about him all the time. The last time there was a riot it was on the late news. I didn't know a thing about it. I was lying on the couch, watching the news, and that came on in a big way. I thought I'd die. I tried calling the prison but all the lines were tied up. He finally called me about an hour after and said that he would be home early in the morning. But, oh, my God. Who could sleep?"

When Shirley is out of earshot, Carvalho acknowledges her worrying. "I know it affects my wife. I'll tell her, 'I'm not going in today.' and she'll say, 'Oh, good, good. Call in sick.' And then I tell her I'm only kidding. And I trudge in there. But I must like it because I keep goin' back."

"It has its good days and its bad. Today, was a good day," he says.

The plexiglass protective shield remained unused. No inmate had refused to return to his cell. None of the young officers had urine or excrement thrown at them. The fire extinguishers remained in their places.

Shirley nods in agreement. Today, Phil Carvalho came home in a good mood.

Chapter 6

PRISON GUARD CONCEPTIONS

G. L. WEBB AND DAVID G. MORRIS

THEMSELVES

IT is not unusual to hear a first-time visitor to Mid-State Penitentiary comment, "Why, it's like a little city in here." Within this minature community, as one guard stated, "the guards are the police force." The identification with police roles is such that many of the guards are active members of police organizations. The image of guards as policemen is also conveyed by the inmates in whose specialized language guards are referred to as "the police," "the man," and "pigs," just as are policemen in major cities throughout the United States. In fact, the term police is used quite regularly by inmates at Mid-State when referring to guards.

The management of guards, as with police officers, is regulated in a military manner. Guards wear uniforms, follow orders, relieve one another at assigned "posts," practice on firing ranges, place people "on report," may be promoted to sergeant, lieutenant, captain, or major and in earlier times even saluted guards and officials of "superior rank."

Key concepts in this para-militaristic culture are the terms "security" and "discipline." Maintaining security is the guards' function, as seen by the guards. They view the prison as a place that serves to protect their communities by confining lawless and oftentimes dangerous men, and they see themselves as "the back-bone" of the institution — the ones who see that the day-to-day operations of the prison are carried out.

Security is viewed as the end result of their roles, the means to that end is expressed as "discipline." Guards frequently comment on "the need for discipline."

From G. L. Webb and David G. Morris, *Prison Guards: The Culture and Perspective of an Occupational Group*, 1978. Courtesy of Coker Books, Austin, Texas and the authors.

"We all need rules and regulations."

"If these men had had discipline, they would't be here today."

"Strict discipline is good for them."

Despite the above quotes, rigidity is disvalued, guards are quick to point out "you can't go strictly by the book," "rules are made to be broken." They argue that one must take a common-sense approach in "enforcing discipline."

"None of the rules are enforced all the time, I guess," a lieutenant with considerable experience confided. "They have to be ignored at times. Rules aren't absolutes."

In an institution such as Mid-State, there is an absence of informal communication between those who establish procedures and those who carry them out. Thus, administrative regulations are subject to interpretation. And, it is in this area of interpretation that the guard draws his power. He decides whether a disciplinary report is required or if an incident can be handled "by other available means." The administrative regulations, as pointed out by one of our respondents, contain an abundance of ambiguous phraseology, e.g. "minimum force" and "normal conditions."

For the past few years, there has been considerable pressure for changes in the management of correctional institutions, and to the guards what appears as an atmosphere of constant change provides even greater room for circumvention of policy. It is not uncommon to hear guards complain about the labyrinth of prison rules. Written rules are not viewed as the ultimate authority to check when the correct or official procedure is not known. In such cases, fellow guards or those of superior rank are consulted.

The guards believe that through their work experience and daily interaction with inmates they have a better understanding of inmates than do "dumb-ass experts in cozy offices who wouldn't know an inmate if one fell through the ceiling." As is reflected by the quoted comment, guards tend to be adamant about their self-perceived superior understanding of inmates.

Which rules are strictly enforced and which aren't? "Each guard interprets the rules a little different. I even interpret the rules differently on different days," one guard commented. The following comment from a guard provides some insight:

> I've met some inmates who will actually help you. If you're on a job where you don't know what the hell you're doing, they'll tell you what has to be done, even who to watch out for. They know what kind of officer you are. They'll try to keep you straight. If they have a good job, they don't want a lot of heat, so they aren't going to let you get things messed up. Oh sure they do some conniving. What the heck. I would too.

This guard is expressing a belief shared by many guards that bartering or trading among inmates is not a serious breach of discipline.

In this regard, the first author (while in guard training, dressed as a guard) was assigned to escort approximately forty inmates to the commissary.[1] Since currency is not allowed, all transactions at the commissary are conducted by ledger.[2] Therefore, it is impossible for a guard to purchase a soft drink at the commissary.

Noticing the absence of money, but experiencing some thirst, the first author asked an experienced guard about the procedure necessary to acquire a soft drink. The guard simply walked to the commissary counter and spoke with an "inmate commissary employee;" seconds later the inmate handed the guard two Cokes®. The guard returned and as we stood drinking our Cokes, he explained that it was impossible to pay for them but that he would do the inmate a favor someday like fixing a ticket.[3] That is to say he would "fix" the ticket in the same sense that a police officer would fix a traffic ticket.

Many guards feel that gambling is not a serious breach of discipline. Some even feel that an inmate who is guilty of being intoxicated has not committed a serious breach of discipline. In fact, during the first author's guard experience, an experienced

---

[1]The term commissary at Mid-State Penitentiary refers to the store, i.e. a retail establishment where goods such as food stuffs (ice cream, soda, potato chips, etc.) and toilet articles (hair dressing, deodorant, combs, etc.) are purchased by inmates.

[2]A record of all money transactions is kept including credits and debits. Inmates are not allowed to make a purchase unless they have enough money on the ledger to pay for the items they select. The amount of their purchase is deducted from their balance.

[3]The term "ticket" at Mid-State refers to disciplinary reports written on inmates by guards for violating prison rules. The term has probably evolved in part because the disciplinary report forms are small (approximately twice the size of a pack of cigarettes) and resemble "traffic tickets."

guard commented that a certain inmate was "alright" because he caught an inmate fellating this inmate's penis and the inmate referred to as "alright" (the recipient of the act) later thanked him for not reporting the incident. Generally considered as the more serious inmate offenses are physically assaulting or threatening a guard, impudence or disrespect toward a guard, or refusing to work or to comply with an order.

Regulations governing inmate behavior are not the only regulations subject to circumvention by the guards. Some guards fail to follow rules governing their own conduct. Most guards tell that they would not traffic with inmates and deplore the fact that others do. But, it seems highly probable that because of their loyalty to one another they would be most reluctant to inform on a "fellow guard."

A stereotypical image of the prison guard is seen by them as unrealistic and serves to intensify their perspectives and conceptions of themselves as protectors of an unappreciative society. The stereotyped image of a prison guard as brutal and sadistic particularly irritates them. Guards are quick to point out that they did not take their positions because of a desire to fulfill such a role.[4] Rather most guards tell that they took their jobs because it was the best available in the area, the highest paying job available, or because it was steady work, not subject to the layoffs they had experienced elsewhere.

"I did it (accepted a guard position) with the full intent of finding something else as soon as possible," one guard, who started in 1963, stated. Another guard accepted his position ten months ago with apparently a similar attitude. He says he plans to obtain employment at a coal mine in the near future.

Most guards indicated what they liked most about their jobs was being able to remain in the rural area where the prison is

---

[4]In fact, anyone familiar with the restrictions placed upon guards at Mid-State would hardly suspect them of brutality or sadism. Guards are not allowed to carry saps, sticks, or even penknives. A weapon of any kind is not allowed. The only armed guards are in the gun towers. Guards at Mid-State are not even allowed to carry mace. Guards are armed only with a pen or pencil to record the number of an inmate who misbehaves. In essence, a guard is helpless in larger part if attacked by an inmate. He has only his bare hands and the help of fellow unarmed guards as a defense, with the exception of assaults occurring near gun towers. Needless to say guards are assaulted with some regularity.

located or the companionship of their fellow guards. They dislike the lack of advancement opportunities, the perceived role played by "politics," the constant pressure for change, the physical conditions of the institution, and above all else, recent administrations, which have been viewed as lacking experience or insight, prone to coddle inmates, and "out to get us" ("us" referring to guards).

There is discontent over being assigned on manhunts when an inmate escapes, but this has been relieved somewhat by the recently implemented policy of paying overtime to participants. Surprisingly, the seemingly monotonous tasks of supervising line movements, the perpetual locking and unlocking of doors, and the constant watching of inmates elicits very little complaining. However, most guards do express a decided preference for working on the group as opposed to working in a gun tower. Interestingly, guards assigned to tower duty generally have less status among the guards.

SOCIAL SERVICES PERSONNEL

The world of the custodial officer is of course not limited to guards and inmates. Many employees fill noncustodial roles, including: psychiatrists, doctors, sociologists, psychologists, counselors, chaplains, teachers, vocational instructors, nurses, dieticians, secretaries, and clerks.

At Mid-State, all employees are divided into two groups; one is said to work in either security or in treatment. The guards are thought of as the security staff and play the more dominant role in the institution. Although the first employee to be designated as a counselor was not hired until 1970, nonuniformed personnel are generally thought of by older guards as counselors, no matter what their position might be.

The treatment and security categories are treated as somehow divorced from one another. A strong belief exists throughout the institution that these categories are incompatible, even detrimental, each to the efforts of the other. They are separate but unequal. The second author remembers one of the wardens telling a group of counselors to stay away from the guards. "You have your job to do, and they have theirs," he said.

In April of 1973, inmates seized control of the commissary and took a guard hostage. A local newspaper ran a related story on May 3, 1973 (Sec. 1, p. 1), citing "... a high degree of unrest among the inmates at (Mid-State) for several months, according to security officers." This story continued: "The atmosphere in the prison stems from coddling the prisoner, inmate counselors who have become in fact inmate advocates in almost every disciplinary action by the security force, and an overemphasis on social and educational programs within the prison."

How representative of the guard force was the phrase, "according to security officers?" We can never know for certain. Most of the guards with whom we discussed nonguards, expressed the belief that counselling and educational services are needed and that those persons assigned these roles are for the most part "alright," which is the ultimate respect afforded a "treatment employee." But of course, due to our status as "treatment employees" their remarks are necessarily subject to propriety, as well as to honesty. Indeed, many guards speak disdainfully of "counselors" and graciously exclude the authors of this paper. Most guards, while indicating that rehabilitative programs are necessary, indicate that they believe they are ineffective because they are "overloaded." Some guards seem to possess considerable insight into the goals, functions, and problems of social service personnel, while others seem to have little, if any, idea of why such employees are even in the prison.

. "I think the programs here are crap. Very few enable the inmate to get a job on the street. The programs right now serve as recreational periods to get the men out of their cells and keep them busy. If the programs are not stiff and worthwhile, they're a waste of time," one guard commented.

Because of the two-staff approach, most guards and most nonguards aren't too familiar with one another. Also, as conveyed by the two-staff concept, most guards see their jobs as unrelated to the rehabilitative process. However, most also see their jobs as more utilitarian than those of the nonguards.

Guards frequently express the belief that they are by the nature of their roles tougher than "counselors" (who are viewed as permissive) and therefore better able to relate to inmates. Several guards noted that in the past, guards were required to do many of the things presently handled by counselors, and they indicate a measure of resentment because of this.

In conclusion, gaining acceptance by the guards is the responsibility of the nonguard employee, for he is the newcomer to the microcosmic world within the prison walls. He becomes "alright" with the guards first by getting to know them. No matter how much he might be like the guards philosophically, they will regard him as an outsider if they do not know him. Then, of course, he must reflect an attitude of sympathetic support for them, value discipline, and naturally, become "conwise."

ADMINISTRATORS

"The administrators are drunk with power. Their idea is to have us do whatever they say. We have no input; we can't relate to them. They radiate the idea that they're a controlling force. I don't like the feeling of so much power over my head." These comments made recently by an experienced guard express the sense of fear conveyed by many others.

Though subject to superiors in a hierarchy, a prison warden does in fact have at his command discretionary use of dictatorial powers in administering his institution that are similar to the authority of the captain of a sea-going vessel. It is this aura of absolute authority that creates an atmosphere of fear, as exemplified by the guard who stated, "They seem to be out to get everyone. After thirty-four years, I find myself worrying about holding onto my job."

Wardens are generally viewed as outsiders. At Mid-State they are not subject to civil service requirements, as are their counterparts in federal prisons; and, wardens have traditionally been appointed on the basis of political patronage.

The view of the warden as an outsider is especially true in the case of recent wardens. Recent wardens have had little prior experience in prison work. Key administrative posts have been assigned to the warden's associates, further alienating the staff, who not only see these administrators as outsiders but as "Johnny Come Latelies." Guards and nonguards alike feel "stalemated" in terms of advancement and it is generally felt that promotion is dependent on one's political contacts.

Most guards say that they believe administrators should work their way up and be subject to civil service requirements that emphasize experience. They favor "a prison man," as they put it. The last warden at Mid-State considered to be a "prison man" was replaced in 1973. He began as a guard approximately thirty years before, was stabbed and nearly died trying to quell a riot, and worked his way up the promotional ladder. He was eventually named assistant warden and then acting warden upon the resignation of his predecessor. He served as warden for approximately six months.

The guards greatly admired this man. "He was the best. The guards would do anything for him. The inmates respected him, too."[5] There is general agreement that it will take someone like him to "put the place back together again."

Of course, the warden is not the whole administration, and the guards understand this. "It's run by remote control. Somebody in the capital says to do this, and it's relayed to us."

The "somebodies" in the state capital are viewed as unknowledgeable about prisons in general and about Mid-State in particular. The guards witness "a trial and error approach" and become frustrated. But mostly, the guards see the administration as politically motivated. As one guard commented, "They all use statistics to make themselves look good." Guards see the purchase of expensive office machinery as political graff and question the rationale for such purchases in view of existing shortages of foodstuffs and toilet paper. Rumors of "tapped" telephones and suppressed information are rampant.

In short, guards see prison administrators at all levels as outsiders with political connections and arbitrary power determined to "look good." They lack the guards' knowledge of the institution and its population. They are viewed as a necessary evil; something that in good times may support them and in bad times will blame them when things go wrong. "When some dumb-ass expert dreams up a new theory, we're the ones

---

[5]Interestingly, the inmates also respected this man a great deal as evidenced by literally hundreds of unsolicited comments offered by approximately 2,000 inmates the authors of this paper have interviewed during the past five years.

who have to try it out. And, if it backfires, it's a guard that gets
hurt. Then these bastards in their plush offices in — — — [6] or
up in front of the double gate (reference to the wardens) sit
back and defend their stupid theories and place the blame
for their failures on us overreacting guards." And, in the
guards' final analysis of the administrators, "They all come
and go."

INMATES

There is, of course, no such thing as an average inmate, nor
is there such a thing as an average conception of inmates. Each
guard brings to his encounters within the walls a world view
that is uniquely his own, but due to the commonality of their
relationships with one another and with the other people
present in the institution, their views tend to become rather
uniform in many areas.

This uniformity of perception becomes most splintered in
the areas of what inmates are like. While there may be a consensus that inmates are evil, there is no consensus on how or
why they are evil or to what extent they are evil. A guard asked
to tell what inmates are like is going to predicate his answer to
a great degree on his personal knowledge of inmates, what he
has heard others say about inmates, his ability or inability to
get along with people in general, and, of course, on his most
recent dealings with inmates.

Guard's views of inmates may be seen as resting between two
hypothetical poles; at one extreme would be the concept that
inmates are just like the guards. On the other extreme would be
the concept that inmates are the exact opposite of guards.
"I'd say 80 percent are no different personality-wise than the
people you meet on the street. Moral-wise, they're different."

"Inmates aren't like anybody else. That's bunk. They're different. No doubt about it. Their feelings of right and wrong are
different than most people's."

The comments above reflect the disparity between two
guards' views, and yet an area of consensus.

----

[6]The name of the State Capitol has been deleted.

Some guards indicate that they dislike inmates and manifest a critical attitude:

"Most (inmates) don't take too much pride in their personal appearance."

"These guys are like kids, always butting into someone else's business."

"They think they're better than everybody else."

Some guards indicate that they like inmates and manifest a tolerant attitude:

"There's some decent ones down there. The majority just want to do their time and get the hell out."

"Out of 2,000 people, you're bound to find some you like. I like the way some of them are very outgoing and uninhibited."

"Just because they're inmates doesn't keep me from liking them as people. Some people on the outside I like; some I don't. It's the same with inmates."

How do you make friends with inmates if you are their keeper? "How do you make friends with people you meet anywhere?", one guard answered. He pointed out that in time, you come to see the inmates as people, rather than "oddities." Remember how when you first started you automatically wondered, whenever you had any dealings with an inmate, what's he in for? And, then eventually you just don't wonder about it anymore."

It seems probable that the opposite effect also occurs with the passage of time, i.e. a dehumanization process going from a view of inmates as people to a view of them as work, cases, or numbers. This process may be viewed as a natural outgrowth of becoming "con-wise." A young experienced guard commented, "I guess I was like everybody else. My heart bled for them when I first started at the prison. Gradually, you feel less sorry for them and more like they're responsible for their being here."

The relationship between guards and inmates is peculiarly intimate. When interacting with inmates, guards are bound to have favorites, no matter how diligently they might try not to. This is not a condemnation, but a fact common to all interpersonal relationships. Coaches have favorite athletes, teachers have favorite students, parents even have favorite children. And, in prison, this type of relationship is labeled as a father-son situation. "He's his kid"[7] is said about an obvious favorite inmate of any given guard. Similarly it might be said that the guard is the kid's "dad," or "daddy."[8] The term "kid," "dad," "daddy," and the like, used in this fashion imply no disrespect, unless applied to a proinmate guard.

One important factor involved in the guard's view of inmates, which shall be discussed at greater length in the next section, is their fear of them. When asked what he disliked most about inmates, one guard answered, "The fact that they can smile at you and stab you in the back." This statement is very representative of a guard's fear in that it may be viewed as a metaphor (as is the most common usage of the phrase by guards) or it may be used literally. In a literal sense, many guards are afraid of inmates and are very concerned with their safety. In a figurative sense, many guards fear "being stabbed in the back," i.e. duped or in some way made to look poorly before other guards or the administration.

In describing what inmates are like, some guards allude to what may be termed peer pressure among inmates.

"I don't like the general idea that they have to be sneaky about everything. Most of them take pride in the fact that they were able to obtain some trinkets by illegal means. And, it's catching. If they didn't do it when they first came here, eventually they get around to it."

"I've never found one that was really honest, because he is playing a game. And, he's going to play this game as long as he's inside the institution because they all do." The majority of the guards at Mid-State appear to reflect what might be termed a fundamentally pragmatic conception of inmates. Inmates are regarded as individuals who may or may not be likeable but who are almost without exception untrustworthy.

"Understanding that some thieving, conniving son of a bitch

---

[7]In this sense, the word "kid" has no sexual overtones. However, when it is said that one inmate is another's "kid" the word "kid" does have explicit sexual overtones. Such usage generally refers to a young inmate who is cared for and protected by an older inmate. In exchange, the young inmate "services" the older inmate, i.e. he allows himself to be sodomized and/or fellates the older inmates's penis on a regular basis.
[8]In this sense, the word "dad" or in more common usage, the word "daddy" has no sexual overtones. However, when the term "daddy" is applied to an inmate it refers to the fact that he has a "kid" (a young inmate who services him sexually).

behaves the way he does because he's black and his mother was a whore and he never knew his father and he had to steal to eat — understanding that — is important, but it don't alter the fact the son of a bitch is still a son of a bitch."

Chapter 7

SCREWS VS. THUGS

Anthony L. Guenther and Mary Quinn Guenther

> Almost everyone agrees that something has
> to be done about [convicts]. The question
> concerns what is done, who does it, and the
> nature of the mandate given by the rest of us
> to those who do it. Perhaps we give them an
> unconscious mandate to go beyond anything
> we ourselves would care to do or even to
> acknowledge.
>
> Everett C. Hughes

ACCORDING to Everett Hughes's thesis, once we have dissociated ourselves from the people for whom prisons are designed and have declared them a problem, the next logical step is to let someone else do the dirty work which we would be unwilling to do ourselves. But even when the work of confining prisoners is delegated to specialized functionaries, questions have been raised in a variety of quarters about the effectiveness with which prisons accomplish their objectives. The conventional indictments of prisons attack overcrowding, antiquated facilities, personnel turnover, budgetary limitations and public apathy. Other observers have noted that penitentiaries fail because they must contend with all the shortcomings and malfunctions of prior stages in the criminal justice system. What most critics have overlooked as a major source of prison failure is the set of obstacles faced by correctional officers.

While it is true that numerous treatment activities have recently been introduced within walls, e.g. drug abuse, legal assistance and correctional counselor programs, the most du-

Published by permission of Transaction, Inc., from SOCIETY, Vol. II, No. 5. Copyright© 1974 by Transaction, Inc.

rable and intensive relationships experienced by prisoners are with line correctional officers, an increasingly popular synonym for "guard." The task of creating an atmosphere conducive to prisoner change is, in effect, relegated to these officers, who are ill-equipped and poorly motivated to perform such a duty. The everyday operations of correctional work such as locking grills, making counts, supervising work crews and delivering mail work against prolonged contact between captors and their captives. The presumption that correctional staff have extensive and potentially therapeutic interaction with prisoners, when in fact they don't, may well be an important source of strain in the officer's role. But the most complex and subtle process which can undermine correctional objectives is created by an institutional atmosphere of uncertainty and precariousness.

To study the role of the correctional officer and his perception of both the objectives and realities of his job, data were obtained by the senior author as part of research on custodial staff made over a half-year period at the U.S. Penitentiary in Atlanta, Georgia. Daily contact with officers on all shifts and job assignments as varied as tower duty, the dining hall, the cellhouses, segregation (solitary confinement) and the control center provided opportunity for hundreds of informal interviews. Moreover, all written documents from "jackets" (dossiers) on inmates, records of "incidents" involving theft, assault, escape, etc., to a running log of occurrences during each shift were made available. Supervisors (lieutenants), who were the actual heads of operations for each shift, participated fully in rating all correctional officers on the criteria of technical competence, stability under stress, and effectiveness in dealing with inmates. Additional data were secured through lengthy questionnaires returned by three-fourths of the custodial staff.

Complementary data, volunteered by scores of inmates, gave additional insight into the role of correctional officer. Over a dozen prisoners were known to the investigator from another federal penitentiary in past years, and their provision of contacts with the inmate population was indispensable. In combination, these multiple sources of data provided a dynamic assessment of officer-inmate interaction.

The Atlanta Penitentiary is classed as a maximum-security federal facility, and was built seventy years ago as a sister institution to Leavenworth. Some 2,200 men are incarcerated there within the twenty-eight acres enclosed by a wall ("security perimeter") whose height varies between thirty-two and forty feet. About 170 correctional officers, civil-service employees at levels of GS-7 and GS-8, comprise the basic custodial staff. This is supplemented by eleven lieutenants, a captain and an associate warden. A parallel but much smaller "treatment" staff including caseworkers, correctional counselors, medical personnel and clergymen handles noncustodial functions.

For inmates, doing time at Atlanta is roughly similar to serving a sentence at any large, older prison. If anything, federal institutions, including this one, reflect the few advances identifiable in American corrections. For example, legal aid is readily accessible, visitation facilities are open and unmonitored and even subscriptions to *Playboy* are permitted. By inmate reckoning, doing a "bit" under federal auspices is less dehumanizing than almost anywhere else. Nevertheless, prisoners who "pull" time here can expect denigrating conditions of psychological separation, lack of privacy, unchallenging jobs, potential danger and routinization. Being referred to by correctional officers as "thugs," "thieves" or "convicts" reinforces the notion that prisoners, with few exceptions, should expect a full allocation of indignities conferred upon them by conviction and incarceration.

In many ways, correctional officers "pull" time as well, for their occupation lacks many of the socially rewarding sources of job satisfaction. Officers find that there are relatively few ways to distinguish themselves, and that many job assignments are sheer tedium. Moreover, their occupational self-images hardly benefit from public conceptions of the kind of person who would work in a prison. Within the walls derisive references to officers by inmates as "screws," "hacks" or "cops" are vivid and explicit forms of contempt. Advancement, many officers feel, does not necessarily occur through merit, and the consequences of an error or misjudgment may disqualify them for promotion. The seriousness of committing error is compounded by the uncertainty inherent in prison work; for, at the operational level, it is impossible to predict the behavior of 2,200 men in captive circumstances. Many of the dilemmas encountered by prison correctional officers originate from these unpredictable conditions whose sources and responses are the foci of this study.

SOURCES OF UNCERTAINTY

Outsiders are often surprised and occasionally alarmed to discover that the penitentiary is continually in a state of change. Public stereotypes of the prison as a closed community or total institution convey the image of regimentation, order and control to the extent that any publicized departures from this image suggest incompetence or political corruption. The incidents at Attica, San Quentin and elsewhere in the last three years, for example, invited questions such as: "Why did the guards let the prisoners take over?" and "Have rehabilitative programs for inmates been the victims of legislative apathy?" Officers themselves are acutely sensitive to changes they see taking place on the corrections scene, few of which, from their perspective, are welcome. They cite new challenges such as the reduction in control, and increase in inmate aggressiveness, the incidence of court-ordered policy changes and the new-style inmate (black, inner-city bred, politically aware, articulate and doing "lots of time") as particularly troublesome.

In addition to these recent threats to traditional correctional work, there have always been so many potential sources of incidents in prison that administrators invest a significant portion of custodial manpower in preventive strategies, the objective of which is to anticipate and forestall crises. A lieutenant stated a popular view when he said, "It's hard to believe that we don't get more trouble than we do around here. When you think about how much time these guys are doing and how little experience custodial [officers] have, it scares you half to death." A January 1971 staff report sent to the Bureau of Prisons was more explicit in describing the conditions at Atlanta which confound smooth functioning:

> Conditions at Atlanta would seem to indicate many problems resistant to solution. These are (1) enormous size of the insti-

tution, (2) large inmate population, (3) inmate housing facilities which are antiquated, overcrowded, and present substantial control problems, (4) other physical facilities which are outdated, obsolete, or present unusual supervisory problems, (5) difficulties in providing supervision for many operations because of open-door, freedom-of-movement policies, and (6) a large industry operation which runs at night and on weekends [in addition to the daytime].

A crisis or incident in the penitentiary usually has far greater repercussions than an equivalent episode in the outside community. Broadly defined, "incidents" refer to security breaches, personal endangerment, wide-scale disruption of schedules or destruction of property. Their proportions are magnified by the enforced density of men under physical coercion and by the danger posed by some inmates, if freed, to the staff and the community at large.

Conventional advice passed on to new trainees by experienced officers includes pithy references to incidents forestalled (a fracas in the dining hall that "could have turned into a real 'shit-storm'"), as well as to events which occurred despite the best countermeasures available ("We had information that drugs were coming in but the officers shaking down didn't find them"). From the perspective of both staff and inmates, the atmosphere of antagonism, conflict and compression creates incidents which often defy prediction yet require intervention before getting beyond control.

Data obtained at the Atlanta Penitentiary suggest that only a very small proportion of the 2,200 men imprisoned there may be affected by an incident, yet if the crisis is potentially threatening to strained relationships, it must have prompt attention. If, for example, racial animosities have been running high, an incident involving only one or two blacks and a like number of whites may compel large numbers of inmates to choose sides along racial lines. Uncertainty, then, affects correctional work more than many other occupations, for the artificial role relationships of captives and captors, the aggregate of their physical coexistence and an atmosphere of intensified emotions produce a unique organizational climate. The capacity to reduce uncertainty through accurate predictions is highly desirable in corrections work. Yet there is so much behavioral spontaneity within the prison, often precipitated by outside influences, that only estimates of day-to-day occurrences are possible.

The interaction between custodial staff and inmates is affected, generally speaking, by four sources of unpredictability, all of which require compensatory efforts. These are (1) malfunctions of plant or equipment, (2) problems originating among employees, (3) problems created by inmates, and (4) difficulties produced by the free community.

The first source of unpredictable occurrences in the prison is a failure of plant or equipment, whether resulting from sabotage, natural deterioration or poor maintenance. A utility breakdown in large cellblocks or dormitories, for example, may necessitate the relocation of large numbers of inmates. Similarly, a disruption in food preparation or service, as can be seen in the following case, may cause an alteration of feeding schedules for the entire institution:

> *July 3, 1972.* Complaints by a number of inmates on "short line" (a work crew eating lunch before the "main line") about "spoiled chicken" were quickly investigated by the staff. Although they thought the "strange taste" was caused by over-seasoning, and most inmates showed no ill effects, the Warden ordered that the chicken be removed. Food service personnel had less than a half hour to prepare and serve hot dogs as a substitute meat, rather than risk a dining hall incident.

From a custodial standpoint, serious malfunctions which affect large numbers of inmates demand immediate and decisive remedies, though they may involve curtailment of other activities. Not only are inmates likely to be impatient with departures from institutional routine, but some may seize the chance to implement a personal plan. A power failure, for example, may provide an escape-minded inmate with a long-awaited opportunity to "hit the wall" when guard towers are incapacitated.

There is evidence that malfunctions of equipment and mechanical or electrical services are unusually frequent in older U.S. prisons, and these, like Atlanta, often house the most recalcitrant, long-term offenders. Thus it is not surprising that in a large, complex prison, the most conscientious surveillance cannot prevent tools from disappearing, equipment from being sabotaged and existing utility systems from being disrupted. Experienced officers automatically suspect, first, that the breakdown is intended, and second, that it may be a ploy to divert attention from an escape attempt, assault or other nefarious activity. If, by community standards, correctional officers appear cynical in this respect, it is because their experience in penitentiary work does not suggest that prisoners can be trusted or will act in a conventional manner.

A second set of problems leading to unpredictability in prison work is attributable to the employees themselves. Inmates are made so dependent upon correctional staff for the timing, sequence and direction of events that attrition of personnel on a shift cannot be tolerated. Not only would key positions go unmanned, thus compromising security, but also large numbers of confused prisoners may have no guidance. Thus, there can be such serious consequences of a cellhouse officer disabled by a bleeding ulcer, a tower officer suffering a coronary attack or an employee "flipping out" in reaction to prolonged stress that immediate adjustments are required. The importance of staffing the various shifts in a penitentiary schedule is so critical that tardiness is unacceptable, and there is a permanent position on the custodial roster to cover the jobs of officers who may succumb to illness.

But a unique feature of prison work is its inability to allow the standard indiscretions permitted in most other occupational careers. Correctional officers who overextend themselves financially, have marital difficulties or drink to excess not only raise doubts concerning their commitment to the job; they may also be regarded as undependable. As can be seen in the following memorandum, indiscrete behavior, in turn, often means that an injudicious officer can be compromised by an enterprising inmate. (In this and other memos cited here, fictitious identities are given to staff and inmates.)

> *March 6, 1972.* We became aware that Mr. Sender, a correctional officer trainee, had introduced contraband into the institution for financial gain. He has given a signed affidavit to the F.B.I. admitting he received a package, believed to have

contained marijuana, from Beverly Phillipson, the wife of inmate Phillipson 29623. He delivered this package to inmate Woodruff 62472 inside the institution. [Prosecution resulted in a two-year prison sentence for Mr. Sender, the employee, and a sentence of one year's probation for the inmate's wife.]

Observations made of probationary correctional trainees suggested that the most important judgment experienced personnel make is whether or not a new man is reliable. Training sessions for probationary officers emphasize through analysis of past episodes the ways in which personnel often have to assume absolute dependence upon each other. In contrast to many other occupations which require "team efforts," correctional staff working the yard or cellblock must be positive that they have backing when dealing with an explosive situation. The assumption is tacitly made, then, that a new officer is dependable until he proves otherwise, an arrangement which is not very satisfactory because it may be years before one sees his colleagues under acute stress. Having to make the assumption of reliability is discomforting to some officers, particularly if subjective impressions gleaned from verbal, behavioral or biographical evidence discredit that assumption. As a custodial officer with eight years' experience put it:

> I wouldn't give you a plugged nickel for several officers here. You know who I mean; just look at some of the jobs they have to give 'em so they don't get in trouble. When it really begins to hit the fan around here, they're the ones who'll be hiding out.

This kind of speculative comment, based upon the most tenuous impressions, becomes persuasive when it receives interpersonal validation. Thus one of the functions of assembly-room gossip just before a shift begins is to compare hearsay about peer officers. For an officer to be defined as unreliable by his colleagues is highly discrediting and becomes a virtually ineradicable stigma.

Field observations indicated that a third source of unpredictability is deliberate action or inaction by inmates, by far the most frustrating to custodial staff. A lieutenant close to retirement commented.

> The toughest part of this job is the anticipation that goes

with each watch. You're constantly under stress because you don't know what will happen, much less what you can do about it until it breaks. No one can remain alert, month after month, year after year, to all the things that can go wrong in this old place.

An officer reporting for duty in most penitentiaries is unlikely to be briefed about the activities of the previous two shifts, and he may even have recently been sick or have had a period of annual leave. Only in exceptional cases, such as alleged imminence of an escape attempt, escalation of racial tensions or abundance of serious contraband, will a shift supervisor have a special briefing for his staff. Thus an officer may take up his assignment in the dining hall or on the yard unaware that "home-brew" has been consumed, a homosexual triangle has evolved or several inmates have just received parole denials. The capacity for handling any events which may follow is nearly always impaired by the attention which must be given to routine details of a job assignment. Besides, many officers would prefer to avoid discretionary matters.

As in other prisons of its type, the Atlanta staff can anticipate during a "normal" day that a number of inmates will become ill, that others will violate regulations by refusing to work and that the behavior of others will be influenced by personal problems. In each instance, a correctional officer or other employee will be involved with an incident whose origin, location, timing and duration are unpredictable. This type of repetitious uncertainty takes as great a toll in strain and apprehension among staff as the more episodic occasions when notorious inmates become assaultive, get inebriated on home-brew or burn out another prisoner's cell. Incidents that reinforce staff beliefs about the capriciousness of prisoners occur almost daily, and, as can be seen in the following illustrations, no amount of training or surveillance can be preventive.

December 9, 1969. At approximately 11 AM, Rackley 33265 was assaulted with a club by Guilford 32007 and was subsequently treated for head injuries. It appeared that Guilford felt Rackley had "put the voodoo" on him, and that he took this action because Rackley had placed a rag doll in his bed with pins stuck in its head. Rackley stated that he "hardly even knew" Guilford.

December 12, 1969. Inmate Tyberson 27222 became inebriated [on home brew beer] and went berserk in B cellhouse on the evening shift. He was swinging at any inmate near him until restrained and held down by other prisoners. Then he was taken to the hospital and placed in restraints until he sobered up and calmed down.

An additional feature of the second case should be mentioned. It is not at all unusual to find other inmates taking control for they reason that one or more persons may suffer bodily harm, or that unwanted attention ("heat") will be focused upon their domain unless official notice is averted.

Another type of incident, intended to harrass or intimidate officers, takes place just often enough to convince the officers that they are "at war" with prisoners:

January 26, 1970. At approximately 5:15 PM the officer on duty in C cellhouse was standing just inside the office door when an iron weight of about five pounds was dropped from an upper range. It landed on the metal screen covering the office. It is believed this was a measure of retaliation against the officer who was performing his job in a manner seen as "overzealous" by inmates. We were unable to identify the person(s) who dropped the weight.

February 8, 1968. An electric motor weighing approximately sixty pounds was dropped from the top tier onto the office of D cellhouse. It crashed through the expanded metal roof of the office and struck the officer's desk, causing considerable damage. The officer, Mr. Billingsley, was barely missed and had the drop hit its intended mark, the officer surely would have been severely injured or killed.

Again, it is clear that a conspiracy to vanquish an officer is exceedingly difficult to forestall and may, in fact, be entirely spontaneous. It makes little difference to staff that only a minority of inmates gets involved with assaults; their preconceptions of custodial work include the notions that most inmates have poor impulse control, little tolerance for stress and inherent hostility toward authority.

The correctional officer's orientation to prisoners is structured basically in terms of the axiom that if he does not know a man personally, there is little he can assume about him. This rule determines much of the content and style of interaction with offenders in the cellhouses, the dining hall, on the yard and elsewhere. During interviews officers often emphasized their interest in establishing and maintaining working relationships with inmates — a task made difficult by quarterly job rotations and high inmate-to-officer ratios — for they felt that their ultimate control over inmates during crises was a close function of these associations. The smallest personal knowledge, such as an inmate's name or the job he has in the institution, can be used by an officer to initiate a verbal exchange suggesting trust and a fair settlement.

In addition to these three sources of uncertainty in correctional work, a fourth category of incidents arises from events in the world outside the walls. The man sentenced to a term in federal court and designated for the Atlanta Penitentiary typically comes from those segments of the general population characterized by job instability, poor health, financial crises, emotional disturbance and lack of opportunity. Imprisonment often exacerbates an already tenuous relationship between the new inmate and elements of the outside community. In fact, employees who handle prison casework tasks devote much of their time to the enormous numbers of documents each day which attest to the disruptive effects of incarceration. It is these problems, communicated to the prisoner through visits or correspondence, which are one source of uncertainty precipitated from outside the wall.

Letters from the outside which refer to financial strife or which convey frustrations or even vengeance can be particularly disturbing to the man whose opportunities for response are severely curtailed. Perhaps greatest impact follows a letter from a son or daughter, often written under the guidance of a disillusioned wife:

Daddy

I hope you never get out of there. When you get out stay 15 miles away from us.

I want a father than can stay out of Jail. You never gave me 22 dollars from working on the truck and I'm going to get it.

Like it or not.

I want a father than can teach me how to be a good man and show me the right way to do things.

I think I can do better than you are in staying out of trouble.

Your a lousy father I never like you.

I don't work for nothing you know. I hope you like our letters. HA HA HA. You better answer all the letters.

Nicky

HA HA HA

Officers who have supervisory responsibility over inmates rarely examine prisoners' dossiers or consult their caseworkers although knowledge of inmates' problems might prevent an incident. There is an understandable reluctance among officers to get involved in "amateur counseling"; yet they may confront an inmate who has just been sued for divorce, has learned of a death in the family or has just received notice that a detainer (for legal action following the immediate sentence) has been lodged against him. Few correctional officers at the Atlanta institution felt that inmates could cope with these setbacks in a rational or conventional manner.

A second exogenous source of uncertainty originates in decisions made at high administrative levels, many of which call for modifications in existing local policies. In the minds of many officers, too little thought is given to the consequences of a new policy statement or to the ramifications of a court decision. Within the federal prison system, directives to institutions are formulated in Washington, a procedure prompting one lieutenant to observe:

> It's hard to know what you can or can't do with a prisoner these days. If the Bureau [of Prisons] isn't always changing its mind about how we handle these guys, then the courts make us change things just because some character got tired of bellyaching and threw a writ.

Some changes in institutional policy, then, are a reaction to "jailhouse lawyering," or to court-ordered changes brought about by "writ-writers." The percepiton that "the goddamned courts are running the prisons these days," widely shared among staff, is reinforced by the following episode:

February 7, 1972. Judge Forbes awarded $3,000.00 to Plaintiff [Carruthers 21793] on his complaint of negligence on the part of U.S. Penitentiary officials in failing to provide adequate protection resulting in his being injured (stabbed by another inmate) in A cellhouse on September 8.

The judge stated that there was an inadequate number of officers assigned to A cellhouse to provide proper protection and supervision of inmates living there. He also stated that although the perpetrators were known to penitentiary officials as an enforcer and gambler, respectively, they were permitted to remain in the general [prison] population rather than be put in Segregation. The judge also stated that although Carruthers had reported to prison officials threats made toward him by other inmates, and had requested transfer to another institution, this was unfortunately not done.

Correctional officers predictably have little regard for judicial opinions or operating procedures rendered by "absentee authorities" whose familiarity with local problems may be suspect. In addition, if the courts show favor to suits brought by organizations perceived by officers as radical (the American Civil Liberties Union is everybody's whipping boy), correctional administrators must contend with the feeling among their staff members that the authority for running the prison has been surreptitiously undermined. Thus, influences on institutional life which are generated from outside sources convince correctional workers that their line of work is becoming increasingly precarious.

STAFF RESPONSES TO UNCERTAINTY

The socialization of newly hired officers in the federal penitentiary usually involves a transformation of their occupational ideologies. Initially an officer trainee will have high expectations that he can change the man with whom he comes in contact in a socially acceptable direction. It takes little time, however, for a new employee to become disappointed; he soon learns that numerous features of the correctional officer's role impair his effectiveness as a change agent. Gaining experience, he comes to realize that he doesn't have the "tools" with which to achieve his early objective. Because certain posts, such as the towers and patrol duty, are often used specifically for new trainees, he is likely in addition to have little prolonged contact with inmates during his first year. The recollection of a correctional officer with two years' service dramatizes this shift in outlook:

> You enter the [federal prison] service thinking that you can do a better job than others have in helping inmates. It doesn't take long to find out that you aren't going to change anybody. Officers who've been here ten or fifteen years aren't changing anybody either. Oh, you help out some poor old devil every so often, make him feel a little better. But nothing lasting. On top of it all, you've got almost no incentives to offer a prisoner, so how much can you expect?

The awareness that a transformation of offenders into nonoffenders, ostensibly a goal of corrections, takes place only in spite of confinement at Atlanta was an important contributor to the feeling of precariousness and uncertainty among officers. What, then, are the behavioral consequences of working in an atmosphere of low predictability?

Data from questionnaires completed by correctional officers as well as informal interviews reveal that uncertainty has varied effects upon custodial staff. On the one hand, there are those who are exceedingly threatened by the absence of repetition and pattern. They prefer an orderly watch, one which proceeds without disruption or delay. Occasional references by officers to a "convict guard," or a "stick man," identified this particular type as someone who does not usually care for new policies, rule changes, shifts in the composition of the inmate population or changes in the administrative hierarchy. In an attempt to classify the divergent responses to uncertainty Atlanta officers were asked what advice they would give to new trainees. Those subscribing to the "stick man" ideology — about two-thirds of the custodial staff — supported the view that they should expect the worst from the inmate population and would be well-advised to adopt a style which minimizes uncertainty: "Learn all about the inmates who are 'hot'"; "Be nosy: check the unusual *and* the usual"; "Give an order and then enforce it at all costs"; and "Say what you mean; mean what you say."

About a third of the staff, however, thrives upon the nonre-
petitive, unsystematic features of correctional work. These officers look forward to quarterly job changes, the introduction
of new treatment programs, new regulations affecting inmate
conduct and a fluid, upwardly-mobile staff. This is not to suggest that they are foolhardy adventurers; on the contrary, they
have as great a distaste for disarming an assaultive inmate,
coping with a food strike, in short, unstable or dangerous situations, as the others. Their distinctive preference, though, is for
a job in which initiative, challenge and ingenuity are required,
and they are likely to tailor decisions about inmates individu-
alistically rather than categorically. According to these officers,
staff members should anticipate more change, uniqueness and
individuality. To the question concerning advice for new trainees, these men replied: "Listen to an inmate's problem with an
open mind"; "Be prepared to change jobs and directions
often"; "Treat each inmate as an individual and act accordingly"; "Stay flexible with the type person you are dealing
with"; and "Consider the varied personalities [staff and inmate]
you are dealing with."

One of the unanticipated field observations made during this
research arose while recording the operating styles employed by
two and sometimes three officers doing the same job. For example, "Quarters Post Orders" which cover the supervision of
an inmate housing unit provide the following work description
for these officers:

> The most important function of the unit [cellblock] officer is
> the maintenance of proper security and control in his quar-
> ters. In order to achieve success in this goal, the officer should
> at all times strive to develop a good working relationship
> with each inmate. This can only be accomplished by frequent
> individual personal contacts.

Further, he is directed to "maintain continuous accountability for all inmates," to "conduct daily security inspections,"
enter information of interest in a log book for officers on other
shifts such as "rumors of trouble between inmates, suspicious
activities [like] plotting escapes, strong-arm gangs and homo
activity." Similarly the quarters officer must "supervise the
formation and movement of all inmates to and from the cell-

house," and must "screen carefully all individual inmate requests to leave their assigned area."

It was surprising to discover that this job and many others were performed in markedly dissimilar ways despite the existence of uniform instructions. A closer look at the officers involved made it apparent that these behavioral contrasts were important indicators of the polarized correctional ideologies discussed above. For instance, a "stick man" arranges the priorities of his job so that his role is essentially accusatory: anyone entering or leaving the cellblock does so only with his permission; small groups of inmates conversing over a period of time are reprimanded and dispersed; and departures from the schedule of cellblock routine become sources of grave concern. He maintains considerable social distance between himself and inmates and develops a highly structured cellblock environment. The other type of officer, instead, may feel that keeping himself and fellow cellhouse officers accessible to inmates for counsel and assistance takes precedence over attention to out-of-bounds prisoners, cluttered cells and strict adherence to a schedule. He is more apt to "negotiate" rules and to draw the boundaries around permissible conduct more loosely. Thus an inmate often finds that he must adapt to quite varying custodial expectations, even on a given day, because the officers' conceptions of their roles are markedly different.

MINIMIZING LOSS OF CONTROL

Largely in response to their belief that a prison term can be tailored to effectively manage deprivations, a strategy Erving Goffman calls "working the system," inmates adjust in fairly standardized ways. For some, of course, the constraints of imprisonment are nullified only through physical flight; for others, there is psychological escape through fantasy or drugs. Most inmates in Atlanta, however, know how to do time, and the one predictable feature of their existence is the pervasive goal of making-do by manipulating the environment. Compensating by illicit means becomes a game in which prisoners try to "beat" or "con" the staff, who are ostensibly in control. From the inmate perspective making-do by chicanery is rewarding because it reinforces the belief that correctional officers are fallible, it shifts some of the power theoretically held by the staff to inmates and it allocates spoils to the underdog.

Knowing in advance that the prisoners value activities which will reduce the constraints of imprisonment, correctional personnel employ counterefforts to protect themselves against being defrauded or otherwise victimized. There was consensus among Atlanta officers that certain procedures were necessary to minimize uncertainty and inmate opportunism, yet many felt that the steps taken to ensure custody and security were at best a holding action. Nearly every member of the staff commented upon the futility of maintaining control over such a large inmate population in a mega-institution like Atlanta.

Despite a generalized suspicion among custodial staff that the prison's fate is largely indeterminate, several means have evolved over the years to cope with uncertainty. These almost exclusively concentrate upon problems created by inmates since most other sources of unpredictability are beyond staff intervention. The following strategies, therefore, are employed in the penitentiary to minimize loss of control:

The Shakedown. A central task of correctional personnel is to locate and confiscate goods which are not officially issued to inmates and thus qualify as contraband. Shakedowns hopefully identify persons responsible for the theft, exchange, fabrication or possession of illicit goods, but in practice the zeal with which those responsible are sought is usually contingent upon the nature of the goods. Shaking down can be routinely conducted or it may appear advantageous to vary both the time and location for a search. Experienced officers contend that however productive a shakedown may appear it uncovers only a fraction of the contraband circulating at any given time. The staff use two advantages, information given by informers and judicious timing, to survive in a contest against inmates who have in their favor an almost unlimited number of stashes, including some that are specially engineered, hired lookouts ("jiggers"), a policy of keeping goods moving and, though rarely, the compliance of an intimidated employee.

Shaking down is calculated to reduce the availability of goods which are considered a nuisance or which may pose more serious threats to the welfare of the institution. But the regular appearance of contraband is an unwelcome reminder to officers that many inmates have almost unlimited ingenuity and that the struggle for control can easily shift in favor of the captives.

Information. It has long been a practice in prison setting to solicit and use secret testimony from inmates about clandestine activities in the institution. Despite the fact that the informer is held in contempt by other prisoners and is derisively referred to as a "snitch," "rat" or "squealer," information is readily available about nearly all matters. An effective means for locating contraband or for coping with trouble such as potential assaults, escape attempts or work strikes is to develop an information system in which prisoners find it profitable to cooperate. They may hope thereby to preclude bodily harm, receive amnesty for their own indiscretions or retaliate against real or imagined aggressors. Even if a large proportion of the information available inevitably has little or no value, as appears to be the case at Atlanta, supervisory personnel hold that the whole system is worth it if just one crisis is averted.

It was apparent during interviews with the Atlanta staff that they were unconcerned with ethical problems associated with prisoner-volunteered testimony. Most correctional officers and their supervisors contended that inmates are going to snitch anyway, in exchange for the obvious benefits to them, and that the welfare of the total prison community is enhanced if trouble is averted.

The Count. There are several issues in the management of inmate activity which require that choices be made among alternatives. For example, if a prison administrator were to decide that knowing the whereabouts of prisoners at any given time (accountability) had become unacceptably lax, improvements would almost certainly require redeployment or expansion of manpower and curtailment of some treatment programs. In this instance, supervisory personnel must weigh the benefits of accountability, thus increased predictability, against possible costs incurred by manpower changes and decreased inmate satisfaction. Accountability is such an important concept that an elaborate ceremony, the "count," is performed at regular intervals to ensure that a full complement

of prisoners can be located. An enumeration in the prison is so
critical that nearly all activities are suspended until the count is
"cleared." Among custodial officers, moreover, one of the most
visible signs of incompetence or carelessness is to submit an
erroneous count, and for an inmate to interfere with the count
is an exceedingly serious offense.

Officers in the institution nostalgically recalled the "sun-
down count" that was made in past years after inmates completed the evening meal and then returned to their quarters or
went to the yard. Their comments reflected an uneasiness in
presuming full accountability during the critical hours when
the work day had ended, few custodial staff were on duty and
darkness could conceal indecorous activities.

The Siphon. Atlanta correctional officers contend that
"trouble" is the product of a relatively small proportion of the
population, and that if it were possible to eliminate troublesome inmates the custodial task would be materially simplified.
In the absence of any known screening device or psychological
test for trouble-prone inmates, officers invoke conventional
stereotypes of problem cases: offenders who are escape risks, are
serving long sentences, have committed violent crimes, are
known homosexual aggressors, are assaultive or have demonstrated a proclivity for narcotics or other drugs. In Atlanta it is
standard procedure to keep a "Hot Book" (referred to by inmates as the "Hunting List") of selected records on those inmates whose potential for trouble is felt to merit the special
attention of employees. Theoretically, staff members consult
this volume from time to time, but in practice most officers
find out who is "hot" through hearsay. Officers are expected to
make informal counts of hot prisoners particularly after the
yard is closed or following an entertainment event.

When trouble occurs or conspiracies are detected, suspected
prisoners can be detained in a separate facility ("Administrative
Segregation") pending a hearing. Knowing that certain notorious inmates have been removed from the population is a
source of encouragement to officers whose effectiveness with
large numbers of prisoners is compromised by the presence of a
few who are belligerent or manipulative. Also included in Segregation are men who need protective custody, that is, who
must be secured from intimidation or exploitation by other

inmates. Of these, a sizeable number are locked up in Atlanta's prison-within-a-prison at their own request.

For particularly chronic cases, authorization can be obtained from the Bureau of Prisons for a transfer to another penitentiary. In such "separation cases," often instances of one inmate killing another or testifying against another in court, transfer is most frequently made to Leavenworth (Kansas) or Marion (Illinois) where he can be reintegrated with the general prison population. In turn, hot cases at those maximum-security penitentiaries may be transferred to Atlanta. A few inmates whose reputations for trouble have achieved national proportions are said to be kept "on the circuit" between Atlanta, Leavenworth, Marion and McNeil Island (Washington).

Contingency Planning. Any institution must anticipate the occurrence of breakdowns in essential goods and services. For penitentiaries, extensive preparations are made to cope with the disruptive effects of power, heat or water stoppages, fire, natural disaster or widespread sickness. Advance planning is made at Atlanta for another type of acute uncertainty as well: the crisis of an escape, attempted escape, riot or strike. In these instances officers must not only identify suspected prisoners and take them into custody, but the rest of the inmate population must be secured and provided with essential services. Field observations in Atlanta during two escapes and two attempted escapes verified the importance of continuing the normal schedule. Delaying the evening meal, recalling the population from their jobs for a special count or cancelling an entertainment event because a manhunt was underway met with little understanding and sympathy among the 2,000 uninvolved prisoners.

Officers with long experience in these matters hold that no two riots are alike, although, of course, there are significant patterns in all, nor are reactions to any two escapes alike. As in many other staff perceptions of inmate behavior there is the implicit suggestion among correctional officers that even the most extensive contingency planning cannot anticipate all possible outcomes, for whoever gains control is in part a matter of fate, chance or fortuitous circumstance.

Those persons who argue that prisons have historically failed to achieve the multiple objectives given them can find ample reasons for their failure. The problems seem so numerous, in fact, that former governor Lester Maddox was moved several years ago to propose "a better class of inmate" as the solution.

Public expectations of correctional institutions make custody implicit and treatment explicit, but the realities of prison work support a reversal of these objectives. In spite of the introduction of correctional counselors and legal aid assistance, the most immediate and continuing influence upon prisoners is still the custodial staff. Therefore, it is important to understand the nature and the demands of this role. At present, the reality of prison life makes unpredictability a salient feature. Although theoretical expectations about the goals of prisons may emphasize the rehabilitative aspects, the daily task of containing the prisoner, conforming to the latest directive and continuing daily routine forces the average officer to place emphasis upon the custodial rather than the rehabilitative function of his job. This knowledge is essential to any realistic assessment of our objectives for prisons. The whole matter is probably reducible to what we want done within the walls, for what we presently give lip service to is demonstrably more than we currently are willing to invest.

Chapter 8

PRISON GUARD

JAMES B. JACOBS AND HAROLD G. RETSKY

UNLIKE the police who have been the subject of considerable attention in recent years, the role and person of the prison guard systematically have been ignored. Neither Clemmer (1958) nor Sykes (1966) in their classic studies of prison communities pauses long to consider the *career* of the guard. What others have said about guards is mostly by way of lament over their meager education, poor training, provincial world view, and sometimes sadistic personality traits. The more complimentary treatments cite the difficulties of the work and the subsistence wages, recommending that censure be withheld in light of the circumstances (see Roucek, 1935).

Surely there is a need to develop a fuller literature on the prison guard, not only because of their crucial importance to all questions of prison reform, but also because of their significance as social control agents organized within a paramilitary regime. In addition, close attention to this occupation may sensitize us to the moral division of labor as well as to the organization of "dirty work" (Hughes, 1958) within formal organizations. We offer an ethnographic picture of the prison guard gained from the scarce literature on the subject, our own substantial contact with maximum-security prisons, and formal interviews with more than thirty prison guards at various stages of their careers at Stateville Penitentiary, Joliet, Illinois.[1]

The original version of this article appeared under the title "Prison Guard" by James Jacobs and Harold Retsky published in URBAN LIFE, Vol. 4, No. 1, April, 1975, pp. 5-29 and is reprinted herewith by permission of the Publisher, Sage Publications, Inc. and the authors.
[1]When this paper was originally published, J. Jacobs has been conducting research at Stateville Penitentiary and at other maximum-security prisons for two years. H. Retsky had served two years as a guard at Stateville and was serving as a clinical counselor at that institution.

THE ROLE

While it is a central theme of this report that guards can be distinguished according to the kind of work they are assigned, their rank within the paramilitary organization, and their length of service, it is necessary to examine the dimensions of the role common to all prison guards.

The prison guard's role immediately can be distinguished from the role of those who guard objects in order to protect them. Brinks guards, military sentinels, Secret Service Agents, and those who guard nuclear materials are concerned with external threats to the objects they are protecting. The situation is radically different for the prison guard whose task involves protecting the surrounding community from the possibility of contamination by exposure to convicted men. While the Secret Service Agent enjoys a community of interest with the individual whom he is guarding, the prison guard from the outset owns an interest diametrically opposed to the inmates left to his charge.

The inmate rarely will see restrictions on his freedom within the prison as necessary or legitimate, while such measures as counts, shakedowns, and controlled inmate movements may be essential if the small number of guards is to successfully manage the vastly greater number of inmates among the hodge-podge of buildings, tunnels, corridors, yards, and gates that characterize mega-prisons like Stateville.

The prison's primary goal is to contain securely those convicted men assigned to its charge. The plain fact is that the inmate does not want to be in prison. Indeed, a small number are likely to be frequently reassessing opportunities for escape. Prisoners cannot be treated or trained if they cannot be held. The public will not tolerate escapes. In fact, escapes and riots are the only two occurrences likely to focus momentary public attention on the prison.

Prevention of escape and riot is the primary task around which the role of the guard is organized. Closely related is maintenance of a modicum of internal order and security. In recent years chilling stories of gang rapes and assaults among inmates have been reported in the press and before Congress. Such developments call attention to the fact that the guard is involved in adjudicating claims over residual freedom among conflicting groups (Werthman and Piliavin, 1967).

Aside from these primary goals the prison as a total institution necessarily generates several subsidiary goals connected with people-processing (Goffman, 1961). In any large-scale total institution, there is a whole range of maintenance tasks that must be carried out under staff supervision of inmate laborers. In the prison, new inmates must be processed, clothing must be laundered, medicine must be distributed, food must be prepared, lavatories must be kept clean, dining rooms and living quarters must be cared for; in short, the institution must be kept running. In the great mega-prisons plagued by low budgets and high turnover, this requires no small amount of organization and coordination of human energies.

To the primary goal of preventing escapes, riots, and predatory behavior, rehabilitation has been added. That these primary and secondary goals are fundamentally incompatible is the subject of considerable comment (for example, Janowitz and Vinter, 1959). It is not surprising that contradictory organizational goals have caused conflict in such organizational micro-units as the guard role. Under the role prescriptions dictated by the rehabilitative ideal, the guard is to relax and to act spontaneously. Inmates are to be "understood," not blamed, and formal disciplinary mechanisms should be triggered as infrequently as possible. These are vague directives. Cressey (1960) argues that no more precise rules concerning the "how" of rehabilitation can be formulated since the essence of rehabilitation work, as practiced by "professionals," lies in treating each individual as unique according to professional judgment, which belies adherence to hard and fast rules. What is allowed one prisoner may be denied another depending on evaluation of individual needs.

Where guards have attempted to follow these vague role prescriptions, they have often met with frustration. Inmates themselves believe that differential treatment based on individual needs requires professional competence. While competency and proficiency may be imputed to psychologists and social workers based on academic credentials, inmates are quick to point out that they will grant no such discretionary authority to "screws." The very essence of the professional's authority lies in his claim to charisma while the guard's only basis for authority is his rank within the caste system.

The rehabilitative ideal has no clear directives for the administration of a large-scale people-processing institution. In order to carry out primary tasks and to manage large numbers of men and materials, bureaucratic organization and impersonal treatment are necessary. Furthermore, to distinguish between inmates on the basis of psychological needs leaves the non-professional open to charges of gross bias, discrimination, and injustice.[2]

Treatment personnel in their administrative capacities are likely to hold guards responsible for preventing escapes and riots, ensuring order, and maintaining the prison as a smoothly functioning institution. The consequence of these contradictory demands on the guard is evidenced by the extremely high rates of staff turnover. At Stateville the turnover is greater than 100 percent per year and much higher among new guards since there does exist a sizeable proportion of guards with long years of service.

The old-timers complain about not knowing what is required of them and look back nostalgically to the "old days" when they knew what their job entailed and how they would be evaluated.[3]

> During Ragen's days you knew every day what you were supposed to do and now you are in a position where there are too many supervisors and too many changing rules. First one will come and tell you its got to be done this way and then somebody else comes along and says to do something different. In the old days we knew what our

---

[2]The same tension between equal treatment and recognition of the "special case" is discussed in the mental hospital context by Stanton and Schwartz (1954).

[3]The Morrises (1963, p. 84) make a similar observation about nostalgia among the guards in their classic study of an English prison.

job was.

Guards are more likely to fall back on their security and maintenance role because it is the only one on which they can be objectively evaluated. No guard will be reprimanded or dismissed for failure to communicate meaningfully with inmates. On the other hand, the guard whose carelessness smooths the way for an escape or whose lack of vigilance contributes to opportunity for a stabbing or rape will most likely find himself out of a job.

THE CAREER

Individuals do not grow up aspiring to become prison guards. Only 1 percent of teenagers surveyed by Lou Harris indicated that they had given any consideration to a career in prison. Our data indicate that the decision to seek employment as a guard usually came after a period of unemployment (the State Office of Employment Services regularly refers applicants), a layoff, or a physical accident that made previous work (e.g. mining) impossible.

> Well they had this piece in the paper, see I'm from Hamilton County; that's about 300 miles south of here. And they was wanting guards. I knew several fellows used to work here from down there at the time. The dust — the corn dust — I'm allergic to it and the lint offa cattle. So there's this place to go to Vermont to take a civil service examination. So I just drove up there that day and I took that civil service examination and in about 3 weeks, why they called me up to the Menard Penitentiary.

In spite of the fact that the State of Illinois has no residency requirement, does not demand a high school diploma, will accept men from eighteen to fifty-five years of age, has even dropped the written civil service examination (substituting an oral examination to determine the ability to communicate rules and orders), and has substantially increased its pay scale (approximately $10,000 after certification) there remains a chronic shortage of applicants. If, as Bittner suggests, "police work is a tainted occupation" (Bittner, 1970), then prison guard work is utterly polluted.[4] While Secret Service Agents and Brinks guards may achieve esteem from their contact with the objects they are guarding, close contact with convicted felons seems morally profaning for the guard. Even close friends do not know what to make of the prevailing belief that prison guards are sadistic, corrupt, stupid, and incompetent.

The stigmatization of the job, the peculiar working hours, and the frequent isolation of the prisons in out-of-the-way places make for a certain esprit and solidarity among the guards. Like the police, guards may sometimes view themselves as a society apart. This is especially true where the prisons have supplied dormitories and other facilities for living quarters. Stateville Penitentiary maintains both a dormitory for bachelors and a trailer park for married couples on prison property beyond the walls. The subculture which develops in these closed communities promotes a parochial and defensive world view.

The shortage of guards and the high turnover rate have important consequences. The chief guard needs bodies to fit into work slots and around the prison and tends to see those who do not show up for work for any reason as spiting him and the institution. The constant pressure to fill the gaps in the various institutional assignments out of an unreliable work force causes the captains to view subordinates as objects. At Stateville, absenteeism is staggering, sometimes approaching 40 percent. In a job that has few objective criteria for evaluating performance, simply reporting for work is likely to become the most important factor on which the new guard will be rated.

---

[4]Attempts to ease the stigma by upgrading the job usually suggest placing more treatment responsibility on the guard according to a "collaborative model" of corrections. As prisons have been renamed Correctional Centers to improve their public image, so guards have been rechristened Correctional Officers, although they continue to refer to themselves as guards. The importance of the name as a symbol of the work is evident in the following communication received from Stateville's former warden, Joseph G. Cannon, after reading an early draft: "It bothers me a bit to see the term 'prison guard' utilized in reference to such a study. Most people, I am sure, understand who the correctional officer is and certainly, with the changing of terminology from penitentiary to correctional centers, it would seem consistent to work on the image of the staff by adopting correctional officers as a reference to those men and women who wear the uniforms and play the initial roles which they do. Why does 'guard' die such a slow death. . . . The self concept we're trying to create at Stateville is certainly not of a 'guard' vintage."

Being a prison guard is a dead end. To date no career ladders have been built to reward those guards who have shown particular promise on the job. The skills necessary for guarding usually are not transferable to other situations except to lower-paying jobs in private security. While a few individuals have been promoted through the ranks to sergeant, lieutenant, and captain (and even warden), these opportunities often close early in the guard's career and the increasing professionalization of prison administration makes the availability of such administrative opportunities in the future even less likely. Without an outside sponsor or an immediate acceptance into the dominant clique, the guard will have to wait many years for promotion to sergeant, if indeed he is ever promoted at all.

Claims of favoritism in promotions are a common complaint and another cause of resentment.

> I think most of the supervision personnel is unqualified, they got their position through friendships, and I think some example of what I am talking about is you have a man over you. You've been here three weeks and you can see the man is inefficient. Why can't his supervisor see that he is inefficient? And you can see it. And if you will check some of the supervisors' educational background and go to their personal files; you will come up with something else. I've met a lot of people who've started from the time that I've been here and I think we've wasted a lot of time and the main gripe that we've had is that supervisory officers have a way of degrading men; treating men like they're beneath them and causing difficulty.

The social distance between higher-echelon guards and the new recruit parallels the social distance between the recruit and the inmates he is assigned to guard. At Stateville this organizational distance is reinforced by the different backgrounds of the high-ranking guards and old-timers and the vast majority of new recruits. The former have traditionally been recruited from rural southern Illinois while the latter increasingly are being drawn from the minority population of Chicago. There are many illustrations in the literature of the difficulties in becoming accepted in the closed prison community (Cronin, 1967: 114). Because most guards do not stay beyond the first year or two, old-timers will tend to remain aloof until the end

of this period.[5] This informal probationary period may be more
trying than the formal one.

The social distance between lower- and higher-level guards is
further reinforced by the paramilitary organization which
passes information upward while initiative and decisions flow
in the reverse direction. The line officer is often under the same
kind of scrutiny as the inmate under his surveillance. Alleged
trafficking in contraband is held to justify periodic shakedowns
of the line officers. In addition, it is not unusual to have a
lieutenant inspect both guards and inmates at an assignment to
see that they are working. Just as guards are required to write
tickets (disciplinary reports) on inmate rule violators, so too do
superiors (and sometimes inmates) make written reports on
guard infractions of the rules. Guards also are encouraged to
write tickets on each other. The disciplinary board for guards is
quite similar to the tribunal that hears inmate cases.

> I was disciplined once because I took a shoeshine in the
> barber shop and which only takes about six minutes. There
> was a sign in the shop which had fallen down forbidding
> this. But I did not see it. A captain spotted me and wrote me
> up, which was only his job and for which I hold no grudge,
> but I do feel he could have warned me that he was writing me
> up. I had no knowledge this had happened until I got a letter
> two weeks later telling me I had to go before the review
> board. They gave me three days off without pay. I think I was
> dealt with harshly. One man shouldn't take food from you.

The advent of the union movement has served to strengthen
the line officer in his position relative to higher-echelon
guards, although this has been attenuated by the membership
of all levels of guards in the union and by the difficulties of

---

[5]There is an obvious schism among those prison guards who regard their job as a life's
career and those for whom it is only a brief phase. Surveying all prison guards in the
country, the Joint Commission on Correctional Manpower and Training found that 20
percent had three or less years of experience while 36 percent had more than ten years.
For the student of the prison community this fact suggests the existence of distinct
factions. Austin (1973) found that the length of time served as a guard correlates
significantly with negative attitudes toward inmates. If this conclusion held up under
more rigorous testing, it might illuminate a phenomenon similar to the cynicism
attributed to veteran police. In addition, it is highly important to note the points in the
career when guards "drop out." A comprehensive study of prison guards would require
a concentration on drop-outs as well as on incumbents.

developing a viable collective bargaining procedure in the public sector. Unlike the police union, which is closed to supervisory personnel, the guards' union (although not the bargaining unit at the present time) includes all uniformed guards and civilian counselors as well. According to one informant, the attempt to limit union membership to line personnel was unsuccessful because without top-echelon guards there was an insufficient number of men with adequate qualifications to run the union. When one of the line officers who had served as secretary was promoted to sergeant, there was no one else with the educational skills to handle the job, so a decision was made to retain the secretary and to open the union to all.

Not only does the prison guard occupy a low social status in the outside community, he also experiences the disdain and sometimes open contempt of prison professionals. Thomas (1972) argues that in England over the past two decades, the prison administration formed a kind of alliance with inmates. While this has not occurred so dramatically in the United States, it would not be an exaggeration to say that administrators and professional treatment personnel feel more respect and greater affinity for the inmate than they do for the guard.

Increasingly, top prison administrators have come to justify their careers in terms of an ethos of public service. Whether professionals and administrators will be evaluated as successful in their jobs depends on some degree on the statements that inmates make to lawyers, visitors, and the press. Recent court decisions have made administrators doubly conscious of the importance of staff/inmate relations. If riots, work stoppages, and demonstrations are to be avoided, inmates must be somewhat placated. Their demands must be taken, to some degree, into account.

Professionals from the domains of social service and psychology often hold to a view of inmates as individuals with deficiencies that need to be erased so that successful readjustment to the society will be possible. In effect, the success of their career depends on their ability to get along with and to "convert" inmates. Relationships with guards are in no way essential to the careers of treatment personnel. On the contrary, the guards serve as a convenient scapegoat for the lack of success that has attended most efforts at rehabilitation. It always can be argued that the guards have been engaged in subverting the program and plotting against the best efforts of modern penology.[6]

The Work

Many of the principles used to describe continuous mass-production organizations are also applicable to the prison where argot refers to inmates being "worked," "fed," and "housed." The most obvious characteristics about prison work are its routine and boredom. The prison is to a great degree an institution isolated from the day-to-day exigencies of the outside world. It is a closed and timeless society where days, weeks, and months have little to distinguish them. With the exception of infrequent riots, few exceptional happenings are likely to occur. One day's routine is like the next. "Most guards having nothing to do but stand guard; they do not use inmates productively any more than they themselves are used productively by prison managers. Guards manage and are managed in organizations where management is an end, not a means" (Cressey, 1965).

DIVISION OF LABOR

Just as an understanding of the division of labor in the police department is vital for the study of that organization and of the police as an occupation (see Skolnick, 1966), so too it is necessary to note that prison guards are not a monolithic work force, but engage in a variety of tasks that bring them differentially into contact with administrators, inmates, and outsiders. That a single individual may be called on over time to perform many work tasks does not belie the significance of each work assignment in generating unique problems requiring different skills. While prison guards carry on numerous activities ranging from transporting inmates to and from court to sitting on disciplinary boards, we will concentrate here on three broad

---

[6]See, for example, McCleery's (1960) account of the revolt of the old guard power structure at Oahu Prison when a new liberal regime attempted to introduce reform principles.

areas of guard work carried on in living units, work units, and security units.

The cellhouse is the basic living unit of the traditional maximum-security prison. At Stateville Penitentiary, each circular cellhouse holds approximately 250 inmates, supervised by two, three, four, or five guards, depending on the shift and who shows up for work. In the course of a day's work the cellhouse guard, stationed at the gate, is required to open and to close the steel-barred door allowing entrance and exit to inmates whose work or visits require movement in and out of the cellhouse. Another guard may distribute medicine, mail, and laundry, answer telephones, and supervise maintenance activities. A third guard is positioned in a tower in the middle of the cellhouse from where he can see into every cell. The most important responsibility of the cellhouse guard is conducting the "count" whereby the staff determines several times a day if all inmates are present and accounted for. A proper count in a cellhouse is the most important single activity of the daily routine. If there is a miscount (either short or over), all operations and movement cease. Depending on the time it takes to rectify the mistake, the guard may suffer punishment, from reprimand to dismissal.

After the escape of three prisoners in 1972, four Stateville guards were fired. One of these men did not report for work until 3 PM and the escape had occurred at 1:30. He discovered the escape at the 6 PM count, but was fired for not alerting the institution to the escape earlier by checking out the movement chart in the cellhouse.

Not unmindful of the significance of the count, inmates can withhold cooperation in order to place an unpopular guard's job in jeopardy. They may attempt to elude the counting officer by hiding in their cell or by shuffling back and forth if the count is taken while the inmates are in line entering the cellhouse. In either case, the delay and disruption of the prison routine will be attributed to the guard who is responsible, and he will earn both formal censure and informal derision from his colleagues.

The guards who work the cellhouses are the busiest in the institution. The need for cooperation in carrying out maintenance tasks (distribution of mail and medicine, running telephone lines, feeding, overseeing maintenance, and so forth) and in conducting the count brings the guard to increasing reliance on his clerk and the other key inmates.

> I was lucky in that I had a sharp, smart and concerned inmate working for me. Whatever benefits he received from our relationship, it was understood that he had to pay for by helping maintain a correct count. He knew how many left the cellhouse; how many returned and where every man was at a given time. When I finished the count of each gallery and called the number to him he could verify this with his figures. At one particular count, after I had been working with him for eighteen months, I miscounted and he verified the count as correct when in fact it was incorrect. This continued three more times so that I delayed the count over three hours until at the fifth count, I came up with the correct answer. Needless to say, I heard from my clerk, who in spite of the advantage the job offered him, immediately offered to resign and when I turned this down, was apologetic about the affair for months afterward. He made many overtures to keep my good will and prove to me that his error was only a ridiculous one time error that could never happen again. And, in fact, it never did as long as we worked together.

The cellhouse is the most dangerous place for the guard. Inside the cellhouse of a mega-prison, guards are clearly at the mercy of the inmates. In case of emergency there is no fast exit. At any time the guard knows that he could be seized and held hostage. Not only might an unpopular cellhouse guard be treated roughly during a riot, he might at any time be assaulted, thrown off a gallery, or pelted with objects thrown from the upper tiers. During the 11 PM to 7 AM shift, when lights are out, objects such as steel bearings, bed springs, or paper clips are thrown or shot with the aid of rubber bands or spring devices at the guards.

The majority of guards during the day shift are assigned to work areas — the mechanical store, the metal factory, or the yard gang. Some are assigned to maintenance crews in the cellhouse. These guards are somewhat analogous to factory foremen although, as Cressey (1965) points out, the guard really has no counterpart in the business or industrial world.

It is not rare to enter a prison workshop and see no activity whatsoever. The guard may be found sitting in an office or standing in a corner talking to a colleague. The guard at the work area does not need more than a very minimal amount of compliance from the men assigned to him. Even this, however, may place the guard in a position where he is likely to have his authority "corrupted by reciprocity" (Sykes, 1956). In order to meet minimum requirements (boxes have to be warehoused, furniture has to be repaired), the guard may be willing to overlook certain breaches of the rules.

This ultimately may prove an unstable accommodation if inmates continue to demand greater favors for the same conformity. The newly recruited guard's first orientation to the prison invariably includes the warning to remain aloof from inmates lest the cycle of corruption and blackmail destroy the guard's career.[7] Until a recent policy change, guards at Stateville were not allowed either to offer or to accept a light from an inmate on the rationale that any nonessential contact no matter how superficial, ultimately would be corrupting.

It also seems that the guard in the work area establishes the closest relations with inmates. Perhaps men who work together for years often develop a camaraderie. Work assignments usually consist of a reasonably small number of inmates, and conversation between inmates and guards develops spontaneously. It also happens that there are guards assigned to workshops who have skills which they pass along to inmates. Those inmates who learn to weld or to repair a TV set may be grateful to their "teacher." At Stateville, Mr. V., the guard in charge of sheet metal, is among the few men who is held in great respect by the inmates. He is not only considered a good teacher, but is constantly seeking to place inmates in industry upon release.

---

[7]Note the following sober warning presented as a model for guard training by the American Correctional Association (n.d.: 23). "Bribery usually begins as a result of being too intimate with inmates. They offer a cigar, cigarettes, or some trivial article. Each time this is done a closer contact is made and finally they come through with what they really want the officer to do. They may work the officer into a compromising position by securing information from him which may make it appear to his superiors that he has been passing on confidential or department information. Or it may be that an inmate is a witness to some incident involving the officer, and which, if known, would not add to his reputation for efficiency and reliability. Self-protection, being a powerful instinct, the officer might ask the inmate to keep quiet or to falsify his testimony when questioned. This is the beginning of bribery, and it may get the officer on the inmate's payroll from that time on."

It is not unlikely that work assignment guards and their subordinates will sometimes develop friendships and will come to see each other as individuals. One guard noted that it is not rare for a guard "to unburden things to an inmate that he would not tell his wife." It is under the conditions of small work groups in the industries and in the cellhouses that it is most possible for the guard's authority to be "eroded through friendship" (Sykes, 1956).

The work unit guard often may become dependent on his men for the skill and expertise which they have developed over the years. As prisons are chronically understaffed, it seems natural that one small task after another will be delegated by the guard to inmates anxious to ingratiate themselves and to keep busy in an environment where lack of work and boredom are endemic. At times a locksmith, machine operator, or agricultural worker becomes indispensable to the prison regime. This is reinforced by the fact that the turnover rate in many prisons is so great that many work areas will find an inexperienced guard directing an inmate group in a task that he knows nothing about.

There are two security jobs in the maximum security prison that need to be distinguished: the tower and the gate. Traditionally, assignment to the guard towers along the prison wall had been reserved for recruits, old-timers who are partially incapacitated, and guards who are unable to manage inmates or who tend to harass them, although in recent years the increased violence in some prisons has led old-time guards to request transfer to the towers. The position is not likely to attract many volunteers. The loneliness, uncomfortable temperatures, and boredom are calculated to make this task more like a punishment than a viable job assignment.

The guard on the tower pulls a regular shift of eight and often eight and one-half depending on when his relief arrives. At Stateville, his lunch is delivered in a mental cannister which is hauled up to the tower by rope. During the winter, coal for a fifty-year-old, pot-bellied stove is hauled up in the same fashion. The stove is inadequate to heat the tower because of wind leaking through the windows. If you are close enough to the stove for heat, it becomes unbearably hot; if you watch the yard and road running alongside the wall, you have to move away from the stove, thereby exposing yourself to the bitter cold. In the summer, the towers are always intolerably hot; the only relief is being supplied an ice container hauled up along with the food.

The tower guard is alone. Except for telephone or walkie-talkie communication with the security headquarters, he has no contact with other individuals during the eight-hour shift. It is forbidden to bring either a radio or reading matter into the tower. The guard caught reading or dozing is dealt with quite harshly. Indeed, he is liable to be fired on the spot by the shift commander.

Tower work places the guard in a position of confrontation vis-à-vis inmates. If there be any doubt as to the nature of the institution or as to the purpose of the custodial staff, the inmate may merely glance at the walls. The tower guard symbolizes the stern hand of the community that has placed him in exile. The interaction between the tower guard and the inmate is continuous and uncomplicated. For the most part it consists merely in the positioning of the actors. No words are exchanged. The guard always has the inmate under surveillance while the inmate always must take the tower guard into account. One guard noted: "The guard on the tower is so far removed from the human element that it becomes impossible for him to see a man. He can only see a problem and has the immediate solution for this in his hand."

The tower guard himself is placed in an uncomfortable position, both physically and existentially. The rules relating to the use of deadly force are ambiguous. In addition, there are those whose training and experience with firearms are such as to raise doubts about their ability to act decisively at the critical moment. However, with respect to the use of weapons, all guards indicated to us that they viewed this as just another aspect of the job.

> That doesn't bother me in the least. If I had to use the weapons, I would use them. Uh, if a person's whole life was in danger, like say you was in the yard, and if two or three or maybe just one would jump you, and was trying to take your life, I would put a few rounds off in the air to stop them for a warning and then I would do my best to wound him to bring him off of you but if it didn't do any good and I only

wounded him and if he started at you again and then if I had to put him out for good, I would. If his intention is to kill you or any personnel then he's going to do it knowing that he's going to die, knowing that he might lose his own life. He's gotten to the point where he doesn't care. Because it may be me down there some time. And if someone's trying to kill me, I would definitely want to live. I'd want this person off of me. I wouldn't want my life drained out on the ground because somebody's sittin' in the tower and not doing anything about it.

On entering the maximum security prison as an outsider, one is frisked, stamped, and checked by guards standing at gates each successively closer to the heart of the prison. At Stateville, there are four iron gates; each has a guard assigned to it. The guard is not permitted to open the gate unless the visitor is with a staff member or has been approved. The gate is an attractive job for an ambitious individual. It gives one the opportunity to be in constant touch with top-echelon security people and administrators. Assignment to the gate is often a sure indication that sergeant stripes are forthcoming.

It is the guards at the gates and those stationed in the visiting room who actually present the face of the institution to the streams of outsiders (students, relatives, lawyers, legislators, and so on) who enter the prison each day. They have a high number of brief and superficial contacts with staff, inmates, and outsiders. Different social skills are required in this work role than in those roles requiring more sustained contact with inmates. Top staff are sensitive to the fact that the staff often may be judged by the behavior and appearance of those guards in these front-line positions. Conscious efforts are made to choose those who will make the best impression. Even then, however, tension is likely to develop between the guards and visitors who resent having their motives for entering the prison questioned by searches and other security measures.

Inmates passing through the gates are required to have a "pass" and are "patted down" at each gate. For some inmate runners who pass back and forth through the gates many times a day, the patting down may be a particularly humiliating dramatization of their lowly and unworthy status. In order to normalize the interaction between gate keeper and those inmates who move frequently through the gates, the patting down becomes a ritual in which the guard attempts by his detachment, inattention, and speed to show that this is a mere formality, not an impeachment of the inmate's character.

SERGEANTS, LIEUTENANTS, AND CAPTAINS

It is important to emphasize that the division of labor sketched above is applicable only to the lowest-ranking guard — the line officer. In Illinois there are three ranks of guard higher than the line officer — sergeant, lieutenant, and captain. The chief guard recently has been promoted to the new rank of major.

The work of a sergeant is almost identical to that of a sergeant in the army. He is not only directly familiar with the work of the line officer, but often fills in as a line officer, manages the unit he is assigned to, and participates in specific jobs that require special responsibility such as gate keeper at various key points in the institution. In addition, a sergeant is usually in charge of cell houses, work units, and the hospital.

Lieutenants function as a police force within the prison. When there is any kind of disturbance in a cellhouse or on a work assignment, the lieutenants immediately will be called to the scene to deal with the problem. If an inmate must be "walked" to isolation or forcibly removed from his cell, this task will be carried out by the lieutenants. When they are not responding to trouble, the lieutenants roam about the institution making checks and shakedowns on inmates and lower-ranking guards.

There are only a handful of captains among the guards. They rarely have time to exercise first-hand supervision of the general prison area, but instead are assigned either to full-time administrative responsibility or to shift commands. Increasingly, they have been saddled with greater and greater amounts of paper work regarding such matters as personnel evaluations and budgets. At Stateville, during the day shift, one captain sits as chairman of the assignment committee, a second is in charge of the disciplinary committee, and a third functions as head of the security force and operates out of a control room. The power of the captains has dwindled in recent years with increasing responsibility for the management of the prison being assumed by college educated professionals and administrators. The very committee structure alluded to above signifies the loss of an authority that was once both unchecked and unquestioned.

The Guard's World

That man's work tends to shape his view of the world is a common notion in sociology. Similarly, the position of an individual within a social setting goes far in shaping his perceptions and behavior. The total institution is a pervasive organization for guards as well as inmates. The concrete walls which lock the inmate inside also lock society out; the guard's daily contacts are limited to inmates and a few staff members. In this situation, both inmates and guards become deeply committed to their organizational roles.

The guard's world has increasingly come to be pervaded by fear and uncertainty. Within the maximum-security prison, guards carry no weapons because they might be overpowered by the greater number of inmates and have the weapons turned against them. Ironically, many inmates are armed or have easy access to lethal weapons like shivs, razors, iron pipes, bats, and broken glass.

> I was back there on the job when it broke out. I was frightened. I think every officer out there was frightened because we had no weapons. The tower officers — they didn't know exactly what to do. They were firing warning shots. You couldn't see clearly what they were doing, so you didn't know whether to duck, run or stand still — and then you look at the inmates and they are coming with sticks, baseball bats, iron bars and all this stuff. Any man who says he wasn't afraid, I'd have to call him a liar.

Tension continually looms over the prison threatening to explode into assault or even riot. This is drilled into the recruit during his first training classes. The guard's manual stresses the need for vigilance and alertness lest the unexpected take one unaware. Not only is the new guard exposed to the word-of-mouth stories of fellow students and training officers, but at the prison he immediately may be exposed to situations which confirm his worst fears.

> When I arrived, I was almost immediately assigned to "B" house which contained a gallery known as three-gallery lock-up. The inmates here had been under constant lock and key for almost a year. As a result of this, they were acting like animals and their verbal abuse scared the shit out of me. I decided then and there to turn in my resignation but was talked out of it by my supervising officer.

Similar to Skolnick's (1966) findings on the police, few prison guards speak openly about fear, although they attribute such concern to their wives and families. In recent years, assaults on prison guards have become more common. At Stateville in 1973, the first killing of a prison guard in decades occurred when a guard was thrown off a high gallery. Not only has this demoralized the prison staff, it also has made them chronically apprehensive. There are three apparent strategies for dealing with this fear: becoming increasingly repressive, courting acceptance with the inmates, or retreating from duty and responsibility. All three strategies are very much in evidence in Stateville. The first is most common among the lieutenants, the second among new guards, and the third among old-timers.

Not only guards, but inmates too, live with an anticipation of violence. Perhaps awareness of this contributes to a normalization of relationships and a day-to-day accommodation. Inmates and guards share a small, shut-off, physical space as well as common language, diet, and each other's constant companionship. The fact that so much distance separates line officers from top-echelon decision-makers places guards in the same position as inmates with respect to a feeling of powerlessness. Often line officers and the inmates in their charge will share a common definition of administration, and the lieutenants and captains will see their position as being constrained by uninformed and ill-advised superordinates.

> I often put myself in the inmate's position. If I were locked up and the door was locked up and my only contact with

authorities would be the officer walking by, it would be frustrating if I couldn't get him to listen to the problems I have. There is nothing worse than being in need of something and not being able to supply it yourself and having the man who can supply it ignore you. This almost makes me explode inside.

Guards and inmates also share similar socioeconomic backgrounds. Many black guards have known inmates on the streets. White guards, too, are not drawn from the more law-abiding middle class, but usually are drawn from delinquency-prone groups where scrapes with the authorities during teenage years were not uncommon. Where guards and inmates interact in living units and working units day after day, there may be subtle psychological pressures on the line officer to identify with the prisoners unless he can develop a theory to account for his differentness from the inmate population. One important function of the guard's uniform, for example, may be to sharply distinguish him from the inmates (Roucek, 1935).

Goffman (1961: 87) argues that within total institutions there is a tendency for ideology to develop to explain the nature of those under control. "This theory rationalizes activity, provides a subtle means of maintaining social distance, allows a stereotyped view of inmates and justifies the treatment accorded them." In general, prison guards tend to view inmates as morally inferior. Kirson Weinberg, one of the earliest students of the prison community, lends support to this assertion (quoted in Barnes and Teeters, 1943: 721).

> The officials, especially the guards, regard the convicts as "criminals after all"; as "people who can't and shouldn't be trusted," and as "degenerates who must be put in their place at all times." "You can't be too easy with them," states one custodian. . . . "They're on the go to put one over on you. They don't think about us when they try to get over the wall." "There must be something wrong with every man here," states another, "else he wouldn't be here. They're scheming all the time, soon as you give them an inch. That's because there's something wrong with every one of them." Convicts are considered "born bad"; as mentally or emotionally or morally deficient.

This stereotypical view of inmates is more prevalent among the lieutenants and captains, who must be thought of as the

"tradition bearers" of the institution. Their distance from inmates and their long tenure within the institution seem to
insulate them from seeing inmates as individuals. They have
become most firmly committed to an emergent ideology.

This view of the inmate can be distinguished from the police
officer's view of the felon. The latter views the felon as vicious
and evil, while the former sees the inmate as sick, inadequate,
disgusting, and degenerate. The difference is not due to a
greater acceptance of the rehabilitative ideal on the part of the
prison guard, but to the difference in the setting in which the
policeman and guard interact with the criminal.

The police interact with the felon on the street. Unlike the
guard, they are likely to have had a first-hand view of the
victim and to have personalized society's quarrel with the criminal. The guard does not see the inmate until many months (or
even years) after the crime, and he normally is unaware of facts
involved. In addition, the stripping of the inmate's identity, the
drabness of his prison garb, the obliteration of his hair style all
tend to make him less fearsome appearing in prison than he
was on the street.

The prison organization is calculated to reduce the inmate to
a child. With respect to medicine, for example, no more than
one dose at a time is distributed even if the inmate will have to
rely on the guard four times during the day for his pills. No
matter what a man is occupied with in his cell, when count is
called he must stand up and face front. If he is occupied in a
bowel movement, he has to raise a hand and other inmates in
the cell are required to point to him. The guard is likely to
believe that the inmate is not a healthy, competent male, but
stupid and inadequate. This view is reinforced by the behavior
the inmate exhibits on entrance into the prison. No matter how
street-wise the criminal is, commitment to prison will be somewhat of a disorienting experience. Dealing with the regimentation, lack of privacy, and new normative system, the prisoner
may appear clumsy and unsure of himself. Certainly behaviors
such as homosexuality go far in suggesting to the guard that
the inmate is a moral degenerate.

> I think they (homosexuals) are sick. There are a lot of them in
> prison. . . . It's a disease the way I look at it. Maybe the man
> is sick and needs help from a doctor. He should not be poked

fun at or anything like that — he should be helped.

Guards do not view all inmates as degenerate. On the contrary, it is common to hear guards speak of good and bad inmates. Like all others in the criminal justice system, gradations of degeneracy are recognized. Some inmates thought to be wealthy or to have important ties in the professional underworld are respected, even admired.

At Stateville, guards make no distinctions among inmates on the basis of offense. Inmates are judged on how willingly they conform to authority. While the prevailing ideology prescribes abhorrence for the "no good son-of-a-bitch" inmates as a class, exceptions are made in individual cases. The "good inmate," like the "good nigger," cooperates with the guard, knows his place, and keeps to himself — in short, he does his own time. The "no good" inmate causes trouble for the guard by insisting on his rights and privileges: mail, medicine, telephone calls, and the like.

Stateville guards do not openly indicate racist attitudes. Whatever prejudices may exist are kept to one's self. This is in sharp contrast to studies of the police which have found an abundance of openly stated racist comments (Stark, 1972) and to other prison studies which have stressed the blatant racism among guards (Wright, 1973). Even in informal discussions, we have not heard guards refer to black inmates as "niggers" or in other racist terms, although whites continue to be disproportinately represented in better "up front" jobs. We suspect that much that has been explained as racist attitudes toward inmates in the literature stems from the organizationally sponsored conflict between guards and inmates.[8]

---

[8]That the hostility which characterizes interaction between guards and inmates results from the "inherently pathological characteristics of the prison itself" (Situational Hypothesis) rather than from the individual's evil motives (Dispositional Hypothesis) is supported by the well-publicized social psychology experiment by Haney et al. (1973) wherein they simulated the prison situation by creating a "mock prison" in the basement of the psychology building at Stanford University and assigned Stanford University student volunteers randomly to the guard and inmate roles: "many of the subjects ceased distinguishing between prison role and their prior self-identities. When this occurred, within what was a surprisingly short period of time, we witnessed a sample of normal, healthy American college students fractionate into a group of prison guards who seemed to derive pleasure from insulting, threatening and dehumanizing their peers — those who by chance selection had been assigned to the 'prisoner' role."

In a prison like Stateville, where blacks constitute 80 percent of the inmate population, racism may be a dead letter. There are too few whites to make white/black distinctions significant. The guards come to distinguish instead between the good and bad inmates among the blacks. On the other hand, evidence seems to indicate growing racial tension between white and black guards both in the barracks and sometimes on the job.

In general, prison guards are cynical about rehabilitation and the work of treatment agents within the prison. They feel that they see the prisoner twenty-four hours a day and are in a better position to judge the man's sincerity and true commitment to group therapy and other treatment programs. Inmates cannot be rehabilitated if that means that something is to be done to them by outside agents. Instead, they believe that a man can only change if he is motivated to do so — and this appears to be a characteristic of the individual and to have nothing to do with the organization and its therapists. Like the policeman and all those who must assume the capacity of clients to carry out their tasks, the guard adheres to a radical free-will theory of man and human behavior.

REFERENCES

American Correctional Association (n.d.) Correction Officers Training Guide.

Austin, J. (1973) "Attitudinal variation in correctional officers." (unpublished)

Barnes, H. and J. Teeters (1943) New Horizons in Criminology. Englewood Cliffs, N.J.: Prentice-Hall.

Bittner, E. (1970) Functions of the Police in Modern Society. Washington, D.C.: National Institute of Mental Health.

Clemmer, D. (1958) The Prison Community. New York: Holt, Rinehart & Winston.

Cressey, D. (1965) "Prison organization," pp. 1023-1070 in J. March (ed.) Handbook of Organizations. New York: Rand McNally.

———(1960) "Limitations on organization of treatment in the modern prison," pp. 78-109 in R. Cloward et al. (eds.) Theoretical Studies in Social Organization of the Prison. New York: Social Science Research Council.

Cronin, H. (1967) The Screw Turns. London: John Long.

Goffman, E. (1961) Asylums. Garden City, N. Y.: Doubleday Anchor.

Haney, C., C. Banks, and P. Zimbardo (1973) "Interpersonal dynamics in a simulated prison." International J of Criminology and Penology

(January): 69-97.

Hughes, E. (1958) Men and Their Work. New York: Free Press.

Janowitz, M. and R. Vinter (1959) "Effective institutions for juvenile delinquents: a research statement." Social Service Rev 33 (June): 118-130.

Joint Commission on Correctional Manpower and Training (1969) A Time to Act. Washington, D.C.: Joint Commission on Correctional Manpower and Training.

Morris, P. and T. Morris (1963) Pentonville: A Sociological Study of an English Prison. London: Routledge & Kegan Paul.

McCleery, R. (1960) "Communication patterns as bases of systems of authority and power," pp. 49-75 in R. Cloward et al. (eds.) Theoretical Studies in Social Organization of the Prison. New York: Social Science Research Council.

Roucek, J. (1935) "Sociology of the prison guard." Sociology and Social Research 20 (November): 145-151.

Skolnick, J. (1966) Justice Without Trial. New York: John Wiley.

Stanton, A. and M. Schwartz (1954) The Mental Hospital. London: Tavistock.

Stark, R. (1972) Police Riots. New York: Focus.

Sykes, G. (1966) Society of Captives. New York: Random House.

———(1956) "The corruption of authority and rehabilitation." Social Forces 34 (March): 157-162.

Thomas, J. (1972) The English Prison Officer Since 1850: A Study in Conflict. London: Routledge & Kegan Paul.

Werthman, C. and I. Piliavin (1967) pp. 56-98 in D. Bordua, The Police: Six Sociological Essays. New York: John Wiley.

Wright, E. (1973) Politics of Punishment. New York: Harper & Row.

Chapter 9

THE BOOK VS. THE BOOT:
TWO STYLES OF GUARDING IN
A SOUTHERN PRISON

BEN M. CROUCH

PRISON guards are neither the brutes portrayed in popular films nor the one-dimensional background characters implied in most prison studies. Yet data on which to base informed conclusions regarding the behavior and attitudes of this important prison figure are rather limited (Irwin, 1977, p. 36). With few exceptions, e.g. Sykes, 1958; Guenther and Guenther, 1974; Jacobs and Retsky, 1975; Crouch, 1977b), prison researchers typically overlook guards. This general omission leaves open such important questions as how guards behave in various work settings, what shapes that behavior, and how guarding patterns influence a wide range of prison outcomes, e.g. inmate behavior, inmate and guard socialization, and general prison stability. The analysis reported here offers some answers to these questions about guard work by examining two distinct styles of guarding which exist simultaneously within a single prison facility.

Although all of the guards within the prison studied wear the same uniform and answer to the same warden, the general settings in which guards work require, or perhaps allow, particular styles of guarding. The first style emerges within the fenced and gun-towered building compound, where the primary guarding function seems to be keeping inmates secure; here guarding is relatively passive and bureaucratic. The other style of guarding emerges on the extensive agricultural operation that defines the institution as a "plantation prison." Guarding in the "field" is more aggressive and less concerned with formal procedures. In the title of this paper the terms *book* and *boot* symbolize these styles, respectively; these words not only suggest divergent conceptions of prison social order but succinctly hint at how guards ensure order in the two prison settings.

METHODOLOGY

Data for this analysis derive from over six weeks of participant observation in a prison I will call Trinity, one unit in a large southern prison system. Although I followed routine job application procedures, I entered the system for study purposes with the aid and knowledge of top officials in the state's Department of Corrections. Preparation for being a guard was limited. Beyond drawing my four sets of grey uniforms and having my haircut in accordance with prison regulations, I spent one afternoon becoming oriented to the job with the aid of a self-administered slide presentation accompanied by a manual.[1] After my orientation I spent the first part of the observation period working in and around the cellblocks. Throughout this period and during most of the project itself, other officers treated me simply as a new employee learning the ropes and inmates treated me as they would any other "new boot boss." Their perceptions derived from the fact that I performed the duties of any other correctional officer I and did not volunteer my university affiliation or research interests.

After approximately three weeks in the cellblocks, I arranged to be transferred to other work areas on the Trinity unit.[2] In this way I was able to observe guard work in all major areas, inside the building and in the fields. This movement, together with the routine altering of cellblock assignments and officers

[1]Because I was a "summer hire," a guard hired when the system is traditionally short-handed, my training was very abbreviated. Most guards entering the system of which Trinity is a part must undergo two to three weeks of classroom and on the job training.
[2]As a result of being placed in other segments of the prison to get a better perspective on guarding, the degree to which I was directly responsible for inmate supervision diminished. This is because all guards start work in the cellblock as I did and with time and experience move to other posts in the building or perhaps to the field. Thus, during the last two weeks of the project, though still in uniform and still performing some duties, I "worked" in parts of the prison (education, disciplinary committees, field) where a new man with my experience would not likely have been assigned. During this time I began to let it be known that I was studying the prison and that I was a professor. My intent was to blunt the possibility, born of "prison paranoia," that the guards might feel they had been spied on without their knowledge.

on the shift, allowed me to talk informally with at least ten officers for several hours at a time as the work pace permitted. I talked with many other men for shorter periods.

What these men said and did, whether to inmates, to each other, or to me, constituted essential data for this analysis. I attempted to record this information as accurately as possible in a small notebook I always carried. Since scheduled security routines and other activities often kept me busy, I made notations as time and opportunity permitted. When I did update my notes, I wrote as inconspicuously as possible.. At the end of each shift, I tape recorded all notes and general impressions. In addition, interpretation of the data benefited from over 100 hours I had spent in nonparticipant observation in other units in the state prior to the present project and the perspective gained from limited observations and interviews with guards in other state prison systems (Crouch, 1977a). I also submitted initial drafts of my analysis to four key informants at Trinity. Three of these men are uniformed guards in either the building or the field with over thirty years of prison work among them; the fourth is a Trinity administrator with several years experience as a guard on this unit. The reactions of these men provided an important check on the validity of my interpretations.

The discussion that follows is an analytic description (Lofland, 1971) of two guard worlds within one prison. It assumes that the differences between the two styles of doing guard work can only be understood in terms of the immediate environments in which that work is carried out. Thus, I will examine the building and field settings before turning to the guarding styles themselves.

DESCRIPTION OF THE SETTINGS

Enclosed in a double fence, topped with coiled barbed wire, the building is a large and rather imposing structure designed for efficient control of inmates. Built seventeen years ago, for just over 1100 men, it housed approximately 1900 felons during this study. The central feature of the building is a one-quarter mile long hall broken at several points by riot gates. Off this hall in a "telephone pole" design protrude the wings for housing, feeding, curing, teaching and supervising these inmates. Most inmates live in cellblocks containing sixty-eight cells; because of the crush for space all cellblocks but "segregation" contain one-man cells renovated slightly to house two and sometimes three men. There are two dormitories, each containing about one-hundred selected inmates. Movement from one point in the building to another must be through the hall; that movement is controlled by green lines, painted on the floor, that serve to direct inmate traffic much like highway stripes.

Even though the building design emphasizes control, several features of this work setting prevent guards from knowing individual inmates or detecting their rule-breaking behavior. The first of these features is the ratio of inmates to officers. Over the past few years, as in most state prisons, the inmate population at Trinity has grown rapidly. But this growth has not been paralleled by an expansion in the custody staff. Consequently, on the shift I worked, the ratio of inmates to guards was about 150 to 1. A second feature of the building that makes guard work here problematic is low visibility of inmates; the very walls and bars that secure them make inmate transgressions hard to see. The cellblock officer controls the doors of inmate cells from a barred enclosure or "picket" that commands a set of two cellblocks. The problem is that this physical arrangement makes it impossible for the officer to see *into* any cell; he can only see the doors in profile. Except for the purpose of counting inmates (done rapidly, single-mindedly, and always at predictable times) a guard seldom looks into cells.

The third feature of this setting, the frequent movement of officers to different assignments and inmates to different cellblocks, exacerbates the problem of visibility. Cellblock officers, who supervise the blocks and "day" rooms where inmate trouble is perhaps most likely, move from block to block through the course of a week as a matter of routine. At the beginning of each shift, the captain reads down a list of the cellblocks and dormitories and, after each, names an officer; until the shift begins, a man seldom knows where he will work. This strategy presumably prevents close relations between specific inmates and officers permanently assigned to a particular picket or guard station. Inmates also change living assignments due to trouble with their fellows or, more likely, job changes.

Given this shifting of both the keepers and the kept, guards may easily miss clues to impending trouble. For example, a physically and mentally weak inmate told his cellblock officer that several others were going to rape him. The officer told the inmate not to worry, that the aggressors were probably bluffing. However, two days later, an inmate who lived on a different block entirely, entered the weak inmate's block when a large group returned from a meal. He went up to that inmate's cell tier and stood behind him. When the officer rolled all the doors open to allow the men to reenter their cells, the interloper pushed the weaker man into his own cell, cowed, and raped him. The rape, of course, was out of sight of the officer and, since that officer did not recognize all of the men living in that block, he was not suspicious of the transgressor.

The agricultural operation at Trinity provides a very different work setting. This "field" operation produces a wide assortment of food and fiber grown on 4500 acres. Every week day it is not pouring rain or below 42° F, 300 to 400 inmates work there. For about six hours a day, squads of twenty-five to forty inmates labor under the eye and gun of a mounted "field boss." These guards supervise the same squad week after week, regardless of the task.

Features of the field contrast sharply with those of the building outlined above. First, the inmate-guard ratio is more favorable to authorities; there is about one guard for every thirty inmates. Second, unless the inmates are working in broom corn, which is as high as a mounted man, guards can easily see them at all times. And should the immediate squad supervisor not see a breech of security such as an escape attempt, a *highrider* reinforces security. The highrider, also on horseback, stations himself alone, out of handgun range, and watches everything. He carries the only rifle in the field, with orders to shoot any inmate who tries to escape. An ever present pack of tracking dogs also discourages escape.

The building and the field settings differ in regard to two other features as well. The first of these is isolation from prison outsiders. Trinity is a unit primarily for young adults ranging in age from seventeen to twenty-one and, for this reason, contains a wide ranging academic and vocational education program. These particular features make Trinity a frequently visited unit. At least once a week a tour of college students, law students, grand jurors, or bar association members will troop through the halls. Clearly, officials would prefer these visitors leave with as good an impression as possible, a fact that makes a tight, efficient operation all the more desirable. Yet these tours see only the building; they almost never see the field operation. The major reason for this is logistical, in that the field tasks may be two or three miles from the building. But officials may also prefer that the public not see this operation or sense the guarding style there. For example, an employee in the Department of Correction's Public Affairs Office related to me that taking a tour past a group of field officers who happened to be in the building produced a little unease for that employee. The reason was that the hats, spurs, and old west demeanor of these men can produce in the minds of tour members an image of the prison that officials would prefer they not carry out with them.

These settings also differ in the types of inmates officers must deal with. While the field inmates are outside, building officers deal primarily with inmate trusties, men who have at least some "good time" and who have shown good enough records to be assigned to an inside job. However, after about 4:30 PM building officers must deal with all types of inmates. Field officers, on the other hand, deal with three kinds of inmates who may be more troublesome. First, all new inmates must go to the field. The philosophy operating here is that "new boots" should start at the bottom, at the least desirable work in the prison, and earn better jobs by working hard and causing no trouble. If they can demonstrate these abilities, they may be able to move up to jobs in the building (such as the kitchen or laundry, which is only slightly more desirable) after only a few months under the southern sun. Some inmates, however, for whatever reasons, cannot stay out of trouble or work hard enough to suit their field supervisors. These men constitute the second type of troublesome inmate, some of whom spend long periods in that assignment. Inmates constituting the last type are men who had better positions in the building, but who returned to the field as part of disciplinary action. All three types of men have in common the fact that they have relatively little to lose since they are at the bottom of the inmate job hierarchy.

THE GUARDING STYLES CONTRASTED

Degrees of Formality

Because of the size of the inmate population and the extensive division of labor among both guards and inmates, the guarding style in the building is much more bureaucratic and formalized than the field style. The massive movement called for from day to day in the compound precludes a concern for dealing with inmates individually. Since a web of rules holds the organization together, those rules become paramount. Indeed, most building guards do not supervise specific inmate tasks. Instead, their work consists mainly of assuring that inmates abide by the administrative and conduct rules. Thus, building guards regularly admonish inmates regarding talking ("knock off that 'head runnin'"), walking ("get off that South Dallas shuffle . . . "), and dressing ("tuck that shirt in and button it").

The field style, however, does not involve a similar concern for inmate adherence to a wide set of rules. Instead, field officers appear to focus primarily on two fundamental goals: completing the agriculture task at hand and returning to the building the same number of inmates "turned out" at the beginning of the day. Thus inmates may fare relatively well if they do not attempt to escape and if they work hard. This means that field officers care little for the rules of dress and demeanor that so concern building personnel. For example, when inmates file out to go to the fields, they sport a wide assortment of shirts, shoes, and hats, most of which are creatively customized for individuality, comfort, or both. Such creativity is unacceptable in the building. Field officers seem also less concerned about the fights that occur regularly. When a fight begins in the cotton patch, the officer responsible for the squad containing the combatants typically rides up and tells them to stop. While officers stop most fights as soon as possible, especially if hoes become weapons, it is not uncommon for the two inmates to be allowed to "duke it out." This response to fighting is quite different from that observed in the building. There, at the first sign of a fight, the several officers assigned to the hall, and typically the shift captain as well, literally sprint to the scene to break it up. The difference in response may lie in the greater concentration of inmates inside plus the greater ratio of inmates to guards. But for whatever the reason, building guards are well aware of this difference. Several times during the observation period these men complained about how fights allowed to begin and gain momentum in the field were often continued inside. Building officers thus perceive the informality of the field to undermine order in the building, at least to some degree.

The disciplinary hearings held for inmates also show the difference in formality associated with the two styles. Trying inmates for rule infractions falls either to the building or the field disciplinary committees, depending on where the infraction occurred. In order to contrast the conditions under which the committees meet and the procedures employed by each, I will sketch the trials of two inmates charged with "failure to work," a common offense at Trinity. My description here is simply to indicate differences in styles, especially degrees of formality, and not to give a full documentation of prison justice.

Inmate Smith, while working as a porter in the building, fails to please his supervisor with a sweeping job. That supervisor writes an arrest report and files it with the disciplinary committee. That day, or no later than the following day, the inmate finds himself standing outside the building major's office awaiting his turn before the disciplinary committee. He will appear before a tribunal composed of two high-ranking officers and a representative from the treatment staff. When this tribunal calls Smith in, the building major, who typically presides over the hearings, formally reads the offense report written by the arresting supervisor who is never present at the trial. After reading the offense, the major asks the accused if he understands the charge, and if so, tells him to sign his name on the report. The major then asks the accused for a plea — guilty or not guilty — which the inmate himself writes beside his name. The prisoner may then briefly tell his side of the story after which he is sent from the office. In his absence the tribunal deliberates, typically not over guilt or innocence (I never saw an inmate found innocent in over forty trials), but over punishment. Inmate Smith then comes back in and the major states in a somewhat formalized manner that the committee finds the inmate guilty and sentences him to seven days cell "rack up." This means he can leave his cell for meals and work only.

The field disciplinary committee proceedings reveal the greater "looseness" and informality which characterize the style in this work setting. Inmate Jones, while chopping cotton did not please his "boss" with his efforts all morning and had, according to the officer, turned in a poor performance the day before. Thus, Jones must stand trial for failure to work. Although this trial takes place after the work day in the building major's office, similarity to the building proceedings ends there. Jones enters to face not a tribunal seated rather quietly around the table, but the field major and five or six other officers, all wearing hats, boots, and spurs, and all talking, laughing, and drinking coffee. The hearing does not begin with a formal reading of a charge submitted by an absent accuser. The following, a verbatim account from field notes, exemplifies the procedures:

Major: "What's the matter with Jones?"
Officer: "Major, Jones been fuckin' off all week and I'm tired of him draggin' his ass."
Major "You been fuckin' off, Jones?"
Jones: "Major, I been workin', sir."
Major: "I think Jones been fuckin' off. We'll put him on about seven days cell rack up and see if he can't straighten his 'bidness' out."

This informality does not mean that a report of the trial will be left off Jones' record. Later that night or the next day inmate Jones will have to sign an arrest report filled out by his field supervisor and enter a plea. Thus, according to records on inmates Smith and Jones, the trials appear equally formal; in fact, however, they differ greatly.

Competition vs. Paternalism[3]

Interaction between guards and inmates in the building may be described by employing the analogy of a contest, placing the two parties in rather constant competition. Of course, regardless of the work setting in a coercive organization like a prison (Etzioni, 1961), all interaction between the keepers and the kept will be to some degree competitive. My point here then is that the building environment is much more reflective of this competition than the field.

Competition in the building means that what one party wants must be gained at a loss to the other, and so each constantly jockeys to gain the upper hand. This jockeying comprises the dynamics of control in the building. Officers want a predictable environment, one that functions smoothly and efficiently. If all inmates flow from one point to another on time with no stragglers, if no inmate tries to deprive another of a jar of peanut butter or a wristwatch, if all inmates eat all their food and throw none on the floor, if inmates follow these and a hundred more rules, the ideal of smooth functioning can be achieved. But since the desires of most inmates differ markedly from those of officials, inmate compliance with the rules is always problematic and must be enforced. In this competition between officers and inmates to achieve divergent ends, inmates benefit from their numbers as compared to guards and by the low visibility offered by the physical layout of the building. Because of these factors, guards actually see few rule violations beyond minor infractions in the hall, problems on the job, and fights in the open day room. In this competition, then, inmates often win.

In order to control inmate behavior and thereby stay at least even in their contest with inmates, building personnel regularly engage in acts to anticipate rule breaking, to catch inmates in the process, or uncover the particulars of an event after the fact. The most obvious examples in this regard are regular head counts throughout the unit and "shakedowns," thorough searches of cellblocks or dormitories to locate rumored contra-

---

[3]These concepts are loosely adopted from P. Van den Bergh's (1967) ideal types of race relations.

band such as knives or drugs. Periodic cell checks illustrate efforts to catch inmates in the wrong cell. Here the officer, armed with two by three inch cards featuring each inmates' name, number, crime and photograph, goes from cell to cell matching names and faces. Shift captains also urge these cellblock officers to ease unannounced into the cellblock during lulls in the schedule and walk the cell runs just to see what is going on. Invariably, however, an inmate will betray the presence of an officer by shouting, "jigger on the run," in an effort to warn his fellows and keep the contest even.

This competitiveness within the building fosters between inmates and guards a marked social distance. Perhaps the most valuable commodity for either side to possess is information, data on what the other side knows or intends. If information is so valuable, then passing it to a member of the other camp, and even fraternizing with him, should be highly sanctioned among inmates and guards alike. For example, the inmate taboo on "snitching" found at Trinity and in other maximum-security prisons illustrates such a sanction. Should an inmate snitch or pass information about inmate activities to officials, he risks a physical sanction or at least a "snitch jacket," a reputation for betraying other inmates. For this reason most inmates usually try to avoid being overly friendly with or close to officers. Of course, snitching does occur and because of inmate efforts to hide or disguise their rule violation, officers rely on the practice. But even when inmates do pass information, it is done surreptitiously in order to maintain at least the illusion of social distance.

Officers also seek to maintain social distance from inmates in order to avoid giving to inmates any information which could possibly undermine official authority (Sykes, 1958) and thereby place guards at a disadvantage in the contest. One type of information officers learn to protect is information on themselves, their personal life, and background. Officers know from experience that such information could form the basis of inmate stories that might harm an officer's reputation. For example, one officer related to me that he got friendly with an inmate, discussed his personal life and even bought the inmate a Coke. He learned later that this inmate bragged that the officer was "his woman," that they were so close the officer would do the inmate's bidding. The man told me it took some time to reestablish his reputation.

Another kind of information that guards try to keep from inmates is that officials do not always know what to do in given situations. Given the array of administrative, educational, medical, and recreational activities in the building, it is impossible for guards always to know the answer to an inmate's question or the legitimacy of his request. Early in my guard tenure other officers advised me that the standard practice in such a situation is to "send 'em back to their houses [cells]." While this response does not solve the inmate's problem, it does serve to create the impression that the officer might have the answer but just does not want to be bothered right then. Since it also serves to save face for the officer (Goffman, 1967), social distance is quite functional.

In the field, on the other hand, officer-inmate relations reveal a kind of paternalism. Here the roles of the two parties parallel the inequality of parent and child. That is, the inmate is relatively powerless and unable to engage in the conniving possible in the building. He is both highly visible and literally under the gun. Because the field operation emphasizes security and task completion, expectations of guards are clear and involve little negotiation. The possessiveness implied in the parent-child analogy is reflected in the common notion that the inmates do not work for the prison system; they work for their supervisor. Similarly, in Trinity parlance, an officer "carries" an inmate work squad, a term symbolizing his responsibility for and authority over it. Thus, in this field situation, the guard is able to employ, within limits, what means necessary in order to ensure work production from his men. He may, for example, urge his horse to bite a slow inmate or he may have inefficient inmates stand outside against the wall while their fellows eat lunch. He may also allow the other inmates in the squad to "tighten up" a laggert so they can all stay out of trouble.

This paternalism means that the social distance between inmates and supervisors in the field is not as great as that in the building. Unlike building personnel, field officers have the opportunity to oversee the same small squad of men each day and thus can come to know the inmates better and be known by them. Over time, guards and inmates learn the idiosyncracies of each other and a relationship built on some combination of respect and fear may emerge. I heard from several informants that one squad of inmates will only work for a particular officer; if for some reason that man is absent, they will only go through the motions for a substitute. However, while guards come to know their men through daily contact, they by no means become intimate. Officers typically come to know their men only in relation to the work setting; they may not even learn the full names of the bodies they know well. Illustrating this familiarity and closeness without intimacy is the case of the field officer asked about two inmates, Brown and White. He replied he did not know either man, although both had been in his squad for some time. When the inquisitor described the men, the field officer immediately recognized them. To him they were known only as "Gimpy" and "Carrot top."

The Role of Personal Dominance

All officers, to maintain some respect and authority must project some degree of physical competence. Regardless of duty assignment, the man who cannot muster some version of this masculine image before both inmates and his peers is in for trouble. For example, one rather obese young man I worked with had been employed by the unit for several months and had never been able to gain respect from either camp. Inmates, from the anonymity of their cells, called him "Bubbles," a term said was an improvement over earlier inmate epithets. Other officers also referred to him with a sneer; his appearance and behavior did not fit with the informal expectations of this masculine world.

But the need to project this image of personal, physical dominance seems to be less marked in the building than in the field. The routine activities which officers supervise inside involve inmates moving orderly to meals, to work, to movies, to visits, to the commissary, etc. Rule infractions and individual inmate problems aside, the bulk of what goes on under the eyes of the building security staff is known and predictable by inmates and generally considered by them to be, if not altogether legitimate, at least, relatively nonaversive. For this reason, building officers can rely to a considerable degree on the organizational routines to effect order and thus can be less concerned about constantly reminding their charges that they can personally enforce their directives.

On the other hand, establishing and maintaining personal dominion over the inmates in his squad is central to the field guard's style. While most inmates comply with the basic expectations in the field, almost all dislike the work. They must work in the heat or cold, depending on the season, at unpleasant tasks such as harvesting broom corn or reterracing a field with only a hoe as a tool. Thus, field officers unlike their counterparts inside, supervise men in an almost constantly negative and aversive situation.

That inmates consider field work to be a negative experience makes refusal to work an ever present possibility, with personal dominance by officers the primary means of forestalling such refusals. Of the three major rule violations possible in the field — fighting, escaping, and refusing to work — the last is perhaps the most threatening to the maintanence of order. Fighting among inmates does not involve a direct test of the guard's authority. Escapes may be handled in an institutionalized manner, with bullets and dogs; they do not involve a direct, interpersonal confrontation between guards and inmates. Refusal to work, however, involves such a confrontation, one in which the officer or the inmate will win. From the officer's point of view, the refusing inmate cannot be allowed to simply sit down and wait until quitting time when he can be tried for disobedience. This would be an inmate victory and perhaps even the opening salvo of a strike. Since the inmate is reasonably certain he will not be shot for his refusal, and since he is at the bottom of the inmate work hierarchy with perhaps little to lose, a major crisis exists for the field staff. To maximize control and order in the field, the inmate must be made to resume working. Better still, from the officer's point of view, the inmate must be prevented from refusing to work in the first place.

To ensure that inmate refusals to work are few and short-lived, the guard in the field cannot rely upon the authority of his uniform alone. He must add the weight of his personal authority. Indeed his success in this environment depends on how well he is able to dominate his squad and have his expectations met. He may do this by presenting such a tough, abrasive demeanor that his charges will produce because they believe that working for him is more acceptable than the consequences of not working. The field officer may also create in the minds of his squad considerable uncertainty about just what he might do. Many officers believe that "playin' with their heads" or "actin' crazy" are viable means of maintaining control. An informant said of one field officer that "his thieves [squad] aren't sure he won't pop a cap at 'em just to hear the gun go off." This man, and the other field officers, try to style their behavior so that inmates will never doubt they can and will personally back up any directive.

CONCLUSION

Each of the two major settings at Trinity reflects a different conception of social order. In the field, order consists of hard work, minimum negotiation between inmates and officers and, if possible, no confrontations. In the building, order essentially means bureaucratic efficiency in the movement and maintenance of prisoners. The guarding styles discussed above portray these definitions of order.

It follows that guards and inmates alike encounter a somewhat different set of expectations in the two settings, a fact that is important for the prison socialization of all parties at Trinity. For guards, the settings represent two variations of the guard subculture,[4] each with its own role and criteria for success. The building guard role, involving as it does ensuring a smooth daily schedule, is perhaps less demanding than the field role. This is because building custody is more structured, requiring less personal dominance over inmates. This is why all

---

[4]The very limited research on guard subcultures indicates that they significantly influence the behavior and career patterns of custody personnel (Jacobs and Grear, 1977; Jacobs and Kraft, 1978; Duffee, 1974). This is certainly true at Trinity.

men begin their prison work at a post inside the compound. Only after gaining experience can a man move to a field assignment. While transfer to the field does not necessarily mean a promotion (and promotion does not hinge on field experience), it does mean that the man's superiors feel he can mobilize the field style. But since the field calls for a different type of guard behavior, success in the building is no guarantee that a man can effectively "carry" a squad. Failure in the field, and subsequent return to a building assignment, causes considerable difficulty for the man involved. Regardless of the reason for the return, inmates and other officers will define the man as weak and incapable of projecting the tough demeanor called for in the field. The illustration of transfer to and failure in the field indicates how differences in the two work arenas can be consequential for an officer's socialization and prison career. It also underscores the differences in guard role expectations.

The fact of two guarding styles is also important to the socialization of inmates, how they perceive and react to incarceration. For those assigned to the field, daily movement from the building to the field and back again at day's end involves a change in social as well as physical environment. Inmates must learn and adjust to varied official expectations as reflected in the styles of guarding.[5] Moreover, reassignment from field labor to building jobs as trusties certainly alters inmate perceptions of prison. This is because most inmates consider with some justification, field work to be slave labor (Krajick, 1978). In that setting, there is a clear caste line separating guards and inmates and the subordinate status of inmates is such that they must ask (or notify) guards even before smoking ("lightin' it up, boss") or urinating ("pourin' it down, boss"). Transfer from this setting can thus make the prison experience less onerous. And since they are no longer in a field squad, inmates will be perceived by guards as less troublesome. It is a sound hypothesis, therefore, based on the self-fulfilling prophecy, that if officials

---

[5]While such adjustments to variations in informal expectations within different prison contexts are certainly part of the inmate socialization process, they are typically overlooked in the extensive literature on the topic (Thomas and Petersen, 1978). Looking at such adjustments to guard expectations would seem particularly important in light of evidence that guards may have the most significant positive or negative influence on inmates (Glaser, 1969, pp. 85; also Giallombardo, 1966, pp. 29).

expect inmates to be less troublesome then they just might be.

In addition to shaping socialization outcomes, patterns of guard behavior also contribute to the quality of control at Trinity. This unit, along with others in the state's prison system, has a reputation for a safe,[6] productive, and obedient inmate population. Whether outsiders view this reputation for effective control as good or bad,[7] it appears to be well deserved. I contend that this reputation is due in large part to the styles of guarding described above, especially the field style. That is, the field style has an initial and important impact on inmate behavior, and subsequently on control in the prison generally. The field experience sets the tone for how inmates will do time at Trinity. Since all incoming inmates labor in the fields for many months, it is here that they learn (or, if "busted" from the building, learn again) quite literally who is "boss." The guards here more forcefully and directly communicate to prisoners the *status quo*, that they are in a subordinate position and subject to the dictates of officials. When inmates understand this message and behave accordingly, all guards view them as "good inmates." Such inmates work hard, say "sir," follow orders and keep a low profile. These characteristics do not necessarily foster success on the outside, but when they describe the overt behavior of the inmate population, the result is a highly controlled, efficient prison.[8] Thus, not only are there variations in guard behavior across prison settings, but these variations can

---

[6]For example, with respect to inmate violence and death, Sylvester, Reed and Nelson (1977) report that prison deaths by homicides in the prison system containing Trinity was .75 per 10,000 inmates and staff. This figure compares with a high of 48.90 (Hawaii) and a national average of 7.44. The Trinity system had the lowest homicide rate of all prisons with over 200 inmates and reporting at least one homicide.

[7]This reputation prompts many emissaries from other state prisons to visit and examine the operations at Trinity and her sister units. In my own travels to prison institutions in other states, officials there often speak with admiration of the control reflected at Trinity (Crouch, 1977a). This reputation is not viewed positively in all quarters. In a recent profile on the Department of Corrections of which Trinity is a part, the Editors of *Corrections Magazine* (1978) asked, somewhat rhetorically, whether that system is "the paragon of prison systems or a slave plantation."

[8]Since I collected the data for this analysis, the inmate population at Trinity has grown considerably. This growth means that currently fewer inmates go to the field and those that go may do so only two or three days a week. Officials at Trinity view this situation as unfortunate precisely because incoming inmates do not experience the "shaping up" process of the field. The result, according to both building and field officers, is a marked decrease in control.

be consequential for careers of guards and inmates as well as the stability of the prison itself.

REFERENCES

Crouch, B.: *A Selective Comparison of Prisons in Louisiana, Arkansas, Mississippi, Oklahoma and Texas.* Unpublished manuscript, 1977a.

————: *On Guard: The Problem of Managing Inmates and Impressions.* Presented before the Southwestern Sociological Association, Dallas, 1977b.

Duffee, D.: The correctional officer subculture and organizational change. *Journal of Research in Crime and Delinquency,* July, pp. 155-172, 1974.

Editors: *Corrections Magazine.* 1 (March): 1978.

Etzioni, A.: *A Comparative Analysis of Complex Organizations.* New York, Free Pr, 1961.

Giallombardo, R.: *Society of Women.* New York, Wiley, 1966.

Glaser, D.: *The Effectiveness of a Prison and Parole System.* Indianapolis, Bobbs, 1969.

Goffman, E.: *Interaction Ritual: Essays on Face to Face Behavior.* Garden City, Doubleday, 1967.

Guenther, A. and Guenther, M.: Screws vs. Thugs. *Society, 1:* 42-50, 1974.

Irwin, J.: The changing social structure of men's prisons. In Greenberg, D. F. (Ed.): *Corrections and Punishment.* Beverly Hills, Sage, 1977.

Jacobs, J. and Grear, M.: Drop-outs and rejects: an analysis of the prison guard's revolving door. *Criminal Justice Review, 2(2):* 57-70, 1977.

Jacobs, J. and Kraft, L.: Integrating the keepers: a comparison of black and white prison guards in Illinois. *Social Problems, 25, 3 (February):* 304-318, 1978.

Jacobs, J. and Retsky, H.: Prison guard. *Urban Life, 4 (1):* 5-29, 1975.

Krajick, K.: They keep you in, they keep you busy, and they keep you from getting killed. *Corrections Magazine, 1 (March):* 4-8; 10-21, 1978.

Lofland, J.: *Analyzing Social Settings.* Belmont, Wadsworth Pub, 1971.

Sykes, G.: *Society of Captives.* Princeton, Princeton Pr, 1958.

Sylvester, S., Reed, J., and Nelson, D.: *Prison Homicide.* New York, Spectrum Pub, 1977.

Thomas, C. and Petersen, D.: *Prison Organization and Inmate Subcultures.* Indianapolis, Bobbs, 1977.

Van den Berghe, P. L.: *Race and Racism: A Comparative Perspective.* New York, Wiley, 1967.

Chapter 10

THE DEFECTS OF TOTAL POWER

GRESHAM M. SYKES

"FOR THE NEEDS of mass administration today," said Max Weber, "bureaucratic administration is completely indispensable. The choice is between bureaucracy and dilettantism in the field of administration."[1] To the officials of the New Jersey State Prison the choice is clear, as it is clear to the custodians of all maximum-security prisons in the United States today. They are organized into a bureaucratic administrative staff — characterized by limited and specific rules, well-defined areas of competence and responsibility, impersonal standards of performance and promotion, and so on — which is similar in many respects to that of any modern, large-scale enterprise; and it is this staff which must see to the effective execution of the prison's routine procedures.

Of the approximately 300 employees of the New Jersey State Prison, more than two-thirds are directly concerned with the supervision and control of the inmate population. These form the so-called custodian force which is broken into three eight-hour shifts, each shift being arranged in a typical pyramid of authority. The day shift, however — on duty from 6:20 AM to 2:20 PM — is far the largest. As in many organizations, the rhythm of life in the prison quickens with daybreak and trails off in the afternoon, and the period of greatest activity requires the largest number of administrative personnel.

In the bottom ranks are the wing guards, the tower guards, the guards assigned to the shops, and those with a miscellany of duties such as the guardianship of the receiving gate or the

From "The Defects of Total Power," in Gresham M. Sykes, *Society of Captives: A Study of a Maximum Security Prison* (copyright© 1958 by Princeton University Press; Princeton Paperback, 1971), pp. 40-62. Reprinted by permission of Princeton University Press and the author.
[1]Max Weber, *The Theory of Social and Economic Organization*, edited by Talcott Parsons, New York: Oxford University Press, 1947, p. 337.

garage. Immediately above these men are a number of sergeants and lieutenants and these in turn are responsible to the warden and his assistants.

The most striking fact about this bureaucracy of custodians is its unparalleled position of power — in formal terms, at least — vis-à-vis the body of men which it rules and from which it is supposed to extract compliance. The officials, after all, possess a monopoly on the legitimate means of coercion (or, as one prisoner has phrased it succinctly, "They have the guns and we don't"); and the officials can call on the armed might of the police and the National Guard in case of an overwhelming emergency. The twenty-four-hour surveillance of the custodians represents the ultimate watchfulness and, presumably, noncompliance on the part of the inmates need not go long unchecked. The rulers of this society of captives nominally hold in their hands the sole right of granting rewards and inflicting punishments and it would seem that no prisoner could afford to ignore their demands for conformity. Centers of opposition in the inmate population — in the form of men recognized as leaders by fellow prisoners — can be neutralized through the use of solitary confinement or exile to other state institutions.[2] The custodians have the right not only to issue and administer the orders and regulations which are to guide the life of the prisoner, but also the right to detain, try, and punish any individual accused of disobedience — a merging of legislative, executive, and judicial functions which has long been regarded as the earmark of complete domination. The officials of the prison, in short, appear to be the possessors of almost infinite power within their realm; and, at least on the surface, the bureaucratic staff should experience no great difficulty in converting their rules and regulations — their blueprint for behavior — into a reality.

It is true, of course, that the power position of the custodial bureaucracy is not truly infinite. The objectives which the officials pursue are not completely of their own choosing and the

---

[2] Just as the Deep South served as a dumping-ground for particularly troublesome slaves before the Civil War, so too can the county jail or mental hospital serve as a dumping-ground for the maximum-security prison. Other institutions, however, are apt to regard the Trenton Prison in somewhat the same way.

means which they can use to achieve their objectives are far from limitless. The custodians are not total despots, able to exercise power at whim, and thus they lack the essential mark of infinite power the unchallenged right of being capricious in their rule. It is this last which distinguishes terror from government, infinite power from almost infinite power, and the distinction is an important one. Neither by right nor by intention are the officials of the New Jersey State Prison free from a system of norms and laws which curb their actions. But within these limitations, the bureaucracy of the prison is organized around a grant of power which is without an equal in American society; and if the rulers of any social system could secure compliance with their rules and regulations — however sullen or unwilling — it might be expected that the officials of the maximum-security prison would be able to do so.

When we examine the New Jersey State Prison, however, we find that this expectation is not borne out in actuality. Indeed, the glaring conclusion is that despite the guns and the surveillance, the searches and the precautions of the custodians, the actual behavior of the inmate population differs markedly from that which is called for by official commands and decrees. Violence, fraud, theft, aberrant sexual behavior — all are commonplace occurrences in the daily round of institutional existence in spite of the fact that the maximum-security prison is conceived of by society as the ultimate weapon for the control of the criminal and his deviant actions. Far from being omnipotent rulers who have crushed all signs of rebellion against their regime, the custodians are engaged in a continuous struggle to maintain order — and it is a struggle in which the custodians frequently fail. Offenses committed by one inmate against another occur often, as do offenses committed by inmates against the officials and their rules. And the number of undetected offenses is, by universal agreement of both officials and inmates, far larger than the number of offenses which are discovered.

Some hint of the custodial bureaucracy's skirmishes with the population of prisoners is provided by the records of the disciplinary court which has the task of adjudicating charges brought by guards against their captives for offenses taking place within the walls. The following is a typical listing for a one-week period:

CHARGE	DISPOSITION
1) Insolence and swearing while being interrogated	1) Continue in segregation
2) Threatening an inmate	2) Drop from job
3) Attempting to smuggle roll of tape into institution	3) 1 day in segregation with restricted diet
4) Possession of contraband	4) 30 days loss of privileges
5) Possession of pair of dice	5) 2 days in segregation with restricted diet
6) Insolence	6) Reprimand
7) Out of place	7) Drop from job. Refer to classification committee for reclassification
8) Possession of home-made knife, metal, and emery paper	8) 5 days in segregation with restricted diet
9) Suspicion of gambling or receiving bets	9) Drop from job and change Wing assignment
10) Out of place	10) 15 days loss of privileges
11) Possession of contraband	11) Reprimand
12) Creating disturbance in Wing	12) Continue in segregation
13) Swearing at an officer	13) Reprimand
14) Out of place	14) 15 days loss of privileges
15) Out of place	15) 15 days loss of privileges

Even more revealing, however, than this brief and somewhat enigmatic record are the so-called charge slips in which the guard is supposed to write out the derelictions of the prisoner in some detail. In the New Jersey State Prison, charge slips form an administrative residue of past conflicts between captors and captives, and the following accounts are a fair sample:

This inmate threatened an officer's life. When I informed this inmate he was to stay in to see the chief deputy on his charge he told me if he did not go to the yard I would get a shiv in my back.
Signed: Officer A———

Inmate X cursing an officer. In mess hall inmate refused to put excess bread back on tray. Then he threw the tray on the floor. In the Center, inmate cursed both Officer Y and myself.
Signed: Officer B———

This inmate has been condemning everyone about him for

going to work. The Center gave orders for him to go to work this AM which he refused to do. While searching his cell I found drawings of picks and locks.
Signed: Officer C———

Fighting. As this inmate came to 1 Wing entrance to go to yard this AM he struck inmate G in the face.
Signed: Officer D———

Having fermented beverage in his cell. Found while inmate was in yard.
Signed: Officer E———

Attempting to instigate wing disturbance. When I asked him why he discarded [sic] my order to quiet down he said he was going to talk any time he wanted to and ——— me and do whatever I wanted in regards to it.
Signed: Officer F———

Possession of home-made shiv sharpened to razor edge on his person and possession of 2 more shivs in cell. When inmate was sent to 4 Wing, Officer H found 3″ steel blade in pocket. I ordered Officer M to search his cell and he found 2 more shivs in process of being sharpened.
Signed: Officer G———

Insolence. Inmate objected to my looking at papers he was carrying in pockets while going to the yard. He snatched them violently from my hand and gave me some very abusive talk. This man told me to ——— myself and raised his hands as if to strike me. I grabbed him by the shirt and took him to the Center.
Signed: Officer H———

Assault with knife on inmate K. During Idle Men's mess at approximately 11:10 AM this man assaulted Inmate K with a homemade knife. Inmate K was receiving his rations at the counter when Inmate B rushed up to him and plunged a knife in his chest, arm, and back. I grappled with him and with the assistance of Officers S and V, we disarmed the inmate and took him to the Center. Inmate K was immediately taken to the hospital.
Signed: Officer I———

Sodomy. Found inmate W in cell with no clothing on and inmate Z on top of him with no clothing. Inmate W told me he was going to lie like a —— — —— ——— to get out of it.
Signed: Officer J———

Attempted escape on night of 4/15/53. This inmate along with Inmates L and T succeeded in getting on roof of 6 Wing and having home-made bombs in their possession.
Signed: Officer K———

Fighting and possession of home-made shiv. Struck first blow to Inmate P. He struck blow with a roll of black rubber rolled up in his fist. He then produced a knife made out of wire tied to a toothbrush.
Signed: Officer L———

Refusing medication prescribed by Doctor W. Said, "What do you think I am, a damn fool, taking that ——— for a head-ache? Give it to the doctor."
Signed: Officer M———

Inmate loitering on tier. There is a clique of several men who lock on top tier, who ignore the rule of returning directly to their cells and attempt to hang out on the tier in a group.
Signed: Officer N———

It is hardly surprising that when the guards at the New Jersey State Prison were asked what topics should be of first importance in a proposed in-service training program, 98 percent picked "what to do in event of trouble." The critical issue for the moment, however, is that the dominant position of the custodial staff is more fiction than reality, if we think of domination as something more than the outward forms and symbols of power. If power is viewed as the probability that orders and regulations will be obeyed by a given group of individuals, as Max Weber has suggested,[3] the New Jersey State Prison is perhaps more notable for the doubtfulness of obedience than its certainty. The weekly records of the disciplinary court and charge slips provide an admittedly poor index of offenses or acts of noncompliance committed within the walls, for these form only a small, visible segment of an iceberg whose greatest bulk lies beneath the surface of official recognition. The public

---

[3] *Ibid.*, p. 324.

is periodically made aware of the officials' battle to enforce their regime within the prison, commonly in the form of allegations in the newspapers concerning homosexuality, illegal use of drugs, assaults, and so on. But the ebb and flow of public attention given to these matters does not match the constancy of these problems for the prison officials who are all too well aware that "incidents" — the very thing they try to minimize — are not isolated or rare events but are instead a commonplace. The number of incidents in the New Jersey State Prison is probably no greater than that to be found in most maximum-security institutions in the United States and may, indeed, be smaller, although it is difficult to make comparisons. In any event, it seems clear that the custodians are bound to their captives in a relationship of conflict rather than compelled acquiescence, despite the custodians' theoretical supremacy, and we now need to see why this should be so.

II

In our examination of the forces which undermine the power position of the New Jersey State Prison's custodial bureaucracy, the most important fact is, perhaps, that the power of the custodians is not based on authority.

Now power based on authority is actually a complex social relationship in which an individual or a group of individuals is recognized as possessing a right to issue commands or regulations and those who receive these commands or regulations feel compelled to obey by a sense of duty. In its pure form, then, or as an ideal type, power based on authority has two essential elements: a rightful or legitimate effort to exercise control on the one hand and an inner, moral compulsion to obey, by those who are to be controlled, on the other. In reality, of course, the recognition of the legitimacy of efforts to exercise control may be qualified or partial and the sense of duty, as a motive for compliance, may be mixed with motives of fear or self-interest. But it is possible for theoretical purposes to think of power based on authority in its pure form and to use this as a baseline in describing the empirical case.[4]

---

[4]*Ibid.*, Introduction.

It is the second element of authority — the sense of duty as a motive for compliance — which supplies the secret strength of most social organizations. Orders and rules can be issued with the expectation that they will be obeyed without the necessity of demonstrating in each case that compliance will advance the subordinate's interests. Obedience or conformity springs from an internalized morality which transcends the personal feelings of the individual; the fact that an order or a rule is an order or a rule becomes the basis for modifying one's behavior, rather than a rational calculation of the advantages which might be gained.

In the prison, however, it is precisely this sense of duty which is lacking in the general inmate population. The regime of the custodians is expressed as a mass of commands and regulations passing down a hierarchy of power. In general, these efforts at control are regarded as legitimate by individuals in the hierarchy, and individuals tend to respond because they feel they "should," down to the level of the guard in the cellblock, the industrial shop, or the recreation yard.[5] But now these commands and regulations must jump a gap which separates the captors from the captives. And it is at this point that a sense of duty tends to disappear and with it goes that easily-won obedience which many organizations take for granted in the naïveté of their unrecognized strength. In the prison, power must be based on something other than internalized morality, and the custodians find themselves confronting men who must be forced, bribed, or cajoled into compliance. This is not to say that inmates feel that the efforts of prison officials to exercise control are wrongful or illegitimate; in general, prisoners do not feel that the prison officials have usurped positions of power which are not rightfully theirs, nor do prisoners feel that the orders and regulations that descend upon them from above represent an illegal extension of their rulers' grant of government. Rather, the noteworthy fact about the social system of the New Jersey State Prison is that the bond between recognition of the legitimacy of control and the sense of duty has been torn apart. In these terms the social system of the

---

[5]Failures in this process within the custodial staff itself will be discussed in the latter portion of this chapter.

prison is very similar to a *Gebietsverband,* a territorial group living under a regime imposed by a ruling few.[6] Like a province that has been conquered by force of arms, the community of prisoners has come to accept the validity of the regime constructed by their rulers but the subjugation is not complete. Whether he sees himself as caught by his own stupidity, the workings of chance, his inability to "fix" the case, or the superior skill of the police, the criminal in prison seldom denies the legitimacy of confinement.[7] At the same time, the recognition of the legitimacy of society's surrogates and their body rules is not accompanied by an internalized obligation to obey and the prisoner thus accepts the fact of his captivity at one level and rejects it at another. If for no other reason, then, the custodial institution is valuable for a theory of human behavior because it makes us realize that men need not be motivated to conform to a regime which they define as rightful. It is in this apparent contradiction that we can see the first flaw in the custodial bureaucracy's assumed supremacy.

III

Since the officials of prison possess a monopoly on the means of coercion, as we have pointed out earlier, it might be thought that the inmate population could simply be forced into conformity and that the lack of an inner moral compulsion to obey on the part of the inmates could be ignored. Yet the combination of a bureaucratic staff — that most modern, rational form of mobilizing effort to exercise control — and the use of physical violence — that most ancient device to channel man's conduct — must strike us as an anomaly and with good

---

[6] *Ibid.,* p. 149.

[7] This statement requires two qualifications. First, a number of inmates steadfastly maintain that they are innocent of the crime with which they are charged. It is the illegitimacy of their particular case, however, rather than the illegitimacy of confinement in general, which moves them to protest. Second, some of the more sophisticated prisoners argue that the conditions of imprisonment are wrong, although perhaps not illegitimate or illegal, on the grounds that reformation should be the major aim of imprisonment and the officials are not working hard enough in this direction.

reason. The use of force is actually grossly inefficient as a means for securing obedience, particularly when those who are to be controlled are called on to perform a task of any complexity. A blow with a club may check an immediate revolt, it is true, but it cannot assure effective performance on a punchpress. A "come-along," a straitjacket or a pair of handcuffs may serve to curb one rebellious prisoner in a crisis, but they will be of little aid in moving more than 1200 inmates through the mess hall in a routine and orderly fashion. Furthermore, the custodians are well aware that violence once unleashed is not easily brought to heel and it is this awareness that lies behind the standing order that no guard should ever strike an inmate with his hand — he should always use a nightstick. This rule is not an open invitation to brutality but an attempt to set a high threshold on the use of force in order to eliminate the casual cuffing which might explode into extensive and violent retaliation. Similarly, guards are under orders to throw their nightsticks over the wall if they are on duty in the recreation yard when a riot develops. A guard without weapons, it is argued, is safer than a guard who tries to hold on to his symbol of office, for a mass of rebellious inmates may find a single nightstick a goad rather than a restraint, and the guard may find himself beaten to death with his own means of compelling order.

In short, the ability of the officials to physically coerce their captives into the paths of compliance is something of an illusion as far as the day-to-day activities of the prison are concerned and may be of doubtful value in moments of crisis. Intrinsically inefficient as a method of making men carry out a complex task, diminished in effectiveness by the realities of the guard-inmate ratio,[8] and always accompanied by the danger of touching off further violence, the use of physical force by the custodians has many limitations as a basis on which to found the routine operation of the prison. Coercive tactics may have some utility in checking blatant disobedience — if only a few

---

[8]Since each shift is reduced in size by vacations, regular days off, sickness, etc., even the day shift — the largest of the three — can usually muster no more than ninty guards to confront the population of more than 1200 prisoners. The fact that they are so heavily outnumbered is not lost on the officials.

men disobey. But if the great mass of criminals in prison are to be brought into the habit of conformity, it must be on other grounds. Unable to count on a sense of duty to motivate their captives to obey and unable to depend on the direct and immediate use of violence to insure a step-by-step submission to the rules, the custodians must fall back on a system of rewards and punishments.

Now if men are to be controlled by the use of rewards and punishments — by promises and threats — at least one point is patent: The rewards and punishments dangled in front of the individual must indeed be rewards and punishments from the point of view of the individual who is to be controlled. It is precisely on this point, however, that the custodians' system of rewards and punishments founders. In our discussion of the problems encountered in securing conscientious performance at work, we suggested that both the penalties and the incentives available to the officials were inadequate. This is also largely true, at a more general level, with regard to rewards and punishments for securing compliance with the wishes of the custodians in all areas of prison life.

In the first place, the punishments which the officials can inflict — for theft, assaults, escape attempts, gambling, insolence, homosexuality, and all the other deviations from the pattern of behavior called for by the regime of the custodians — do not represent a profound difference from the prisoner's usual status. It may be that when men are chronically deprived of liberty, material goods and services, recreational opportunities and so on, the few pleasures that are granted take on a new importance and the threat of their withdrawal is a more powerful motive for conformity than those of us in the free community can realize. To be locked up in the solitary confinement wing, that prison within a prison; to move from the monotonous, often badly prepared meals in the mess hall to a diet of bread and water;[9] to be dropped from a dull, unsatisfying job and forced to remain in idleness — all, perhaps, may mean the

---

[9]The usual inmate fare is both balanced and sufficient in quantity, but it has been pointed out that the meals are not apt to be particularly appetizing since prisoners must eat them with nothing but a spoon. Cf. Report of the Governor's Committee to Examine the Prison and Parole System of New Jersey, November 21, 1952, pp. 74-79.

difference between an existence which can be borne, painful though it may be, and one which cannot. But the officials of the New Jersey State Prison are dangerously close to the point where the stock of legitimate punishments has been exhausted and it would appear that for many prisoners the few punishments that are left have lost their potency. To this we must couple the important fact that such punishments as the custodians can inflict may lead to an increased prestige for the punished inmate in the eyes of his fellow prisoners. He may become a hero, a martyr, a man who has confronted his captors and dared them to do their worst. In the dialectics of the inmate population, punishments and rewards have, then, been reversed, and the control measures of the officials may support disobedience rather than decrease it.

In the second place, the system of rewards and punishments in the prison is defective because the reward side of the picture has been largely stripped away. Mail and visiting privileges, recreational privileges, the supply of personal possessions — all are given to the inmate at the time of his arrival in one fixed sum. Even the so-called Good Time — the portion of the prisoner's sentence deducted for good behavior — is automatically subtracted from the prisoner's sentence when he begins his period of imprisonment.[10] Thus the officials have placed themselves in the peculiar position of granting the prisoner all available benefits or rewards at the time of his entrance into the system. The prisoner, then, finds himself unable to win any significant gains by means of compliance, for there are no gains left to be won.

From the viewpoint of the officials, of course, the privileges of the prison social system are regarded as rewards, as something to be achieved. That is to say, the custodians hold that recreation, access to the inmate store, Good Time, or visits from individuals in the free community are conditional upon confor-

---

[10]The law of New Jersey stipulates that each prisoner may reduce the sentence he receives from the court by (a) earning one day per week for performing work assignments conscientiously (Work Time); and (b) earning commutation of his sentence, up to sixty days during the first year of imprisonment and in increasing amounts for subsequent years for orderly deportment and manifest efforts at self-control and improvement (Good Time). Cf. New Jersey Department of Institutions and Agencies, Research Bulletin No. 18 "Two Thousand State Prisoners in New Jersey," Trenton, New Jersey, May, 1954.

mity or good behavior. But the evidence suggests that from the viewpoint of the inmates the variety of benefits granted by the custodians is not defined as something to be earned but as an inalienable right — as the just due of the inmate which should not turn on the question of obedience or disobedience within the walls. After all, the inmate population claims, these benefits have belonged to the prisoner from the time when he first came to the institution.

In short, the New Jersey State Prison makes an initial grant of all its rewards and then threatens to withdraw them if the prisoner does not conform. It does not start the prisoner from scratch and promise to grant its available rewards one by one as the prisoner proves himself through continued submission to the institutional regulations. As a result a subtle alchemy is set in motion whereby the inmates cease to see the rewards of the system as rewards, that is, as benefits contingent upon performance; instead, rewards are apt to be defined as obligations. Whatever justification might be offered for such a policy, it would appear to have a number of drawbacks as a method of motivating prisoners to fall into the posture of obedience. In effect, rewards and punishments of the officials have been collapsed into one, and the prisoner moves in a world where there is no hope of progress but only the possibility of further punishments. Since the prisoner is already suffering from most of the punishments permitted by society, the threat of imposing those few remaining is all too likely to be a gesture of futility.

IV

Unable to depend on that inner moral compulsion or sense of duty which eases the problem of control in most social organizations, acutely aware that brute force is inadequate, and lacking an effective system of legitimate rewards and punishments which might induce prisoners to conform to institutional regulations on the grounds of self interest, the custodians of the New Jersey State Prison are considerably weakened in their attempts to impose their regime on their captive population. The result, in fact, is, as we have already indicated, a good deal of deviant behavior or noncompliance in a social system where the rulers at first glance seem to possess almost infinite power.

Yet systems of power may be defective for reasons other than the fact that those who are ruled do not feel the need to obey the orders and regulations descending on them from above. Systems of power may also fail because those who are supposed to rule are unwilling to do so. The unissued order, the deliberately ignored disobedience, the duty left unperformed — these are cracks in the monolith just as surely as are acts of defiance in the subject population. The "corruption" of the rulers may be far less dramatic that the insurrection of the ruled, for power unexercised is seldom as visible as power which is challenged, but the system of power still falters.[11]

Now the official in the lowest ranks of the custodial bureaucracy — the guard in the cellblock, the industrial shop, or the recreation yard — is the pivotal figure on which the custodial bureaucracy turns. It is he who must supervise and control the inmate population in concrete and detailed terms. It is he who must see to the translation of the custodial regime from blueprint to reality and engage in the specific battles for conformity. Counting prisoners, periodically reporting to the center of communications, signing passes, checking groups of inmates as they come and go, searching for contraband or signs of attempts to escape — these make up the minutiae of his eight-hour shift. In addition, he is supposed to be alert for violations of the prison rules which fall outside his routine sphere of surveillance. Not only must he detect and report deviant behavior after it occurs; he must curb deviant behavior before it arises as well as when he is called on to prevent a minor quarrel among prisoners from flaring into a more dangerous situation. And he must make sure that the inmates in his charge perform their assigned tasks with a reasonable degree of efficiency.

The expected role of the guard, then, is a complicated compound of policeman and foreman, of cadi, counsellor, and boss all rolled into one. But as the guard goes about his duties, piling one day on top of another (and the guard too, in a

---

[11]Portions of the following discussion concerning the corruption of the guards' authority are to be found in Gresham M. Sykes, *Crime and Society*, New York: Random House, 1956.

certain sense, is serving time in confinement), we find that the system of power in the prison is defective not only because the means of motivating the inmates to conform are largely lacking but also because the guard is frequently reluctant to enforce the full range of the institution's regulations. The guard frequently fails to report infractions of the rules which have occurred before his eyes. The guard often transmits forbidden information to inmates, such as plans for searching particular cells in a surprise raid for contraband. The guard often neglects elementary security requirements and on numerous occasions he will be found joining his prisoners in outspoken criticisms of the warden and his assistants. In short, the guard frequently shows evidence of having been "corrupted" by the captive criminals over whom he stands in theoretical dominance. This failure within the ranks of the rulers is seldom to be attributed to outright bribery — bribery, indeed, is usually unnecessary, for far more effective influences are at work to bridge the gap supposedly separating captors and captives.

In the first place, the guard is in close and intimate association with his prisoners throughout the course of the working day. He can remain aloof only with great difficulty, for he possesses few of those devices which normally serve to maintain social distance between the rulers and the ruled. He cannot withdraw physically in symbolic affirmation of his superior position; he has no intermediaries to bear the brunt of resentment springing from orders which are disliked; and he cannot fall back on a dignity adhering to his office — he is a *hack* or a *screw* in the eyes of those he controls and an unwelcome display of officiousness evokes that great destroyer of unquestioned power, the ribald humor of the dispossessed.

There are many pressures in American culture to "be nice," to be a "good Joe," and the guard in the maximum-security prison is not immune. The guard is constantly exposed to a sort of moral blackmail in which the first signs of condemnation, estrangement, or rigid adherence to the rules is countered by the inmates with the threat of ridicule or hostility. And in this complex interplay, the guard does not always start from a position of determined opposition to "being friendly." He holds an intermediate post in a bureaucratic structure between top prison officials — in his captains, lieutenants, and sergeants — and the prisoners in his charge. Like many such figures, the guard is caught in a conflict of loyalties. He often has reason to resent the actions of his superior officers — the reprimands, the lack of ready appreciation, the incomprehensible order — and in the inmates he finds willing sympathizers: They too claim to suffer from the unreasonable irritants of power. Furthermore, the guard in many cases is marked by a basic ambivalence toward the criminals under his supervision and control. It is true that the inmates of the prison have been condemned by society through the agency of the courts, but some of these prisoners must be viewed as a success in terms of a worldly system of the values which accords high prestige to wealth and influence even though they may have been won by devious means; and the poorly paid guard may be gratified to associate with a famous racketeer. Moreover, this ambivalence in the guard's attitudes toward the criminals nominally under his thumb may be based on something more than a *sub rosa* respect for the notorious. There may also be a discrepancy between the judgments of society and the guard's own opinions as far as the "criminality" of the prisoner is concerned. It is difficult to define the man convicted of deserting his wife, gambling, or embezzlement as a desperate criminal to be suppressed at all costs, and the crimes of even the most serious offenders lose their significance with the passage of time. In the eyes of the custodian, the inmate tends to become a man in prison rather than a criminal in prison and the relationship between captor and captive is subtly transformed in the process.

In the second place, the guard's position as a strict enforcer of the rules is undermined by the fact that he finds it almost impossible to avoid the claims of reciprocity. To a large extent the guard is dependent on inmates for the satisfactory performance of his duties; and like many individuals in positions of power, the guard is evaluated in terms of the conduct of the men he controls. A troublesome, noisy, dirty cellblock reflects on the guard's ability to "handle" prisoners and this ability forms an important component of the merit rating which is used as the basis for pay raises and promotions. As we have pointed out above, a guard cannot rely on the direct application of force to achieve compliance nor can he easily depend on threats of punishment. And if the guard does insist on constantly using the last few negative sanctions available to the institution — if the guard turns in charge slip after charge slip for every violation of the rules which he encounters — he becomes burdensome to the top officials of the prison bureaucratic staff who realize only too well that their apparent dominance rests on some degree of cooperation. A system of power which can enforce its rules only by bringing its formal machinery of accusation, trial, and punishment into play at every turn will soon be lost in a haze of pettifogging detail.

The guard, then, is under pressure to achieve a smoothly running tour of duty not with the stick but with the carrot, but here again his legitimate stock is limited. Facing demands from above that he achieve compliance and stalemated from below, he finds that one of the most meaningful rewards he can offer is to ignore certain offenses or make sure that he never places himself in a position where he will discover them. Thus the guard — backed by all the power of the state, close to armed men who will run to his aid, and aware that any prisoner who disobeys him can be punished if he presses charges against him — often discovers that his best path of action is to make "deals" or "trades" with the captives in his power. In effect, the guard buys compliance or obedience in certain areas at the cost of tolerating disobedience elsewhere.

Aside from winning compliance "where it counts" in the course of the normal day, the guard has another favor to be secured from the inmates which makes him willing to forego strict enforcement of all prison regulations. Many custodial institutions have experienced a riot in which the tables are turned momentarily and the captives hold sway over their quondam captors; and the rebellions of 1952 loom large in the memories of the officials in the New Jersy State Prison. The guard knows that he may some day be a hostage and that his life may turn on a settling of old accounts. A fund of good will becomes a valuable form of insurance and this fund is almost sure to be lacking if he has continually played the part of a martinet. In the folklore of the prison there are enough tales about strict guards who have had the misfortune of being cap-

tured and savagely beaten during a riot to raise doubts about
the wisdom of demanding complete conformity.

In the third place, the theoretical dominance of the guard is
undermined in actuality by the innocuous encroachment of the
prisoner on the guard's duties. Making out reports, checking
cells at the periodic count, locking and unlocking doors — in
short, all the minor chores which the guard is called on to
perform — may gradually be transferred into the hands of
inmates whom the guard has come to trust. The cellblock
runner, formally assigned the tasks of delivering mail, house-
keeping duties, and so on, is of particular importance in this
respect. Inmates in this position function in a manner analogous to that of the company clerk in the armed forces and like
such figures they may wield power and influence far beyond
the nominal definition of their role. For reasons of indifference,
laziness, or naïveté, the guard may find that much of the power
which he is supposed to exercise has slipped from his grasp.

Now, power, like a woman's virtue, once lost is hard to
regain. The measures to rectify an established pattern of abdication need to be much more severe than those required to stop
the first steps in the transfer of control from the guard to his
prisoner. A guard assigned to a cellblock in which a large
portion of power has been shifted in the past from the officials
to the inmates is faced with the weight of precedence; it requires a good deal of moral courage on his part to withstand
the aggressive tactics of prisoners who fiercely defend the patterns of corruption established by custom. And if the guard
himself has allowed his control to be subverted, he may find
that any attempts to undo his error are checked by a threat from
the inmate to send a *snitch-kite* — an anonymous note — to
the guard's superior officers explaining his past derelictions in
detail. This simple form of blackmail may be quite sufficient to
maintain the relationships established by friendship, reciprocity, or encroachment.

It is apparent, then, that the power of the custodians is defective, not simply in the sense that the ruled are rebellious, but
also in the sense that the rulers are reluctant. We must attach a
new meaning to Lord Acton's aphorism that power tends to
corrupt and absolute power corrupts absolutely. The custo-

dians of the New Jersey State Prison, far from being converted into brutal tyrants, are under strong pressure to compromise with their captives, for it is a paradox that they can insure their dominance only by allowing it to be corrupted. Only by tolerating violations of "minor" rules and regulations can the guard secure compliance in the "major" areas of the custodial regime. Ill-equipped to maintain the social distance, which in theory separates the world of the officials and the world of the inmates, their suspicions eroded by long familiarity, the custodians are led into a *modus vivendi* with their captives which bears little resemblance to the stereotypical picture of guards and their prisoners.

V

The fact that the officials of the prison experience serious difficulties in imposing their regime on the society of prisoners is sometimes attributed to inadequacies of the custodial staff's personnel. These inadequacies, it is claimed, are in turn due to the fact that more than 50 percent of the guards are temporary employees who have not passed a Civil Service examination. In 1952, for example, a month and a half before the disturbances which dramatically underlined some of the problems of the officials, the deputy commissioner of the Department of Institutions and Agencies made the following points in a report concerning the temporary officer of the New Jersey State Prison's custodial force:

1. Because they are not interested in the prison service as a career, the temporary officers tend to have a high turnover as they are quick to resign to accept more remunerative employment.

2. Because they are inexperienced, they are not able to foresee or forestall disciplinary infractions, the oncoming symptoms of which the more experienced officer would detect and take appropriate preventive measures.

3. Because they are not trained as are the regular officers, they do not have the self-confidence that comes with the physical training and defensive measures which are part of the regular officers' pre-service and in-service training and, therefore, it is not uncommon for them to be somewhat timid and inclined

to permit the prisoner to take advantage of them.

4. Because many of them are beyond the age limit or cannot meet the physical requirements for regular appointment as established by Civil Service, they cannot look forward to a permanent career and are, therefore, less interested in the welfare of the institution than their brother officers.

5. Finally, because of the short period of employment, they do not recognize the individual prisoners who are most likely to incite trouble or commit serious infractions, and they are at a disadvantage in dealing with the large groups which congregate in the cellblocks, the mess hall, the auditorium, and the yard.[12]

At present, the guard at the New Jersey State Prison receives a salary of $3,240 per year when he is hired and he can reach a maximum of $3,840 per year; and there is little doubt that the low salary scale accounts for much of the prison's high turnover rate. The fact that the job of the guard is often depressing, dangerous, and possesses relatively low prestige adds further difficulties. There is also little doubt that the high turnover rate carries numerous evils in its train, as the comments of the deputy commissioner have indicated. Yet even if higher salaries could counterbalance the many dissatisfying features of the guard's job — to a point where the custodial force consisted of men with long service rather than a group of transients — there remains a question of whether or not the problems of administration in the New Jersey State Prison would be eased to a significant extent. This, of course, is heresy from the viewpoint of those who trace the failure of social organizations to the personal failings of the individuals who man the organizational structure. Perhaps, indeed, there is some comfort in the idea that if the budget of the prison were larger, if higher salaries could be paid to entice "better" personnel within the walls, if guards could be persuaded to remain for longer periods, then the many difficulties of the prison bureaucracy would disappear. From this point of view, the problems of the custodial institution are rooted in the niggardliness of the free community and the consequent inadequacies

---

[12]See New Jersey Committee to Examine and Investigate the Prison and Parole Systems of New Jersey, *Report*, November 21, 1952.

of the institution's personnel rather than flaws in the social system of the prison itself. But to suppose that higher salaries are an answer to the plight of the custodians is to suppose, first, that there are men who by reason of their particular skills and personal characteristics are better qualified to serve as guards if they could be recruited; and second, that experience and training within the institution itself will better prepare the guard for his role, if greater financial rewards could convince him to make a career of his prison employment. Both of these suppositions, however, are open to some doubt. There are few jobs in the free community which are comparable to that of the guard in the maximum-security prison and which, presumably, could equip the guard-to-be with the needed skills. If the job requirements of the guard's position are not technical skills but turn on matters of character such as courage, honesty, and so on, there is no assurance that men with these traits will flock to the prison if the salary of the guard is increased. And while higher salaries may decrease the turnover rate — thus making an in-service training program feasible and providing a custodial force with greater experience — it is not certain if such a change can lead to marked improvement. A brief period of schooling can familiarize the new guard with the routines of the institution, but to prepare the guard for the realities of his assigned role with lectures and discussions is quite another matter. And it seems entirely possible that prolonged experience in the prison may enmesh the guard deeper and deeper in patterns of compromise and misplaced trust rather than sharpening his drive toward a rigorous enforcement of institutional regulations.

We are not arguing, of course, that the quality of the personnel in the prison is irrelevant to the successful performance of the bureaucracy's tasks nor are we arguing that it would be impossible to improve the quality of the personnel by increasing salaries. We are arguing, however, that the problems of the custodians far transcend the size of the guard's paycheck or the length of his employment and that better personnel is at best a palliative rather than a final cure. It is true, of course, that it is difficult to unravel the characteristics of a social organization from the characteristics of the individuals who are its members; but there seems to be little reason to believe that a different crop of guards in the New Jersey State Prison would exhibit an outstanding increase in efficiency in trying to impose the regime of the custodians on the population of prisoners. *The lack of a sense of duty among those who are held captive, the obvious fallacies of coercion, the pathetic collection of rewards and punishments to induce compliance, the strong pressures toward the corruption of the guard in the form of friendship, reciprocity, and the transfer of duties into the hands of trusted inmates — all are structural defects in the prison's system of power rather than individual inadequacies.*[13]

The question of whether these defects are inevitable in the custodial institution — or in any system of total power — must be deferred to a later chapter. For the moment it is enough to point out that in the New Jersey State Prison the custodians are unable or unwilling to prevent their captives from committing numerous violations of the rules, which make up the theoretical blueprint for behavior, and this failure is not a temporary, personal aberration but a built-in feature of the prison social system. It is only by understanding this fact that we can understand the world of the prisoners, since so many significant aspects of inmate behavior — such as coercion of fellow prisoners, fraud, gambling, homosexuality, sharing stolen supplies, and so on — are in clear contravention to institutional regulations. It is the nature of this world which must now claim our attention.

---

[13]Those who are familiar with prison systems such as those of the federal government or the State of California might argue that I have underestimated the possibilities of improvement which can be won with well-trained, well-paid, well-led guards. They might be right, but I think it is important to stress the serious, "built-in" weaknesses of the prison as a social system.

Chapter 11

WHERE STAFF AND PRISONERS MEET

TERENCE P. MORRIS AND PAULINE J. MORRIS

ONE of the focal points in Sykes' analysis of the New Jersey State Prison is his consideration of the notion of "total power." The maximum-security prison with its comprehensive rules, its staff who are prosecution, judge and jury in their own cause, and its ability to mobilize, in extremity, the coercive machinery of the wider society, its courts or even its guns, bears a remarkable resemblance to a totalitarian social system. In reality, as Sykes argues, there are major defects in the structure of total power:

> The lack of a sense of duty among those who are held captive, the obvious fallacies of coercion, the pathetic collection of rewards and punishments to induce compliance, the strong pressures toward the corruption of the guard in the form of friendship, reciprocity and transfer of duties into the hands of trusted inmates — all are structural defects in the prison's system of power rather than individual inadequacies.[1]

Some of these issues have already been discussed, particularly those which relate to the imperfections of bureaucratic administration; our concern here is to examine those aspects of the relationships between staff and prisoners which bear fundamentally on the problem. It would be quite erroneous to accept at face value the statements of prisoners that "all screws are bastards" and of the staff that "all prisoners are liars and not to be trusted." If these stereotypes were consistently held throughout the prison community and were given substance in overt behaviour, the level of tension, and possibly physical conflict, between staff and prisoners would rise to such a level

---

From Terence P. Morris and Pauline J. Morris, *Pentonville: A Sociological Study of an English Prison*, 1963, London, Routledge and Kegan Paul Limited. Courtesy of Terence P. Morris and Pauline J. Morris.
[1]Gresham Sykes, *Society of Captives*, Princeton University Press, 1958, p. 61. That these defects are structural and not "individual" in origin cannot be too strongly emphasized.

that the prison would be perpetually on the threshold of crisis. Whatever staff and prisoners may *say* about each other, the fact remains that neutrality is more characteristic of most relationships than hostility, and that in some instances relationships between staff and prisoners may be characterized by considerable warmth. The two most important phenomena to be studied here are:

(1) the configuration of inmate-staff hostility;
(2) the "corruption of the staff" and the consequent erosion of the face of total power.

STAFF ATTITUDES TO PRISONERS

Because the senior, nonuniformed staff of the prison come into comparatively limited contact with the mass of inmates, their attitudes towards them tend to be different from those of the discipline and workshop staff who are in continuous face-to-face relations with them. It is precisely these latter relationships which are crucial, and in recent years they have been subject to more fundamental change than relationships between inmates and senior prison personnel. For the prisoner, the personalized symbol of his captivity is the "screw" who makes up the bulk of the staff. Principal officers, chief officers, deputy governors and governors are, in the last analysis, no more than varying species of "super-screws." Of the Trenton staff, Sykes writes:

> . . . the administrators of the New Jersey State Prison have no great interest in inflicting punishments on their prisoners for the crimes which they have committed in the free community. . . . There is no indication in the day-to-day operation of the prison that the officials have any desire to act as avenging angels. . . . [2]

Whatever prisoners may argue to the contrary when they repeat the stylized myths of cruelty and victimization, which abound in the prison, it remains that this proposition holds substantially true for Pentonville. While there are both particular prisoners and particular crimes, which individual officers may detest, it is broadly true to say that amongst the Pentonville staff it is

---

[2]Sykes, *op. cit.*, p. 31.

despairing cynicism that characterizes their attitudes towards their captives rather than hate or dislike. In particular, it is the fact that prisoners recidivate that the staff find intolerable — "However much you do for them, however decently you treat them, they still come back." The idea that recidivism is an expression of base ingratitude is continually reinforced by the constant repetition of the statement that "so much is done for prisoners, but nothing is done for the staff."

A view expressed by many officers at Pentonville was that "an officer who runs his feet off for the sake of prisoners is a bad officer. A good officer sees that a prisoner gets exactly what he is entitled to, no more, no less." Statements like "there should be a treadmill here" and "prisoners should be sterilized to prevent them breeding children who will come to prison" can often represent bewilderment and confusion as much as outrage or moral indignation towards the offender. Undoubtedly some personnel with cruel and sadistic leanings slip through the selection mesh. There is a desire to treat men consistently, not only because of its innate fairness but because it simplifies the custodial task. Pentonville, however, is a prison in which reformist, punitive and apathetic attitudes are quite fantastically confused. Thus, while some officers agree that "even if soft treatment doesn't help the men it does help the officers," they also feel that "prisoners have it altogether too easy." Those who have served long years in Pentonville or prisons like it tend to settle for a degree of tolerance beneath which lies an impenetrable layer of cynicism. Those who have recently been exposed to the Wakefield experience find that its ideology is unacceptable in Pentonville. In particular, those who go for refresher courses may be unmoved by what they learn. Thus two officers recently returned indicated that all the information they had been given on the etiology of crime — family, environment, unsatisfactory childhood experiences, and so forth, had in no way altered their attitudes towards prisoners. In spite of all these factors, it was still the prisoner's fault that he was in prison, and the prisoner was still seen as contemptible and unhelpable. A third officer who had been to Wakefield, however, expressed frustration at having to work in Pentonville:

"Officers here have the wrong approach — too much chasing and too little understanding."

Another on his return commented that since he had been to Wakefield he had been particularly discontented with Pentonville and realized that

" . . . if ever I am to achieve what is now expected of prison officers I shall have to get away from a place like this where the only attitude appears to be either 'bash 'em or 'top 'em'."

THE PROBLEM OF CONTAMINATION

One principal officer commented to the research worker:

"Every so often the staff should be moved around because they get too like the men in their ways of behaving. Influences work both ways."

Not only do officers and prisoners share large areas of an urban, proletarian culture, but the officer finds that his closest social contacts in the work situation are with his captives. He can choose to remain aloof, but this in effect means a degree of social isolation, for his superiors will be hierarchically remote and his peers often physically distant. Alternatively, he can choose to seek integration in day-to-day situations. That the latter solution is normally chosen is scarcely surprising, but it means that he must in effect develop three distinct behavioral systems, one for relationships off-duty with his family and friends, one for his peers, and one for his actual work situation.

Because he already shares much of the culture of the community with his prisoners, and, like them, is subject to authoritarian discipline, the average officer, now that personal relationships with prisoners are no longer prohibited but actively encouraged, can make the adjustment fairly easily. This may, to some extent, explain the free use that officers make of swear words in speaking to prisoners and which is a matter of concern to the senior staff. One officer, when asked why he thought the staff swore so much, if, as suggested, none of them swore outside and certainly not in front of their wives, replied:

"It's inevitable in any large community of one sex . . . factory, forces, prisons. It's partly because it's the only way men can express their true feelings, and partly because it's the only language a prisoner understands. If you give him an order without reinforcing it with swear words he doesn't take you seriously."

Swearing is in fact part of the normal pattern of relationships in the prison, between staff and prisoners, and among themselves. For some groups, verbal execrations are a norm of expectation. One winter afternoon the earliest receptions contained a disproportionately large number of alcoholics and derelict vagrants. After a procession of these had been dealt with, one last human wreck shuffled in. Having taken off his two ragged overcoats, he emptied the pockets of the various jackets and pullovers he was wearing into a nauseating pile. His nose was streaming with a heavy cold but he made no attempt to do anything about it. In desperation the reception officer bawled at him,

"If you've got a handkerchief among all that f—— s—— down there, blow your nose!"

PHYSICAL VIOLENCE BETWEEN STAFF AND PRISONERS

The prison officer at Pentonville knows only too well that violence is seldom far below the surface of prison life, and that while there is some certain knowledge about what kinds of handling will or will not provoke violence on the part of prisoners against the staff, there is a considerable area of uncertainty. The mentally disordered may become violent at any time; furthermore, the objects of their aggression need not be the martinets on the staff at all, but may be selected from among the quiet, inoffensive officers, many of whom have a genuine sense of vocation and go to considerable trouble to help prisoners in various ways. Although most officers realize that the greatest threat comes, typically, from the unpredictable psychopathic inmate, the vast majority are utterly convinced that it is only the threat of a flogging which prevents assaults on the staff from rising to an intolerable level. More tangible, however, as a comforting symbol of protection is the officer's "stick" or truncheon. According to Sykes, the stick — in Trenton — is intended to *raise* the threshold of the use of force and eliminate the casual cuffing which might provoke violent retaliation.[3] In Pentonville, the stick is (1) a practical weapon which, in theory, gives the officer an advantage in hand-to-hand combat, and (2) an important symbol of the officer's superior status. Although the staff are supposed to be skilled in judo, very few of them employ it when handling a physically aggressive prisoner.

But because the vast majority of prison officers believe almost all their charges to be potentially violent it does not follow that they are all equally agreed that the most satisfactory method of maintaining order is to be ready to use violence themselves. Many officers in fact go out of their way to handle prisoners in the way *which they believe* to be the most likely to avert trouble. It was impressive during individual staff interviews how each officer thought that not only was *his* method the best but that however much other officers might be disliked, prisoners certainly liked *him*.

"Fairness" but "firmness" was a frequently quoted maxim, based on the belief that prisoners would respect these qualities — an attempt to create in their captives the sense of inner, moral obligation to obey for which the formal authority structure of the prison community can make no provision. To yield indiscriminately to prisoners' demands is generally recognized to be unwise and to invite manipulation; on the other hand, the "gruffness" of some officers is a deliberately chosen veneer intended as a form of self-protection.

Not all officers had inhibitions about the use of physical force. Thus one officer told one of the research workers:

> " . . . in some cases it may be necessary to use force and knock a man about, but you (the research worker) would never understand that such might be a necessity. I've been knocked about in my life and I know what it is like."

It was noticeable that the temporary response of certain psychopaths to punishment deceived members of the staff at all levels. There are few offenders whose psychopathy is so gross that they are *wholly* impervious to the initial impact of punishment. But this is quite ephemeral and is in no way a learning experience.

---

[3]Sykes, *op. cit.*, p. 29.

The fact that many prisoners are by no means averse to using force themselves — and not only those actually imprisoned for violent crimes but those convicted of other offenses as well — makes it difficult for the average officer to recognize that the rule of law which prohibits the use of violence against prisoners in retaliation is absolute, not relative. Somehow it seems grossly *unreasonable* that a vicious and undisciplined criminal should enjoy any rights, least of all exemption from having to taste his own medicine. Comparatively few officers can effectively discriminate between the restraint which their own Code of Discipline demands and the out-and-out pacifist position which they regard with a mixture of bewilderment and contempt.[4]

The Code of Discipline on this question is less definite than at first appears. Part I, Section XI, states that an officer commits an offense against discipline if he is guilty of:

Unlawful or unnecessary exercise of authority, that is to say if he
(1) deliberately acts in a manner calculated to provoke a prisoner, or
(2) in dealing with a prisoner uses force unnecessarily or, where the application of force to a prisoner is necessary, uses undue force.

Although (2) appears to counsel, "Never use force unless you must, and then only as much as you need to use," it is not clear how either the conditions in which force must be used, or the *degree* of force, can be readily identified. Those few officers who have developed some skills based upon insight are often able to persuade even refractory prisoners to accompany them either back to their cells or to the punishment cells without recourse to force. The remainder, however, tend to use it as a matter of course, not because they are necessarily sadistic but simply because they are at a loss to see that there is an alternative. When a staff member has been assaulted it invariably follows that force is used to convey the prisoner to the punishment cells. Only in one instance during the research did a

---

[4]Cf. many officers' attitudes to those who wish to abolish capital and corporal punishment. They cannot understand how others are not so revolted by violent crime, that they too do not subscribe to a retributive theory of punishment.

prisoner who had assaulted a staff member not receive some physical injury. Whenever it was known that an assaulting prisoner was in the punishment cells he was visited by the research worker and in every case there was evidence of some physical injury having been sustained by the prisoner.

In conversation, officers do not normally deny that force is used in such circumstances. Prisoners believe that anyone who assaults an officer will get a terrible beating, and although exaggerations undoubtedly occur they are distortions of fact rather than fantasy. Both prisoners and officers see the situation as an example of the *lex talionis* — "if you knock a screw about you will get knocked about yourself." Apart from prisoners who actually assault staff members the other prisoners who tend to be handled by force are those who smash up their cells.

The noise of a man smashing up can be quite terrifying, particularly when, as is generally the case, prisoners in surrounding cells begin to shout and bang their tin plates as well. It is against the prison rules for an officer to enter a prisoner's cell alone, so that at least two must open the door. Because it is a very real possibility that the staff may be injured either by flying pieces of furniture or by the prisoner wielding a chair or table, the normal procedure is for the door to be opened suddenly and for one officer to rush the prisoner holding a mattress in front of him, his colleagues immediately behind him with their sticks at the ready. When this happens, prisoner and officers often go down in a heap, and the prisoner, all control gone, lashes out with arms and feet. When he has been overpowered he has to be carried or dragged, still struggling, to the punishment cells. It is in the negotiation of the narrow landings and stairways that injuries tend to be sustained.

In Pentonville it is an unwritten maxim that force is necessary when the prisoner offers physical resistance; the definition of "undue force" is more difficult, but as a general rule the force employed would seem to depend not upon conscious reasoning, but upon the accident of circumstances. There is reason to believe that in the heat of the fray both prisoners and officers behave at an instinctual level; certainly from one incident observed it was abundantly clear that the staff were frightened and bewildered.

At 11:25 AM, just as the men were getting ready for dinner, a principal officer rushed across the Center into the passage through the Administration block. Along it five officers were half-carrying, half-dragging a man who was screaming incoherently what sounded like "Murder! Murder!" As he was dragged across towards C Wing and down the stairs to the punishment cells, prisoners began to congregate on the upper landings and other officers shouted at them to get back in their cells. The uproar by this time was deafening, and both staff and prisoners were bewildered and confused as the shouts and screams reverberated round the galleries.

The prisoner was taken down into one of the stripped cells which have an inner and outer part. One of the research workers followed but the outer door was slammed in his face by an officer. As the door was opened again the research worker managed to enter and saw the prisoner's clothes being thrown out from the inner cell. His tobacco tin, which had fallen on the floor, was deliberately kicked into a corner, its precious contents spilling in the process.

By this time the prisoner was quiet, and it was discovered that he had been caught attempting to escape, and that the discipline officers had only just learned that the man was a hospital patient who had broken away from the hospital exercise yard. It was decided therefore to take him over to the hospital, so he was swathed in two blankets and carried kicking up the stairs from the punishment cell again. At the top he kicked off the blankets altogether as he again began to scream incoherently. Virtually naked and kicking, the five or six officers tried to get him to stand, but without success, and he was pulled along by the legs at an angle of forty-five degrees. Everyone tried to cover him with the blankets, and one officer pulled the only clothing he had on — a woolen jersey — over his head to muffle his cries.

As he was being carried up the stairs a group of officers, aroused by the further outburst of noise, rushed up A Wing, but by the time they had reached C Wing the prisoner was well on his way back to the hospital.

Subsequently it transpired that the prisoner had spent no fewer than fourteen years in institutions for defectives, including Rampton, and that his cries of "Murder!" were actually cries of "My ankle, my ankle." The whole incident was characterized by the crude use of force, panic and confusion, and although in this instance the prisoner's struggles were of little consequence and probably the force used was not "undue," the noise certainly reinforced other prisoners' beliefs that the man was being deliberately injured by the staff. The noise and the confusion combined with the degrading aspect of the prisoner's public nakedness underlined the unsettling quality of the experience for both staff and prisoner observers.

PROVOCATION

That section of the discipline code which forbids an officer "deliberately to act in a manner calculated to provoke a prisoner" is in one sense even more vague than that which seeks to define the legitimate use of force. Not only does the threshold of provocation vary from one prisoner to another, but the notion of what constitutes provocative behaviour varies from one officer to another.

The commonest form of provocation is undoubtedly the ignoring by officers of cell bells. When locked up, the bell is the only effective method available to the prisoner by which he may communicate with the staff. A ringing bell may mean that a prisoner is ill, needs to go to the lavatory, or merely wishes to attract the attention of the staff for some other reason. During the time when prisoners are locked away there is often a great deal of frantic bell ringing and banging on doors. If it goes on for long, other prisoners begin to join in the banging, or swell the shouting. The attitude of the staff on duty to prisoners when they are locked away is rather like that of parents, who, having put their children to bed, are irritated by their failure to settle down to sleep and tend to put off answering the children's call until they can be endured no longer. Just as the more the parent procrastinates, the more fuss the child makes, so the longer the landing staff delay "opening up" the more noise the prisoner makes. When the cell is opened up, it is not uncommon for the prisoner to be abusive and obstreperous, nor is it uncommon for the officer, irritated by the persistent ringing and by the final necessity of having to toil up to the cell, to put the prisoner on report for causing a disturbance.

There is little doubt that a good deal of bell ringing during the middle periods of the day is connected with requests either to empty chamber pots or to use the recess in order to defecate, the latter being particularly important to men in "three cells." Although in the workshops and on the exercise yards men may relieve themselves, they must normally obtain permission by the formula, "Fall out, sir?" Having to do this is yet one more aspect of the prisoner's enforced regression to infantile status.[5] In the cells, however, the situation is more acute, and the frustration of the bell-ringing prisoner by the officer who deliberately withholds permission reduces the relationship to a primitive level, the unconscious aspects of which may be potentially explosive when the prisoner's tolerance threshold is low.[6]

It is of course important to stress that by no means all Pentonville officers intentionally frustrate and provoke their captives, and that even among those who do so, the primary motivation may well be unconscious rather than deliberate. That some officers ask for all they get is well recognized by those of their colleagues with greater experience and insight. Thus officers recounting how a principal officer had a dinner thrown at him said:

> " . . . he handled the situation very badly and got all he deserved."

Later the incident was discussed with senior officials, and although there was substantial evidence to suggest that provocation *had* been an important element, the fact that the prisoner was a gang lieutenant was sufficient for them to regard the prisoner as wholly to blame.

One "toilet" incident illustrates how personality factors, combined with administrative incompetence, can lead to physical

---

[5]Of which the "potty" is the unambiguous symbol.

[6]Bettelheim's account of the concentration camp guards' control of their prisoners' elimination, though far more extreme, bears a remarkable structural resemblance to the prison stiuation, in particular the relative shortage w.c.'s and their open aspect which results in the prisoner's elimination (especially on the exercise yards) being conducted in semi-public. Cf. Bruno Bettelheim. *The Informed Heart.* Glencoe, Illinois: Free Press, 1960, pp. 132-133.

violence. An aggressive prisoner with a record of violence against the staff (and who had spent a period in Broadmoor) rang his bell furiously after dinner without being opened up. His account was that he had an upset stomach and badly needed to use the recess. When he was finally opened up he became abusive, so that the officer concerned threatened to put him on report. The prisoner then demanded to see the wing principal officer, who sent back word that he was not at the beck and call of prisoners, and that the man should be taken down to the punishment cells. According to the prisoner, when interviewed by the research worker, this produced the response,

"If you want me down chokey you'll have to f—— drag me!"

whereupon the officers who had been detailed to take him down drew their sticks and began to lay about him.[7]

"The ability to handle men" is regarded as an important criterion by the Pentonville authorities when interviewing applicants for the prison service; what appears to distinguish the really efficient officer from his less able colleague is the ability to discriminate between those situations which are better handled with tact and those which can be handled with authoritarian commands. As one very intelligent trade assistant put it:

"I think assaults on officers are often caused by bad handling. Such has been the case three times as far as I am concerned"
(viz., in three instances known to him).

Much of the research material gathered about assaults on staff related to unfortunate "handling," either as a consequence of lack of skill, or as a result of the officer himself being worried and "touchy." By no means all provocation is gross, but even for able officers with positive orientation towards "treatment" there are pitfalls. Thus a prisoner with a reputation for toughness was put on report for assaulting an officer in the library. It appears that he had asked the officer for a jig-saw as he could not read, whereupon the officer in somewhat sarcastic tones replied that it was about time that he learned. This was said in front of a number of other prisoners and caused the prisoner in question to become very angry and pour execrations

---

[7]He was seen by one of the research workers later that afternoon with his head swathed in bandages.

on the officer's head.

The officer did not put him on report but went to consult the man's wing principal officer, who said that he was a wonderful worker and very clean and tidy. The officer suggested that the principal officer should call the prisoner and give him a "telling off," but this could not be done immediately as the prisoner had gone over to the hospital for some minor treatment. The principal officer then decided to discuss the matter with the governor and in the meanwhile was to keep the prisoner's cell card.

The removal of the cell card was sufficient to start a rumor (which was inaccurate) that the officer had put the prisoner on report; by unhappy coincidence some hours later the two of them met on one of the bridges across B Wing, whereupon the prisoner lashed out with his fist, breaking the officer's glasses.

The part played by rumor and the element of chance, first in the prisoner being in the hospital and again in the meeting on the bridge, were beyond the officer's control. However, as he subsequently realized, to be sarcastic with a burly man sensitive about his illiteracy is to court trouble. Furthermore, he had become accustomed to relating to the intelligentsia of the prison population with whom he worked in the library, and he tended to forget that the majority of prisoners were less well educated and less able to appreciate the joking and sarcasm that his work élite could tolerate without difficulty.

PRISONERS' ATTITUDES TOWARD THE STAFF

As we have suggested, prisoners tend not to place much importance on the hierarchy of rank among their captors, largely because such distinctions have comparatively little meaning for them. In reality, the power exercised by the discipline officer in, say, granting or withholding a request or privilege is just as great as that exercised by the principal officer or indeed the governor. The "screw" on the landing and the yard and in the workshop is the embodiment of authority. Because he is entrusted with the execution of the decisions of senior officials, he is their immediate and tangible representative. Prisoners tend to rank officers according to certain criteria of merit — fairness, consistency, the degree to which the officer allows privileges, and the decency with which he recognizes a prisoner's feelings. On the negative side the tendency to provoke, pettiness, victimization, untruthfulness and failure to keep promises results in the officer being regarded as a "rat" or "bastard."

About six or seven officers were, at the time of the research, universally disliked on account of their unambiguous hostility to prisoners. The most common feeling, however, was that so many officers were "two-faced." Some undoubtedly lacked integrity in their dealings with prisoners, but others gained this reputation through behaving differently towards different types of prisoner. An officer described by one prisoner as a "rat" may often be described by another as "the best officer on the wing."

Just as the staff see prisoners in one context as fundamentally *bad* because they are criminals, and in another differentiate between them on the basis of crime, personality, race, effort, cleanliness, helpfulness, intelligence and a whole range of individual qualities, so prisoners in the context of the prisoners' code see "all screws are out to trick you" and in another distinguish between them in a variety of ways. There is an advantage it is said in "knowing your officers over a long period," though it is also an article of dogma that "if an officer wants to get you — he will." Likewise, as the staff distribute their favors unevenly between the good and deserving and the bad and undeserving, so prisoners distribute their cooperation unevenly between the "good" officers and the "bad." Thus, one of the prisoners on the prison farm party said:

> "K is not an easy officer, but he's civil and treats you like a man; L is sarcastic and barks. K has quite different ideas from L who's very hard. The men take it out on him by letting the battery (of the prison truck) get low, flat tires, etc.; they're not done against the prison but against L personally. When a man "had it away" just before Christmas the other men on the party who knew of his plans said he mustn't do it on a day when K was on duty. If he had been on duty at the time of the escape the others would have made sure he found out about it in time. L thinks he's getting more done but in fact he's getting less."

"Good" officers are thus protected from getting the rap, whereas "bad" officers have all that is coming to them.

The more mature a prisoner is (in terms of prison experience), the less likely he is to indulge in sweeping generalizations about the staff. A group of Dartmoor men in discussion with the research workers agreed with the statement of one of their number:

" . . . inside there are good and bad screws. The best are those that come from ordinary life, the next best are those that come from the Navy, and the worst are those that come from the Regular Army."

Those prisoners whose attitudes towards authority are implacably hostile, usually those with a record of rebellious behavior stretching back to childhood, have at least an uncomplicated picture. Screws — like policemen, teachers, judges, and fathers — are bad, unreasonable and overbearing objects to be disliked and, when possible, cheated. From prisoners such as these the research collected the most wildly implausible stories of violence, corruption and sexual perversion on the part of the staff. For the less aggressively antisocial, an element of ambivalence creeps in, often making for difficulties in staff-prisoner relationships. Thus one essayist writes:

Their conversation is uninteresting, petty, and at times quite sordid. They do not appear to have one half-penny worth of initiative or imagination. Providing they can rely on each other to offer a bold front to the inmates they are happy to carry on in their dogmatic way, often becoming quite pompous over the years. Lastly they are bone idle in mind and body.

Yet, when I get up out of the other side of the bed I find they are plain, ordinary, decent people, as humane as they can possibly be, often going out of their way to do all sorts of kindnesses that would mean at least a half sheet[8] if caught out. They can listen for hours to tales of woe, putting in an occasional sympathetic word to help some young or old down and out talk things out of his system. When prisoners spirits are at their lowest some screws can often raise a smile or even a laugh.

Prisoners, by projecting undesirable qualities on to the staff, are able to minimize the degradation of their own captive status.

---

[8]The equivalent of a governor's report for a prisoner.

> "They are bone lazy, and couldn't really do a proper day's work. It's no good hoping to train and educate them because a decent man wouldn't want the job."

This speaker, during the same conversation, had described one particular officer as "the best landing officer on the wing," and spoke of how he provided cleaning materials for the prisoners out of his own pocket. The argument appears to run, "if we are the lowest of the low, what kind of men are you that choose to come and work here?" Because the status of a money-grubbing turnkey obsessed by clock-watching on the one hand and the prospects of overtime pay on the other is low, the differences between officer and prisoner appear less. The prisoner denies the existence of any specific custodial skills and argues that "anyone could do the job." Occasionally he argues that if it were not for criminals like himself, prison officers would be either unemployed or having to work far harder in the rough and tumble of industrial and commercial life.

FAVORITISM AND VICTIMIZATION

The discipline officer can in reality make a prisoner's life difficult, and it is undoubtedly true that favoritism and victimization occur. The average discipline officer, however, is in close contact with a comparatively small number of prisoners so that the subtleties of such discrimination are limited; this does not stop some paranoid individuals from making claims that they are victimized. The prison sees such complaints as "false and malicious allegations" and punishes them if need be; it does not see them primarily as manifestations of character disorders. Thus one prisoner claimed that on one occasion he reported "special sick" but instead of being taken to the hospital he was "placed on report for disobeying an order." He must have known that the research staff knew that this story was untrue, for "special sick" requests are always dealt with, and although the prisoner may get into trouble it always comes afterwards. On the other hand, the maxim that "if a screw wants to get you, he will get you" has some basis in reality. Furthermore, the possibility of an officer "planting" unauthorized objects in a man's cell is not out of the question, for the honesty of *all* officers is not unimpeachable, and (during research) no fewer than three officers on the staff of Pentonville were subsequently indicted on serious criminal charges, two of them receiving prison sentences.

POSITIVE RELATIONSHIPS BETWEEN STAFF AND PRISONERS

Probably the most important determining factor in the character of relationships between custodian and captive is the scale of the group situation in which they confront each other. When both are remote — in the large workshops, the great exercise yards, or the long galleries of the cellhouses — prisoners and staff tend to see each other in mass terms. Because the mass situation permits little differentiation the relationship is dominated by the persistent stereotypes which divide the prison community into evil criminals and contemptible screws. As the size of the group increases so stereotypy hampers effective communication and the mutual pursuit of the common task. Where prisoners and officers spend time together in small groups they are compelled to regard each other as individuals. The factor of mutual selection enters in here, for the small groups are invariably work groups which depend for their effectiveness upon mutual tolerance. Thus the officer tends to select certain prisoners towards whom he is well disposed either on grounds of personality or work competence and to reject, or get transferred, those who are unacceptable to him. Similarly, prisoners seek to leave such groups if the officer is unacceptable, or if the advantages stemming from the job do not outweigh such disadvantages.

The nature of Pentonville's social organization, however, creates other face-to-face situations which are not small group situations in the same sense, in that the group is not involved in a collective activity. These situations exist on the landings, between the officers allocated to them, and the prisoners located on them. The routine of locking and unlocking, the prisoner's need to frequent the wing office and to make routine inquiries of his landing officer involves relationships which are often closer than those in the large workshop or on the yards. But the ratio of prisoners to landing officers is high, and staff tend to be frequently moved from one landing to another or to other duties. In such situations, officers and prisoners are brought into face-to-face contact, but without the mutual knowledge and understanding which is the normal by-product of prolonged contact in the small work group situation. It is not without significance that some of the most explosive and violent staff-prisoner conflict occurs in such situations where the group is too small to permit complete depersonalization, small enough to allow emotional involvement, and yet insufficiently permanent for relationships to develop in depth. The development of the "Norwich" system, which seeks to link the individual officer more or less permanently with a group of a dozen prisoners or less, is clearly one solution to this problem. But H Wing in Pentonville exemplifies two limitations of the system: (1) that when the group becomes too large the benefits tend to be lost, and (2) that without specialized staff training, explicit objectives and the use of socio-therapeutic techniques, such as group counselling, officers and prisoners sink into a dangerous tolerance of each other's shortcomings.

While there are some officers who seek to avoid conflict with their captives by simple appeasement, there are others who recognize that the rewards for industry and good behavior in Pentonville (outside H Wing) are conspicuously lacking. Accordingly, they strive to reward prisoners in a variety of subtle ways for work well done, and at the same time achieve compliance not by the crude devices of coercion but by the subtle manipulation of incentives. Further, there are some officers who go out of their way to assist prisoners constructively.

For example, two officers in a fixed post, both men of long service, by the nature of their job were brought into continuous contact with prisoners' domestic problems. Unofficially, men managed to come from all over the prison to discuss problems with them to get a sympathetic, though often firm, hearing. On one occasion a man who kept fainting intended to report sick the next day. Instead, he was taken into the office and given the opportunity to talk over his domestic affairs, about which he was extremely worried, and then taken to the hospital, given a sedative, and another for the night. Although such handling was outside the strict confines of the officer's role, it produced a significant lessening of tension. It was no coincidence that a few days earlier one of these officers had presented to him a tinned metal beaker, which he placed on his desk. It was inscribed:

"J . . . — the best screw in the nick."

On an individual basis other officers are able to handle even difficult men. Once the governor and deputy governor were discussing the case of a mentally sick man who, in the governor's view, ought to have been not in prison but in the hospital. The deputy governor said he was refusing to grant the man's continual applications to leave a particular shop because:

" . . . it's the only place where he can do nothing and not get into trouble — (the instructor) understands him and doesn't put him on report."

The extent to which prisoners and officers can joke together is another measure of the relative stability of their relationships. Providing that the prisoner does not "go over the mark" he can indulge in a joking relationship which assists in the maintenance of cordial relations.[9] Moreover, the officer can do the same providing he does not provoke the prisoner too far. Obscenity may, as in some primitive societies, be present. For example, a man in a workshop asks to go to the lavatory and the instructor replies, "But you went last week!"

The closest relationships between staff and prisoners are those in the smaller work groups — in the elites of the large workshops, in the small groups who work alongside trade assistants doing engineering maintenance and constructional tasks, and in strategic office jobs, such as Reception and the Pay Office. When men are concerned with really useful and constructive work the relationships which emerge are akin to those of workman and foreman. Discussions about the job are

---

[9]The structural-functional significance of joking relationships is much discussed in the literature of social anthropology. Thus A. R. Radcliffe-Brown writes:

"The alternative to (avoidance) is the joking relationship, one, that is, of mutual disrespect and licence. Any serious hostility is prevented by the playful antagonism of teasing, and this, in its regular repetition is a constant reminder of that social disjunction which is one of the essential elements of the relation, while the social conjunction is maintained by friendliness that takes no offence at insult."
Structure and Function in Primitive Society, London, 1952, p. 92.

serious and to the point and indicate a commitment to the task. All over the prison there are small groups of staff and prisoners in which jokes are made, tea is drunk and cigarettes smoked, which are of their very nature paradoxical in the total setting of the prison.

There are, nevertheless, situations in which role reversal tends to occur. The red-band in the library drafts the weekly report on educational classes, an orderly in Reception fills out much of the information on newly received prisoners' files and handles committal warrants, and in the mess the orderly exercises most of the functions of a head waiter. In the officers' mess the complaint, "It's the prisoners that run the prison," could scarcely be more apposite.[10] One of the main activities of the senior waiter was, however, concerned not with food, but with football pools. Each week he would work on a permutation for a syndicate of officers and manage to win them steady, if unspectacular, sums.

It is the essence of the Sykes hypothesis that the prison cannot exert total power by reason of the inherent defects of coercion. The informal rewards and compromises that the prison officer must make in order to secure compliance result in the corruption of his authority. Thus,

> ... the theoretical dominance of the guard is undermined in actuality by the innocuous encroachment of the prisoner on the guard's duties. Inmates in this position ... may wield power and influence far beyond the nominal definition of their role ... the guard may find that much of the power he is supposed to exercise has slipped from his grasp.[11]

Once in this position it is difficult to regain his authority.

In Pentonville, there are situations which bear remarkable similarity, not so much because of the "laziness, indifference, or *naïveté*" which is allegedly characteristic of the Trenton guards, but largely through understaffing. Thus one officer in charge of a fixed office post could say:

[10]During the research period the senior Mess waiter ruled virtually supreme. On one occasion one of the welfare officers ordered a cup of tea which was brought by the waiter, who had a poisoned finger which he put inside the cup. The welfare officer pointed out that this was not hygienic, whereupon the waiter replied:

"If you don't like it, you can go elsewhere."

[11]Sykes, *op. cit.*, p. 57.

"I know for certain that it is quite impossible for me to do the whole job on my own, therefore I have to rely on prisoners doing my job for me. In many ways I am completely in their power. If they want to fiddle things I either have to condone it or report it. If I reported it the work simply wouldn't get done and I also stand the risk of being assaulted."

But although such feelings are widespread (and some officers think that if their colleagues spent less time in the mess drinking tea, it would not be necessary for prisoners to do so much of their work), there are important flaws in the Sykes hypothesis.

It assumes a heterogeneity on the part of the custodial staff which does not exist. It is only those officers who have specialized work tasks to perform that find reward and incentive essential to obtain compliance. Indeed, allocation to a special work task is itself a reward, and there is often a queue of potential successors eager to succeed any incumbent who fails to work well. It is only where the prisoner's skills have a significant scarcity value that the staff are at a real disadvantage. In many situations, crude coercion and physical force are remarkably effective in obtaining at least temporary compliance. Nor are all those officers who seek to provide their captives with incentives "corrupted" for they may well withhold them, or even remove them altogether, without major difficulty. Prisoners individually may, in fact, of their own volition seek to please the staff in hope of obtaining favors, or in the case of some personalities, out of a sense of passive obedience to authority deriving from long years of conditioning in residential institutions of custodial character.

Nor does it reckon with the officer who, by virtue of his personality, accepts every challenge in the contest of wills between himself and rebellious prisoners, nor with the whole range of subtle devices whereby he can make the prisoner's life intolerable. Even the threat of physical violence to him is minimized by the fact that in the process of taking a violent prisoner to the cells "legitimate force" will almost invariably be used. If the physical reprisals which occur informally and the official punishments which follow do not protect him by their deterrent implications, he may at least savour the notion that revenge is sweet. If the bureaucratic devices of social control are ineffective by reason of their complex inefficiency the informal system of rewards and punishments is not.

The Sykes argument does not take into account the fact that in certain circumstances the officer actually cares little about the prisoner's compliance. Cynicism and apathy, at least in Pentonville, are sufficiently widespread to make it a matter of little importance to some officers whether prisoners are clean or dirty, whether their cells are neat or squalid, or whether they work industriously or idle their work time away. For the staff who merely watch the clock anything beyond the performance of the minimal tasks of their role is too much bother and they neither attempt to coerce prisoners nor enter into bargains to secure compliance. Nor is it always true that breaches of the rules are *invariably* regarded as invidious reflections upon the staff,[12] for it is constantly reaffirmed among the uniformed ranks that the staff are grossly overworked, the prison is overcrowded, and the delinquent and deceitful character of prisoners is such that it is hardly suprising that they are always up to some mischief.

Finally, it provides no adequate explanation for the behavior of the truly corrupted official, namely, the "bent screw." The bent screw who trafficks in tobacco or who offers to assist in an escape by letting a prisoner copy his keys, plays an alienative role *vis-à-vis* his peers and his superiors which is not dissimilar from that of the robber baron. He is a man who seeks to manipulate situations for personal gain at the expense of the group of which he is a member and towards whom his loyalties ought logically be directed. Just as the robber baron tends to negate the collective efforts of his fellow prisoners to achieve an equitable distribution of the means whereby his imprisonment may be made less painful, the bent screw negates the collective efforts of his fellow custodians to achieve containment and control.

---

[12]While an officer *would* be criticized for allowing an escape he would probably be praised for discovering some illicit article, notwithstanding that the very fact that it had been obtained was a negative reflection upon the staff's ability rigidly to control every aspect of prisoners' behavior.

PART IV

RESPONDING TO CHANGE

While guard work has always been problematic, it seems recently to be even more so due to a number of changes currently affecting institutional corrections. As I discussed in the introductory essay, some of the most significant changes include shifts in prison goals, the intrusion of the federal courts and the presence of larger and more diverse inmate populations. Since these and other changes directly influence daily prison life, guards are especially vulnerable to them. The purpose of Part IV is to explore several ways in which guards individually and collectively react to changing prison conditions.

The most obvious and individualistic guard response to present institutional conditions is simply to leave prison work. High guard turnover rates, especially in the lower ranks, indicate that custody personnel often opt for this solution to work place problems. That so many men leave prison work raises several questions. For example, are guards who leave just dregs of the work force who could not perform the job in the first place, or are competent, committed people leaving? Is turnover due simply to such factors as low pay or are more fundamental problems of prison organization involved? The first reading by Jacobs and Grear illuminates these and other questions with data from a survey of guard force "dropouts" in Illinois. These researchers found that for the dropouts the most important problems on the job involved superior officers and the paramilitary regime. Significantly, the analysis also revealed that the former officers' race was a factor in determining job experiences and perceptions.

Not all men who become frustrated leave prison work, of course. Most of those who remain meet uncertain prison conditions by trying to adapt and do the best job possible. Some-

269

times, however, these conditions become intolerable from the officers' point of view and draw from them some overt reaction. The last three chapters of Part IV describe and account for quite different types of collective reaction exhibited by guard forces.

The paper by Stotland argues that guards may ultimately resort to violence when their authority is severely and regularly threatened. Stotland takes the Attica riot as his case example. Prior to the riot and lethal retaking of that New York prison, guards felt they were losing control. This situation was made worse in their eyes by federal court rulings and by a warden who seemed more interested in inmates than in staff welfare. These factors, Stotland contends, eroded not only authority but guard feelings of self-esteem and confidence. The active and unofficial participation in the retaking of Attica and presumably the subsequent brutality by officers can be understood as a reaction to a growing feeling of powerlessness. Given such feelings by guards, violence during the riot became a legitimate means to reassert authority.

Carroll's paper examines a specific source of frustration among guards, namely the demand that they support treatment programs and embrace the treatment philosophy. In Carroll's analysis, the problem for guards emerged with the installation of a new, treatment-oriented warden. The warden's efforts to redirect prison efforts toward treatment ultimately involved little more than relaxing custody measures. This move to liberalize procedures and reduce the number of specific rules created for guards lessens not only animosity toward the warden but also considerable frustration. Feeling that they had been sold-out, guards reacted in two ways. First, they engaged in general work stoppages, and second, more formally, in union organization.

Unionization of custody staff is becoming an increasingly important aspect of prison organization. Recent changes in prison goals and operations prompt guards to view themselves as being more and more on their own. Not only must they work in unpleasant and often dangerous settings for little pay, but their superiors seem unable or unwilling to represent their interests. Such feelings have led to unionization by guards in many state prison systems. The final chapter of Part IV, by Jacobs and Crotty, examines the implications of collective bargaining by guards. Specifically, these writers consider the effects of collective bargaining on prison administration and policy in New York. They conclude that while union organization seeks primarily to benefit line officers, it will not retard, and may even foster, prison reform.

Chapter 12

DROPOUTS AND REJECTS: AN ANALYSIS OF THE PRISON GUARD'S REVOLVING DOOR

JAMES B. JACOBS AND MARY P. GREAR

INTRODUCTION

HIGH turnover among rank and file corrections officers is frequently cited as a major problem facing corrections. But the causes of turnover have never been systematically examined. In order to ascertain why correction officers leave their jobs, we conducted interviews with a sample[1] of guards who terminated their employment at Stateville Correction Center, Illinois' largest maximum-security prison, between 1 July 1973 and 30 June 1974 (exclusive of medical discharge).[2] The fifty-five respondents consist of

From James B. Jacobs and Mary P. Grear, Dropouts and Rejects: An Analysis of the Prison Guard's Revolving Door. Reprint permission from the *Criminal Justice Review*, Vol. 2, No. 2, 1977 of Georgia State University, Atlanta, Georgia.

[1]Due to time and financial constraints, we conducted telephone interviews with a 50 percent subsample. Because we anticipated difficulty in contacting respondents, we sent out letters explaining the purposes of the research and asked that the former guards call us if the telephone number we listed from them was inaccurate. Because these letters were mailed before our subsample of 135 was drawn, four individuals outside the subsample contacted us, and we included their interviews with our results, after preliminary inspection revealed nothing unique about their responses.

Eleven letters were returned with the notation that the addressee had moved, leaving no forwarding address. We were unable to obtain phone numbers from prison records for nineteen former guards. Of those individuals in the subsample for whom we had phone numbers, we found that thirty-four phones had been disconnected. Another eleven phone numbers led us to families of former officers who could not (or would not) tell us the whereabouts of the men themselves. In addition, one member of our subsample had died and two refused to be interviewed. Ultimately, we were successful in completing fifty-one interviews (38%). *Respondents do not differ from the entire subsample by age, length of service, residence or race.*

[2]The total number of terminations during this period was 269. In a companion study (Liebentritt, Note 4), we followed a cohort (N=88) of guard recruits who were hired in the summer of 1975. By the end of the six-month probationary period, 63.5 percent had terminated their employment at Stateville.

twenty-seven whites, twenty-four blacks and four latinos; blacks and latinos have been grouped together in our tabulations. Guards from both of these minority groups view themselves (and are viewed by others) as outsiders to a force which has traditionally been dominated by white southern Illinoisians.

DISCUSSION

The imagery which forms the administration view of guard turnover pictures a typical recruit taking the job because nothing else is available and staying only as long as it takes to find a better job. It is believed both that most individuals are not suited to work inside a penitentiary and that alternative job possibilities are almost more attractive. The widely held view that guard turnover is caused by the inability of the average individual to adjust to the peculiar demands of the job supports the position of some of the top guards and administrators that "the situation is impossible" and that demands for radical change in conditions within the prison are totally unrealistic.

The guard recruit's assumed inability to adjust to the prison is reinforced by the informal policy of allowing almost all guards the opportunity to resign, no matter what the real reason for the termination of their employment. Formal records indicate a resignation when, in fact, the guard has been fired. The formal records at Stateville show 24 percent of our respondents as having been discharged while, according to their own reports, 40 percent had been discharged (See Table 12-I). Even this figure may be understated due to reluctance to admit having been fired from a previous employment.

The high percentage of involuntary terminations within the prison turns our attention to the prison organization itself and away from the personal inadequacies of the guards.[3] It may well be that a high proportion of those who enter prison work are unsuited by training and temperament for life behind the

---

[3]Clemmer (1958, p. 182) several decades ago urged students of the prison community to view guards empathetically:

> It is unreasonable and illogical to expect guards to be more social in their thinking than the communities and interest-groups which produce them. . . . The occasional atavism is matched, no doubt, in other prisons and in the free world as well. Guards do not possess the reformers zeal. They have

Table 12-I

Respondents' Reported Reasons
For Terminating Employment

	Whites (N=27)	Non-Whites (N=28)	Total (N=55)
Resigned	59%	39%	49%
Retired	22%	0%	11%
Discharged	7%	39%	24%
Resigned/Discharged*	11%	22%	16%

*This category includes those respondents who indicated that they resigned while a threat of discharge was hanging over them.

walls, but this determination of unsuitability is made as often by the prison elite as by the employee himself.

Why is it that so many guards do not remain on the job longer? Perhaps the high turnover within the first six months reflects the fact that these former guards never intended to remain on the job from the beginning, but merely saw the job as an interim employment? The plausibility of this hypothesis is strengthened by "fishnet" recruitment which requires only that the candidate pass a physical examination and not have any felony convictions.

Yet, although it may be true that very few individuals grow up aspiring to become prison guards,[4] and although four respondents admitted that they had only taken the job as a temporary employment, the former guards whom we interviewed report a surprisingly high commitment toward the guard career. A greater percentage of blacks reported having taken the job with a career in mind. While it may be questionable how accurately a former prison guard can recall how long he in-

their own lives to live; they have their own little frustrations, sorrows, and tragedies, and few people, guards included, have sense of state. The personality problems of employees in prison may be quite as serious as those of the inmates with whose care they are charged. The student of social science does not hate a stupid, brutal guard, just as he does not hate the feebleminded rapist. For the betterment of society both need to be controlled, but the point of view must be kept objective. Perspective is everything.
[4]A Lou Harris poll (Joint Commission, 1969) found that only 1 percent of high school students had ever given any consideration to a career as a guard.

tended to remain when he took the job, it is still most interesting that 58 percent of the guards (N=19) who left within the first six months reported that at the time they took the job they had seriously considered making a career of it (See Table 12-II). Several of the black respondents volunteered that they had prepared themselves for a career in corrections by taking college courses.

Table 12-II

How long did you expect to remain on the job when you were hired?

	Whites (N=27)			Non-Whites (N=28)		
	Discharged	Resigned	Retired	Discharged	Resigned	Retired
	(N=5)	(N=16)	(N=6)	(N=18)	N=10)	(N=0)
5 years or more	11%	15%	11%	43%	14%	0%
At least 'till certified	4%	11%	0%	21%	11%	0%
6 Months	0%	4%	4%	0%	7%	0%
Didn't know	4%	29%	8%	0%	4%	0%

Not only was a very high percentage of our respondents discharged, but the majority of all terminations occurred within the first six months (coterminous with the Civil Service probationary period). Of those who resigned, 41 percent (N=11) did so within the first six months. Twenty out of twenty-two discharges also occurred during the first six months. Thus, 60 percent of our respondents left Stateville for one reason or another before completing the probationary period.[5]

Our respondents describe the process of accommodating to the uncommon world of the prison as a disorienting and stressful experience similar to what the inmate "fish" encounters (Irwin, 1970). Many respondents noted that a major source of strain during this period was the ambiguity of their formal status in the prison hierarchy. Because of what is perceived by the top guards to be a chronic manpower shortage the guard

---

[5]Of 440 individuals hired in 1973, 53 percent did not last beyond six months. For 1974, there were 435 appointments and 267 guards separated before having completed six months of service.

fish are sometimes called upon to act as regular guards, but the scope of their authority is ambiguous. Clothed in a special uniform that dramatized their differentness, the recruits found themselves the butt of ridicule from inmates and fellow officers.

The most serious problem experienced by the new guard is not normalizing face-to-face relations with the convicted felons, but the need to accommodate himself to the strict demands of the paramilitary regime. Fifty-four percent of the former guards (73% of the non-whites) who terminated either by resignation or discharge within the first six months attributed their greatest difficulties to their relationships with superior officers (See Table 12-III). If one counts difficulties with co-workers as a closely related phenomenon, a picture emerges of guard recruits, particularly blacks[6], failing to meet the expectations of old time and top echelon guards or refusing to accept the definition of the situation held by the elite. Culture conflict could be expected to be especially sharp between white veteran guards from southern Illinois who dominate the higher ranks (8 of 9 captains and 17 of 23 lieutenants) and young Chicago blacks who account for approximately 50 percent of the recruits. The increase in the proportion of black recruits in recent years, due to affirmative action pressures, is shown in Table 12-IV. In Table 12-V one can see that the tension between probationary guards and supervisory officers is complicated by the racial dissimilarity between the two groups.

Many recruits, particularly Chicago blacks, indicated that they were attracted to the job at Stateville by a desire to "help" inmates whom they felt were likely being unfairly treated.[7] Their empathy for the inmate was reinforced by the training program which emphasized the socio-economic roots of crime and pictured the inmate as a victim of his environment (Griffith, Note 1; Jacobs and Cohen, Note 2; Liebentritt, Note 4). The trainee was urged to place himself in the inmate's position in order that he might better understand the signifi-

---

[6]While blacks constituted 42.3 percent of the officers appointed in 1974, they constituted 63.7 percent of the short-term (less than 6 months) terminations.

[7]In their study of minority recruitment in the New York City Police Department, Hunt and Cohen (1969) found that "Black and Puerto Rican youths, unlike their white counterparts, find the service aspects of police work more attractive than the pay, fringe benefits or job security" (p. viii).

Table 12-III

With which group did you have *most* trouble?

	Whites (N=26)*	Non-Whites (N=28)	Total (N=54)
Co-workers	19.2%	21.3%	20.4%
Superior Officers	15.3%	57.1%	37.0%
Counsellors	3.8%	0%	1.8%
Inmates	34.6%	3.6%	18.5%
Administrators	3.8%	10.7%	7.4%
No Group	19.2%	7.1%	13.0%
All of them	3.9%	0%	1.9%

*Question not applicable in one case.

Table 12-IV

APPOINTMENTS OF WHITE AND BLACK EMPLOYEES,
AND BLACK APPOINTMENTS AS A
PERCENTAGE OF TOTAL APPOINTMENTS, 1967-1974

Year	White Appointments	Black Appointments	Total Appointments	Black Appointments As A Percentage of Total Appointments
1967	532	25	557	4.5%
1968	491	20	511	3.9%
1969	573	35	608	5.8%
1970	382	34	416	8.2%
1971	295	46	341	13.5%
1972	274	140	414	33.8%
1973	251	193	444	43.5%
1974	251	184	435	42.3%

cance of ameliorating the inmate's hardships wherever possible. Respondents reported with pride how they gained the trust and respect of the inmates "by treating them like men" and explained how they had made special efforts to satisfy requests for such items as toothpaste or toilet paper.

Because several of these former guards had defined their role

Table 12-V

Ranking of Superior Officers

Attitude toward superior	Percentage of Positive Ratings	
officer with respect to:	*Whites*	*Non-Whites*
Job orientation	73.9%	40.7%
Support in meeting job problems	78.3%	45.4%
Support in inmate-related problems	90.9%	47.4%
Fairness in imposing work sanctions	65.2%	40.7%
Praising work accomplishment	65.2%	42.3%
Number of respondents	- - -	- - -

as one of helping inmates, it was a source of bitterness that the characteristic response to their efforts was disapproval. Many reported that while they were taught to be "firm but fair" what superior officers actually expected was only formal contact with inmates which stopped short of kindness and concern. While it is important to remember that these are the perceptions of those who left their prison employment, sometime within six months, nevertheless, it was the consistent opinion of many respondents that success in establishing rapport with inmates was inversely related to chances for certification and promotion. To the extent that new training programs fail to change the attitudes of veteran guards or to prepare idealistic recruits for the traditional attitudes of the veterans toward inmates these training academies may contribute to job frustration.[8]

For guards who terminated their training within six months, the majority of whites responded positively to each of five separate items tapping attitudes toward superior officers (See Table 12-V). The majority of non-whites responded negatively to every inquiry about superior officers. Non-whites showed most dissatisfaction with training and discipline. It is also interesting to note that the small number of non-white respondents who did not leave until after having been certified (N=6)

[8]Apparently the organization is successful in screening out the minority guards who are most sympathetic to the prisoners. A survey of incumbent officers at Stateville (in process) shows no significant differences in the attitudes of black and white officers toward the prisoners (Jacobs and Kraft, Note 3).

replied postively to the question about relations with superiors, although not as positively as whites staying beyond six months.

The difference in minority and white attitudes emerges even more sharply if we look at the total number of positive responses for five questions tapping attitude toward superior officers. For all whites, 75 percent of the total number of responses were positive, while for non-whites, 42 percent were positive. A significant difference remains even when we control for length of service.

What is most arresting about the discharge rate is the significantly higher percentage of minority officers who report leaving Stateville by discharge than whites, 61 percent as compared with 18 percent. Assuming the validity of these self-reports, it might be suggested that a differential recruiting process is operating, and that it imposes higher standards on white applicants. Although quite recently the Department of Corrections has sent recruitment trucks into minority areas of Chicago to recruit applicants for guard positions, none of the individuals in our sample were hired in this manner. For our respondents there is no evidence that would lead us to accept the hypothesis of differential recruitment. Both whites and non-whites are routinely hired upon referral from the Department of Labor and also on a "walk-in" basis.

Even if white and non-white guards are recruited by universal standards, perhaps the minority guards perform more poorly on the job, therefore, accounting for their higher rate of discharge? The data does not sustain this hypothesis (See Table 12-VI). Within the six-month probationary period the guard recruit can be terminated for any reason. The most common reasons for dismissal are failure to come to work, failure to carry out orders, and "trafficking" with inmates. The first reason is perceived by administrators and top guards to be by far the most important. They claim that Stateville functions with a chronic and critical manpower shortage.[9] If 120 men are scheduled to appear on the 7 AM to 3 PM shift, sometimes only

---

[9]There is reason to believe that the claims about staggering absenteeism are somewhat exaggerated. Many of the daily "absences" under closer examination turn out to be rescheduled days off or reassignment to training or escort duty. This, of course, does not alter the fact that the shift commander typically finds himself with insufficient officers to cover all posts.

85 percent show up. This means certain posts will not be covered, certain programs cannot be carried out, and the daily routine cannot run on schedule. Supervisors suggest that the reason men do not come to work is because they do not want to work or because they have a commuting problem or because "they are not suited to prison."

Table VI shows the attendance records for white and non-white dischargees and resignees in our sample and comparable figures for white and non-white guards who began employment in the first six months of 1974 (as did many of our respondents who were discharged) and who are still employed at Stateville. The surprising result is that, contrary to the opinion of the administrators and top guards, overall absenteeism of minority officers, both who have terminated their employment and who are still employed, is *lower* than for whites. On the other hand, minority officers are more often docked (not paid) for their absences. This can only be explained if they less often call the prison to explain their absences or fail to cover themselves in some other way, or if superior officers are more strict in evaluating the validity of the minority guard's excuse for his absence.

Table VI also suggests that the absence record of whites who are discharged is worse than that of non-whites. Perhaps the superior officers are more reluctant to discharge whites? Another explanation might be that a greater percentage of minority guards are discharged for reasons other than absenteeism. Stateville lieutenants and captains in private are not sanguine about the performance of recent minority guard recruits. They suspect that the higher rate of trafficking in contraband with inmates is attributable to the influx of minority employees hired out of the same Chicago neighborhoods from which inmates are drawn. They also object to what they describe as the "shuckin'" and "jivin'" that sometimes goes on between black guards and black inmates. An outside evaluation of the prison observed:

> The new breed who make up the second strata [of guards] are younger, more often black, and come from Chicago. These younger guards have been pouring into the system because it is one job that has opened up to blacks and other minorities. . . . The old guards mistrust and resent the new breed

Table 12-VI

Absenteeism

1. OUR RESPONDENTS (N=55)

	Discharged		Resigned		Total	
	Whites	*Non-Whites*	*Whites*	*Non-Whites*	*Whites*	*Non-Whites*
Median Days DOCKED per month	4.00	.95	.13	1.50	.25	1.17
Median Days ABSENT per month	.67	.46	.82	1.00	.80	.62

II. CONTROL GROUP: Employees who started working at Stateville between Januray 1 and May 1, 1974 and who are still employed as of February 25, 1975

	Whites N=9	Non-Whites N=15	Total
Median Days DOCKED per month	.12	.20	.16
Median Days ABSENT per month	.90	.30	.61

intensely. They feel that the new guards lack discipline, a respect for authority, a sense of importance of maintaining vigilance against the violent and escape-prone convict population. Moreover, and this may be more serious, the old guards feel that the new breed, since they are urban and perhaps from the same neighborhood as many of the convicts, may even identify more, in fact, secretly cooperate with the convicts. (Irwin, 1974, Appendix B, p. B2)

Records of the Employee Review Board, the three-man committee that adjudicates infractions of the rules by guards, also indicate a disproportionate number of black guards being disciplined and a disproportionate number being *severely* disciplined (by suspension). A survey of cases which the board heard between January 20, 1975, to April 14, 1975, (N=137) reveals that 65 percent of the findings (N=83) involved black guards, while only 35 percent (N=44) of the guards who were disciplined by the Board were white. Of the 83 black guards processed by the Board, 55 percent (N=46) received suspensions, the most severe penalty. Of the 45 whites who were disciplined, only 27 percent (N=12) were suspended. The only lieutenant to be suspended was black.

The kind of extreme racism that has been described in some other prisons has not been evident at Stateville (Jacobs and Retsky, 1975; New York State, 1972; Wright, 1973). When we asked our respondents whether they had experienced "racial problems" on the job, 41 percent of the whites and 57 percent of the minority officers answered affirmatively. For those discharged the percentages of affirmative responses were 60 percent and 59 percent respectively. Non-whites who were discharged felt they had experienced racial discrimination no more frequently than non-whites who resigned,

The striking difference between the white and non-white respondents is the group to which they attributed their racial problems (See Table 12-VII). Of the sixteen minority officers who reported experiencing racial problems, eleven named superior officers as a group responsible. Ten of the eleven whites experiencing racial problems named inmates as a group responsible, illuminating the familiar picture of racial and cul-

Table 12-VII

With which groups did you have racial trouble?
(Only those respondents reporting racial problems N=27)

	Whites (N=11)	Non-Whites (N=16)	Total (N=27)
Co-workers	45%	44%	45%
Superior Officers	18%	70%	48%
Counsellors	0%	0%	0%
Inmates	91%	19%	48%
Administrators	0%	0%	0%

tural conflict between a guard force dominated by whites and an 80 percent minority inmate population.

Black recruits expressed an awareness that they departed from the stereotype of a "good prison guard" (Goffman, 1961, p. 87). A few guards, including some young white guards, reported consciously presenting themselves to the inmates in ways that would distinguish them from the traditional guard stereotype. They wore mod clothes, fancy shoes, and long hair, acted in an open and friendly way — chatting informally with inmates while on duty. This adaptation to the prison brought guards into conflict with superiors which, several respondents believed, was "the real reason" why they were forced to leave.

Institutional reaction to the new young black recruits was also felt at a more subtle level, especially by those who lived on the prison grounds. Officers are given the opportunity to live in the dorm for a nominal rent. To avoid the fifty-mile commute, this arrangement is attractive to many single officers who live in Chicago, most of them black. The rules prescribing dorm life are exceedingly stringent. No visitors are allowed in the rooms except other dorm residents. A man's room, (like an inmate's cell) can be "shaken down" at any time by other officers, whose identity and purpose need not be revealed. The fact that the guard himself may have his privacy arbitrarily invaded was viewed by many respondents as a device for maintaining control over non-conformity, especially by black guards. The result of these unexpected shakedowns, usually ocurring while the resident was out of his room, was to create fear, distrust, and suspicion among the line officers. One respondent noted that "a guard is just an inmate with a few more privileges." There was a belief that some officers were spying on others in order to gain promotions.

Even those recruits who did not live in the dorm were amazed to find that as correctional officers, they could be discharged for misbehavior off-duty. Reports of traffic accidents and tickets get back, mysteriously, to supervisors. Upon reporting to work, one respondent was told by the shift commander to return home, "because a man who just had a fight with his wife is in no condition to work." The tower guard sitting above the gatehouse had observed the argument in the parking lot and passed the information on to the commanding officer.

For old-time guards accustomed to working with a majority black inmate population, acceptance of blacks as co-workers of equal status to themselves might be a slow process. This recalcitrance is reinforced by the unwillingness of many new recruits to look upon inmates as different from themselves. Instead, they insist that it is merely fortuitous that the guard is on one side of the bars while the inmate is on the other. Perhaps this failure of the new recruit to profess moral superiority over the inmates in his charge is ultimately most threatening to the prison elite?

RESIGNATION

Why do guards resign? There are two general sets of variables that can be examined. The traditional thinking is that prison guards resign for exogenous reasons like pay, stigma, commuting distance and family problems. On the other hand, some students of the prison have stressed role strain, working conditions, and relationships with superiors and inmates (Jacobs and Retsky, 1975).

Salary dissatisfaction accounts for only a negligible part of the turnover. When respondents were confronted with a list of factors and were asked whether each factor "influenced you to leave," only 26 percent chose "amount of pay" (See Table 12-VIII). Related to the hypothesis that most resignations have to do with salary dissatisfactions is the suggestion that guards resign in order to take better jobs. Twenty-two percent of the resignees in our sample have been unemployed since terminating their employment at Stateville. Fifty-seven percent of the resignees reported working at a job that paid *less* than what they were making at Stateville, and nine percent reported making the same salary. Only 26 percent reported being employed at a better paying job.

Our data indicates that the effect of stigma attached to the guard role may be exaggerated. Indeed, several respondents pointed out that one advantage of being a prison guard was that it frequently made them the focus of conversation among friends and acquaintances (See Table 12-IX). There is a significant difference in which minorities and whites experienced some stigma effect. All but one of the former guards who reported being "embarrassed" about his job was non-white (although this still represented only 37% of all non-whites).

Table 12-VIII

Did the following influence you to resign? N=27

	Yes	No
Amount of pay	26%	74%
Superior officers	44%	56%
Co-workers	22%	78%
Administration	7%	93%
Inmates	22%	78%
Lack of safety	52%	48%
Hours	33%	67%
Commuting problems	22%	78%
Working conditions	37%	63%
Your assignment	22%	78%
Lack of job security	11%	89%
Lack of opportunity for promotion	44%	56%
Desire to return to school	15%	85%
Family responsibilities	37%	63%
Health	7%	93%

Table 12-IX

How did you feel about your job as a guard?

	Whites (N=26)*	Non-Whites (N=28)	Total (N=54)
Proud	34.6%	28.6%	31.5%
Just like any other job	61.5%	35.7%	48.1%
Embarrassed	3.9%	35.7%	20.4%

*Question not applicable in one case.

Other exogenous variables seem no more helpful in explaining the decision to drop out. Despite the widespread impression that commuting is a major cause of resignation, we found that only 22 percent of the resignees reported that commuting even contributed to their decision to resign. The percentage was only slightly higher for minority resignees (27%).

The only exogenous variable with any explanatory power was "family problems" and there is reason to believe that this reason is quite ambiguous. In many cases former guards characterized their wives' fears for their safety as a family responsibility which led them to quit their job. The peculiar problems of physical safety attached to guard work could arguably be considered an endogenous variable. Our respondents may have projected their own apprehensiveness onto family members. This hypothesis is strengthened by the fact that the single factor relating to resignation that received the most attention was "lack of safety." There is a prevailing belief that a guard can be attacked at any time. Fear was intensified by the January 1973 murder of a veteran white guard and by the seizure of eleven hostages on September 6, 1973.

Whites are more likely to express fear than blacks. For many of the rural whites with little exposure to urban blacks and particularly to the street gang culture prevailing among the inmates (Jacobs, 1974), the Stateville experience was frightening. Several of these guards left within the first two weeks.

Of the endogenous variables, unsatisfactory relations with superior officers is a frequently cited factor leading to the decision to quit. If we combine the 12 resignees who reported problems with superior officers with the 13 discharges who expressed a similar difficulty, then 44 percent of the entire respondent group indicated this item as a job strain.

Part of the tension between subordinates and superordinates surrounds the question of promotions. There is a strong belief among the line personnel that "you can't get stripes unless you know somebody." Blacks consistently complained that they lacked entree to the top white ruling clique which determined promotions. Frequently the case of the meteoric rise of a young white guard to sergeant before the rest of his class and was even certified was offered as a prime example of favoritism.

On the other hand, many white respondents, especially those

with several years of experience, complained that "the only way to get anywhere these days is to be black."[10] They reported that one black had been promoted to lieutenant even though he had less seniority than many whites because the prison is under pressure to show that they are not discriminating.

CONCLUSION

We have attempted to displace some of the simplified imagery which informs the attrition among correctional officers at Stateville Penitentiary and suggest that the same racial and cultural conflicts that divide the inmates affect the guards. We are not arguing that turnover can be explained in the same way in all American maximum-security prisons or that it has remained constant over time. To the contrary, our data suggest that like inmates, guards import into the prison the culture of the surrounding society.

We have sampled guard dropouts and rejects rather than guards who are currently employed in order to investigate the strains of the job. We believe that studying dropouts and rejects will have important payoffs in explaining the revolving door syndrome which characterizes the prison's lower participants.

Our results lead us to reject almost every one of the traditional assumptions of prison administrators. It is simply not true that guards are taking the state for a ride until they find a better job. Nor is it true that the turnover situation is explained by "mass resignation" over the issues of low pay and unsatisfactory relationships with inmates.

Turnover is the result of a complex process of interaction between a highly heterogenous and unskilled guard force and a highly in-grown, somewhat inflexible and very demanding prison regime. Race is the most critical variable in accounting for difficulties in adapting to the guard role. If turnover is to be attenuated, then the prison administration will have to discover a more accurate method of identifying and attracting guard recruits who can adjust to the peculiarities of prison or it will have to modify the peculiarities of the prison organization to

---

[10]Precisely the same resentment by whites of the new opportunities opening up for minority employees is documented in the case of the New York City Police Department (Alex, 1976).

accommodate the type of guards being recruited.

Finally, this study suggests that the integration of a previously homogeneous prison work force may lead to a breakdown of the solidarity of the staff. If racial loyalties are carried from the street onto the job then one can expect the same type of developments among black correction officers that has occurred in some cities among black police who have organized their own professional organizations to protest discriminatory hiring and promotion policies as well as discriminatory policies in the enforcement of the law.[11]

REFERENCES

1. Griffith, S. *A training experience as a pseudo guard.* Unpublished manuscript, 1974. (Available from S. Griffith, Illinois Department of Corrections).
2. Jacobs, J. B., and Cohen, J. *The corrections academy: The emergence of a new criminal justice system institution.* Unpublished manuscript, 1977. (Available from J. B. Jacobs and J. Cohen, Cornell University Law School).
3. Jacobs, J. B., and Kraft, L. *Integrating the keepers: A comparison of black and white prison guards in Illinois.* Unpublished manuscript, 1977. (Available from J. B. Jacobs and L. Kraft, Cornell University Law School).
4. Liebentritt, D. *The making of a correctional officer, 1974.* Unpublished manuscript, 1975. (Available from D. Liebentritt, University of Chicago Law School).

BIBLIOGRAPHY

Alex, N. *New York cops talk back.* New York: John Wiley and Sons, 1976.
Clemmer, D. *The prison community.* New York: Rhinehart and Company, 1958.
Goffman, E. *Asylums.* New York: Anchor Books, 1961.
Hunt, I. C., and Cohen, B. *Minority recruitment in the New York City police department.* New York: Rand Corporation, 1969.
Irwin, J. Memorandum of convict and staff relationships at Stateville. In

---

[11]In April 1976, a letter was sent to Governor Walker by an organization calling itself the Afro-American Correctional Officers Movement, complaining a racist oppression of · minority employees as well as inmates at Stateville and other Illinois prisons and enclosing a list of seventeen demands. The demands called, among other things, for the resignation of the warden and several other senior white officials, for the removal of "Ku Klux Klan organizers" from Stateville, and for a review of all guard dismissals that had taken place within the last twelve months.

Program evaluation design of the Illinois Correctional Training Academy. Washington, D.C.: Meta Metric, Inc., 1974.

Irwin, J. *The felon.* Englewood Cliffs, N.J.: Prentice-Hall, 1970.

Jacobs, J. B. Street gangs behind bars. *Social Problems*, 1974, *21*, 395-409.

Jacobs, J. B., and Retsky, H. Prison guard. *Urban Life*, 1975, *4*, 5-29.

Joint Commission on Correctional Manpower and Training. *A time to act: Final report.* Washington, D.C.: U.S. Government Printing Office, 1969.

New York State Special Commission on Attica. *Attica: The official report of the New York state special commission on Attica.* New York: Praeger, 1972.

Wright, E. O. *The politics of punishment.* New York: Harper and Row, 1973.

Chapter 13

SELF-ESTEEM AND VIOLENCE BY GUARDS AND STATE TROOPERS AT ATTICA

Ezra Stotland

WHAT were the psychological forces which lead to the excesses of violence committed by guards and state troopers in the assault on the prisoners at Attica State Prison in 1971? Our purpose here is to answer that question by the application of a general psychological theory concerning violence. The application of the theory does not of course provide an excuse for any wrongdoing that occurred.

The theory stems from the work of Worchel (1958), Toch (1969), Feshback (1964) and is developed in Stotland and Canon (1972). It centers around the concept of the sense of competence, i.e. a person's conception of his competence to control his environment so as to attain goals. The sense of competence is a result of direct and vicarious experiences and of communications from others. Since people tend to value a high sense of competence, a person's self-esteem is in part dependent upon it. Self-esteem is also dependent upon evaluations by others and upon the relative status of a person's reference group.

A person's self-esteem can be threatened by failure, insults, the failures of his reference group, and so on. Among the potential reactions to such threats are efforts to increase the sense of competence. These efforts can sometimes take the form of violence. Among the factors which tend to increase a person's tendency to react violently are the following:

1. Learning from his own experience that violence is often

The original version of this article appeared under the title "Self-Esteem and Violence by Guards and State Troopers at Attica" by Ezra Stotland published in CRIMINAL JUSTICE AND BEHAVIOR, Vol. 3, No. 1, March, 1976, pp. 85-96 and is reprinted herewith by permission of the Publisher, Sage Publications, Inc. and the author.

effective in attaining goals. In certain parts of American society, instrumentally motivated, unemotional violence is a very effective means to attain goals.

2. Perception of the immediacy and directness of the effects of successful violence.

3. Observation of others being successfully violent and being admired for their success, e.g. viewing TV violence.

4. Legitimization of violence committed under some vaguely specified circumstance. This legitimization of violence can be established by leaders and other sources of legitimate authority, by group norms, by justifiably violent identification models, and so on.

5. Reduction of the competence of the victim of violence, thereby enhancing the comparative competence of the person committing the violence.

6. Cessation of the insults by a derogator who is silenced by violence. Since the derogator is also reduced in perceived competence, his credibility as a source of evaluation of others is reduced.

This theory applies to emotionally based violence, in contrast to goal-oriented or instrumental violence, such as that of some combat soldiers. The present theory does not apply to such "cool" violence, although it is clearly related to it, as indicated above. In some situations, both types of motivation may be involved. Actions initially instigated by one motive may become supported by the other as well. At Attica, there doubtless was a mixture of motives for at least some of the guards and state troopers. The present paper shows how self-esteem theory can help to explain some but not all of the motives involved. Nevertheless, our purpose is not to prove the theory, but to show its usefulness in explaining one event.

The events at Attica have been researched thoroughly by the McKay Commission (McKay Commission Report, 1972) whose report provides the basis of the present analysis. As the reader no doubt recalls, the inmates rebelled, seized hostages, gained control of a large part of the prison and held it for several days while they conducted immediate and widely publicized negotiations with prison authorities. Finally, state troopers and a few guards attacked the prisoners' enclave, killed a large number of hostages and inmates, some of them committing acts of violence after the inmates had been overcome.

The McKay Commission reports that much of the violence by state troopers and guards was unwarranted and not necessary to protect any lives, i.e. was not instrumental or goal-oriented. In order to show how the present theory can help explain these excesses, it is necessary to demonstrate that three factors were present. One is that the sense of competence and self-esteem of the state troopers and guards is dependent in part on their ability to be violent when appropriate. The second is that the state troopers and guards perceived violence to be legitimate in the situation. The third is that their self-esteem and sense of competence were threatened.

The relationship between the state troopers' use of arms and their sense of competence is obvious. They are trained in arms, use them when they perceive it necessary, and are evaluated in part on their ability to use weapons. Furthermore, they are trained in unarmed self-defense (McKay Commission Report, 1972: 344).

The guard's professional sense of competence is not as closely tied to their capacity for armed violence as the state troopers'. Nevertheless, the guards were expected to be able to use arms when necessary and had been officially issued arms in previous emergencies. They had been encouraged to use their private weapons if the prison supply was short. In the rural area in which Attica is located, hunting rifles and pride in marksmanship are common. As part of their job, guards are expected to use and did use their clubs on prisoners on occasion. In short, for both troopers and guards, the sense of competence, violence, and self-esteem are significantly linked so that the first factor demanded of the theory was present.

The second factor is that the use of violence against the inmates be perceived as legitimate. This legitimization was probably established first by the fact that the inmates were adjudicated criminals, guilty of serious crimes, and no doubt were perceived to deserve punishment even beyond incarceration. The guards probably perceived them as still dangerous, to be kept in line only by fear of force. Secondly, the majority of the inmates were black or Puerto Rican. The McKay Commission reports many indications of prejudice, despite the troopers' and guards' denials (pp. 300-301, 311). They may not have judged it proper to kill a minority person, but the barriers against such killing were probably weaker than against killing a white. Third, the use of hostages no doubt was perceived as an additional crime. The guards knew the hostages as colleagues and friends with whom the troopers also mingled in the days before the assault, and they knew and talked with their distraught families as well. Rumors of atrocities abounded among the guards and troopers (p. 306). Fourth, the death of one of the guards injured by the inmates additionally legitimized violence against them. Fifth, the shooting lasted fifteen minutes, thus probably permitting guards and troopers who initially hesitated to fire freely to conclude that free fire was in fact acceptable to their peers. A parallel process probably occurred during the violence inflicted on the prisoners immediately after the assault. Thus many indicators indicate the presence of the second factor necessary for the application of the theory, the legitimization of violence against the prisoners.

The third factor is that the self-esteem of the potentially violent people be threatened. In order to show the presence of this factor, the history of Attica in the years preceeding the inmate takeover will be examined to see how the changes that occurred probably affected the guards. Before January 1, 1971, the relationship between the guards and the inmates was fairly clearly a hierarchical one. The power of the guards was a reality that was expressed symbolically in many ways, such as restrictions on the color of the inmates' underwear, wearing of shackles on arrival at the prison, and so on. There can be little doubt that the guards' sense of competence was dependent in part on the exercise of power and on its symbolic expressions. In fact, the McKay Commission reports many ways in which the guards abused the inmates (e.g. pp. 74-75). Doubtless, if a guard was to sense high competence, his orders to the inmates had to be obeyed. An additional source of self-esteem for the guards was no doubt their status vis-à-vis the inmates.

This relatively stable situation began to end when Russell Oswald took over as commissioner of correctional services for New York State on January 1, 1971. He had been appointed primarily because of his long and distinguished career as an enlightened and progressive correctional administrator. In Attica, his new policies soon led to the decline of the power and status of the guards relative to the inmates. In July 1971, he ordered that from then on Moslem prisoners were to be given porkless meals. Prior to March 1971, the director of education alone censored all of the books, magazines, and newspapers the prisoners purchased. After that date, the director was reduced to being chairman of a censorship committee, and the criteria for censorship were made explicit. At about this time, the inmates won a lawsuit to receive copies of *Fortune News*, a prison reform journal.

In 1970, a Federal judge ruled that inmates who were charged with an infraction of the rules are entitled to defend themselves. A special adjustment committee was set up to review serious charges brought by guards, the prisoners being allowed to defend themselves. Hearings before the warden were also provided for. Thus, there was some reduction of the officers' power.

During this period, the inmates both expressed and enhanced their power by forming organizations ranging from purely religious to purely militant. Furthermore, the new independence of the inmates was shown by the development of official and unofficial classes in law and sociology. The inmates even conducted a successful sit-down strike for higher wages in the machine shop. After Jessie Jackson was killed, the inmates showed their organization and strength by a collective, silent fast. The McKay Commission reports:

> Thus correction officers frequently found themselves demanding adherence to rules which inmates would not accept. As the number of confrontations increased during this period, so did the intensity. An officer's orders to stop talking, for example, were first questioned, later ignored, and finally ridiculed. [McKay Commission Report, p. 20]

The punishment for such infractions had been keeplock or isolation, but they lost their effectiveness. Additional court orders precipitated even more regulations giving the prisoners more rights. Oswald's administration of the state correctional system was generally supportive of the new movement in prisoner's rights. He liberalized rules with respect to mail, writing, censorship, and so on. He did not approve of the warden's disciplinary actions against some inmates who had made demands for reform. Furthermore, he replied to these demands by acknowledging that they might have some merit, and promised to work gradually for reform. He indicated that he was also aware of the fact that there was some need to change the attitude of the guards. He appointed a new deputy warden who had a reputation for leniency. The effect of Oswald's policies and promises on the guards was an increasing sense of helplessness, i.e. a loss of sense of competence (McKay Commission Report, p. 125). Some of the older, more experienced guards got themselves transferred to jobs that involved less need to discipline the prisoners, leaving that job to less experienced, less secure officers.

The incident which provoked the uprising epitomizes this trend for guard power to decline relative to the inmates and increased this trend tremendously. An inmate refused a direct order and lightly punched a guard lieutenant in the chest. When the inmate's defiance was supported by other inmates, he stood his ground, and the involved correctional officers backed away, so as to try to handle the problem some other way later. No such sequence of events had ever occurred in Attica before.

The next day, the guards placed the inmate involved in the above incident in special custody. The inmates were angered over what they perceived to be an excess of violence in these and related actions by the guards. The inmates attacked several guards severely and began to take over parts of the prison. After the initial attack on a few officers and after the takeover of only a part of the prison, there was a ten-minute lull in which unattacked guards in the vicinity did nothing commensurate with the seriousness of the outbreak. Furthermore, they were unable to inform the central administration of the prison what was going on. This lull not only reflected the guard's sense of helplessness, it increased it. The lull was ended by the inmates' breaking into an area which controlled traffic through much of the prison, severely attacking guards in this area. In short, the uprising had considerable initial momentum against weak officer resistance. The outbreak thus continued a trend of increasing inmate power and lessening guard power which began long before.

When the central administration finally did get word, reactions were very slow and ineffectual because of "the shortage of personnel, an antiquated communication system, and the absense of an institution-wide control system" (p. 162). Even the warden admitted to being helpless (p. 164). Accordingly, the area under control of the inmates quickly enlarged, as they gained keys from the officers they attacked, and as they found or improvised weapons. In less than two hours, the prisoners had taken forty-two officers and civilians hostage. Several officers were seriously injured in the takeover. Many parts of the prison were on fire or otherwise in a shambles. The guards had lost control of all five cellblocks, some shops, the auditorium, school, and commissary. It was only after all of this had occurred that significant countermeasures were taken. The sense of competence of the guards was doubtless severely threatened.

When off-duty guards began to arrive, many with their own weapons, they were told that they would try to retake the prison immediately. But that order was soon rescinded to await the arrival of state troopers. Nevertheless, small groups of guards, and later, state troopers, began to retake parts of the prison, firing their weapons from time to time, but encountering little resistance, since most of the inmates had congregated in D yard. However, these groups did not get permission to try to retake some critical parts of the prison because of the danger to the hostages, because of the fear of casualties, and because of fear of loss of weapons, since these groups were still small. In fact, one very important, recaptured cellblock was given up to the inmates. This restraint by their superiors caused great bitterness among some officers. Their first efforts to reestablish control were stymied and their sense of competence was no doubt battered again.

On the first day, the troopers assigned to guard secure areas of the prison saw much of the destruction the inmates accomplished, a testimony to their power. Moreover, even at this early period, the inmates had organized themselves and negotiations with them had started. During the next few days, as the negotiations proceeded, it soon became evident to all that the inmates were well organized and had gained enormous power because of the hostages. While the guards and the state troopers stood hopelessly by, the inmates' demands for the intervention of numerous prominent outsiders were met to a large extent; the inmates were on television telling the world about their demands; they began to gain point after point in the negotiations; Oswald and Governor Rockefeller gave in to all but two of the demands. The crescendo of increased power to the prisoners begun years before continued. They were elated at their new found power (McKay Commission Report, p. 299). The guards who saw all this were not only angered at the takeover of their prison and the threat of gross mistreatment of the hostages, but were also angered by all the recognition given to the prisoners, as if they were equals. The guards' and troopers' self-esteem must have suffered by the rise in status and power of the inmates.

On the second day, the guards' problems were compounded by the issuing and rescinding of another order to retake the prison. Furthermore, as the guards watched the inmates denounce them over television, they felt that no one was standing up for them; they were being ignored, suffering a blow to their esteem. At the same time the guards could directly observe the increasing armed strength and organization of the inmates' "citadel." Thus, the second day's experiences magnified the guards' and troopers' problems.

By the fourth day, the state troopers' and guards' fatigue increased so that they felt, and probably were, less competent. They could do little to relieve the stench from the unsanitary conditions in the prison. On the fifth day, the inmates' rejection of the state's proposals was an "added indignity" (McKay Commission Report, p. 310). The problem was aggravated because there was still another aborted order to assume positions for the final assault. In sum, then, the threat to the sense of competence of the state troopers and the guards and thereby the threat to their self-esteem was reaching crescendo proportions just before the final order was given to retake the prison.

Nevertheless, there were additional factors which enhanced the threat to the troopers' and officers' self-esteem. As we indicated above, people generally are not invulnerable to insults, even from strangers. The troopers who were stationed in C

Block guarded a number of prisoners who were recaptured during the first attempts to retake the prison. During the four days in which they guarded the prisoners, there was a constant and rising level of extremely hostile verbal confrontation. Meanwhile, the inmates in D Yard, their main citadel, began the second day shouting insults at the troopers and guards standing in the windows around the yard. Each day the intensity of these insults rose. The guards watched their *de jure* representative, Oswald, on television being insulted by the inmates, without his retaliating. Furthermore, as the perceived power of the inmates rose, no doubt the psychological power of their insults also rose.

Another factor was the implicit rise in stature accorded the inmates due to the simple fact that they were being negotiated with, that Oswald and others in authority were treating them as equals. To the extent that the inmates were given recognition as equals, the troopers and guards could not continue to gain self-esteem by comparing themselves to these "low, black, criminals." Again, this rise in inmate status made their insults even harder to take.

As the McKay Commission Report indicates, there was much for the troopers to fear from the inmates in making the assault to retake the prison: their threats to the lives of the hostages; their criminally assaultive records and behavior; the weapons fashioned and perfected for four days; the barricades they had erected, and so on. Thus, at least some of the behavior of the troopers and officers during the assault was generated by realistic, healthy fear for their lives (p. 345). In fact, the final order given to the troopers was to fire only if an inmate engaged in overt, hostile acts against hostages or troopers. (Some guards took it upon themselves to participate in the assault and employed their own guns. Their unauthorized participation is not surprising in the light of all we have said above.)

Our question here is whether the amount of force used was beyond that justified by honest and realistic fear for one's life or the lives of other people. The McKay Commission examined this question in great detail, painstakingly putting together testimony from troopers, guards, and inmates, examining both still and moving pictures, and studying the physical evidence.

There is no need nor space here to review all of the detailed
material assembled (pp. 366-403), since the commission con-
cludes:

> It is understandable that the great majority of the men in-
> volved in the assault acted with restraint. Had they not done
> so, considering the firepower available to them and the lack
> of controls of their actions, the toll of dead and wounded
> would have been much greater. It is also clear, however, that
> the cellblock, on the catwalks, and in D Yard, there was much
> unnecessary shooting.
> There was no justification for the many instances of shooting
> into tents, trenches, and barricades without looking. The
> twenty-one deaths and more than fifty wounded in D Yard
> cannot all be explained by the incident involving Lt. Chris-
> tian [a trooper attacked by inmates while spearheading on a
> charge to save the hostages] or other hostile acts. Even when
> there was some provocation, such as the assault on Lt. Chris-
> tian, the repeated discharge of "00" buckshot pellets into D
> Yard at ranges far exceeding the weapons intended use un-
> questionably wounded, and perhaps killed, many inmates
> who were not engaged in any acts of hostility or resistance
> whatever. There was clearly indiscriminant firing into con-
> gested areas by men who did not value the inmates' lives.
> Indeed, several witnesses told the Commission they heard
> troopers bragging later in the day about their exploits on the
> morning of the assault (p. 402).

The excessive violence did not cease when the inmates' power
had been destroyed. The McKay Commission reports numerous
instances of brutality and humiliation of the inmates during
the process of assembling the inmates and readying them for
return to their cells. The continuation of this violence against
the inmates, after they no longer presented any threat to
anyone's survival or physical well-being, bespeaks the strength
of the motivations involved of attempting to fend off a threat to
self-esteem.

In short, then, the theory proposed above can help us to
understand the motivations of the correctional officers and state
troopers. There were many factors which led them to perceive
that it was legitimate to be violent against the inmates. They
viewed their ability to be violent when violence is needed as an

important aspect of their sense of competence. And there were many threats to their self-confidence: the power of the inmates; the recognition they received; the insults from the prisoners; the evidence of the guards' and troopers' own ineffectiveness and powerlessness.

REFERENCES

FESHBACK, S. (1964) "The function of aggression and the regulation of aggressive drive." Psych. Rev. 71: 257-272.

McKay Commission Report (Attica, the Official Report of the New York State Special Commission on Attica). New York: Bantam.

STOTLAND, E. and K. K. CANON (1972) Social Psychology: A Cognitive Approach. Philadelphia: Saunders.

TOCH, H. (1969) Violent Men. Chicago: Aldine.

WORCHEL, P. (1958) "Status restoration and the reduction of hostility." J. of Abnormal and Social Psychology 14: 355-359.

Chapter 14

THE FRUSTRATED HACKS

LEO CARROLL

FULLY 70 percent of the institutional staff at ECI have custody as their primary function. Officially these men are correctional officers; they refer to themselves as guards; to the inmates they are "hacks." The hacks stand on one side of a caste line that is the fundamental feature of the prison social structure. They are the lower echelon members of a dominant group possessing a monopoly of the legitimate means of coercion. Supported by the authority of the state, granted the power to punish nonconformity and to reward conformity to their expectations, with their positions buttressed by walls, bars, and weapons, the custodians might appear to be both absolutely and securely dominant. But, as Sykes has shown, the nearly total power of the hacks is more illusion than reality.[1] At ECI the reforms have dispelled even the illusion of total power. In eliminating many of the rules, rituals, and routines by which inmate behavior was regulated, the reforms destroyed many of the symbols and supports of coercive power. In granting inmates access to the legislature and courts, in eliminating censorship of mail, and by extending certain safeguards of due process of law to prisoners, the reforms have provided inmates with the capacity to develop a significant degree of countervailing power. Finally, and of direct concern in this chapter, the changes and reforms of the past few years have induced a state of anomie within the administrative/custodial hierarchy itself.

As anomie has become an increasingly popular concept it also has become increasingly ill-defined. As developed originally by Durkheim[2] and later elaborated by Merton,[3] however,

Reprinted by permission of the publisher, from Leo Carroll, HACKS, BLACKS, AND CONS: RACE RELATIONS IN A MAXIMUM SECURITY PRISON (Lexington, Mass: Lexington Books, D. C. Heath and Company, Copyright 1974, D. C. Heath and Company).

anomie refers to a state of relative normlessness in a group or society.[4] It is in this sense that I shall use the term. At ECI there are two primary sources of anomie. First, the inherent contradiction between custodial and treatment goals has created conflict among the top administrators and resulted in ambiguous role definitions for the lower echelon personnel. Second, the policy of humanitarian reform has undermined the capacity of the officers to maintain security and internal order, a primary responsibility to which they remain committed. The result of these strains has been a fragmentation of social relationships at all levels of the custodial/administrative hierarchy and a rebellion of the officers against the prison administration.

CONFLICT AMONG THE ADMINISTRATORS

The problem of goal conflict had long been present at ECI when this study began. During the period of the study, the clearest manifestation of this problem was the unsuccessful attempt of Charles Knott to solidify his position as warden and to mobilize the staff under his direction.

THE PROBLEM OF ADMINISTRATIVE SUCCESSION

The replacement of administrative personnel often presents problems for bureaucratic organizations. In *Patterns of Industrial Bureaucracy*, Gouldner presents an incisive analysis of these problems and of how they were resolved in one factory.[5] Entering a plant that had been characterized by an "indulgency pattern," a system of lenient and flexible rules and close personal relations and favors between supervisors and workers, the new plant manager, Vincent Peele, was confronted with a number of problems. Among these were the implementation of efficiency goals set by the central office, the resistance of middle management personnel who held ties of loyalty to his predecessor and viewed Peele as an illegitimate heir, the resistance of rank and file workers who derived many benefits from the indulgency pattern, and lastly his own personal anxiety in the face of the challenge he confronted. To cope with these problems, Peele resorted to several courses of action that resulted in a bureaucratization of the plant. He enforced previously dormant company rules, thus eliminating many of the characteristics of the indulgency pattern. He adopted a pattern of close personal supervision of production of both by personal observation and a system of written reports. Most importantly, he made several "strategic replacements." He demoted or fired several of the old lieutenants and replaced them. He filled new positions that opened as a result of new machinery and operations in the plant with new managers who, like himself, were committed to production goals and formalized procedures and who were tied to him by bonds of personal loyalty. Through such means Peele was able to establish his position as manager.

A prison is not a gypsum plant. Nonetheless, the situation faced by Charles Knott at the beginning of this study was analogous to that of Vincent Peele. Like Peele, Knott was a successor to a man who had occupied the position for a number of years, and he was a successor from outside the organization, to some extent a stranger among friends. In assuming the position of warden, he entered an institution that, by virtue of the policies of his predecessor, was characterized by a system of lenient rules and relaxed discipline akin to the indulgency pattern. Moreover, as a result of the disturbances and investigations of the preceding year, Knott was mandated to change the character of the institution, to move it in the direction of a treatment orientation. And finally, in approaching the position, Knott also exhibited a great deal of anxiety. He was a political appointee whose position was dependent upon the maintenance of security and order and the whims of the electorate as much as upon the implementation of treatment programs. That he saw himself in a probationary status was symbolized by the fact that he maintained his residence in his native state some fifty miles from the prison.

Lack of Options

That Knott was unable to establish himself as warden may be understood in terms of several conditions associated with his position that made it different from the gypsum plant studied by Gouldner. First, there exist no bureaucratic rules that Knott could impose to facilitate attainment of the treatment goal. Unlike the production of gypsum board, the process of rehabilitating offenders cannot be precisely defined and specified. It requires professional expertise rather than bureaucratic authority and a relaxed and relatively comfortable atmosphere. The implementation of bureaucratic rules and regulations, then, was not seen by Knott as a means of solidifying his position as it was antithetical to the goals set for him and to which he himself was committed. The priorities Knott set were (1) the procurement of professional treatment personnel and the establishment of treatment programs, (2) the education of his staff in the perspectives of treatment ideology, and (3) a further relaxation of custodial measures.

The first two of these priorities were never realized. As I noted in the previous chapter, soon after he became warden, Knott secured a federal grant to establish a new vocational training program, but he received no additional resources from the state. In the first budget, he submitted to the legislature in 1970, he requested additional funding for several new positions. Among these positions were a psychiatrist, a clinical psychologist, three social workers, two teachers, a deputy warden for treatment services, a drug addiction specialist, and a coordinator of inmate activities. Not one of these positions was funded, and the same response was given to a similar budget request in 1971. Thus, despite his mandate to implement a treatment approach, Knott was unable to secure the essential resources to achieve this objective, and the changes he was able to make were by and large an extension of the policy of humanitarian reform — increased visiting privileges, the permission to form additional inmate organizations, permission for long hair and beards, and so forth.

The lack of resources for new programs and positions had implications beyond the immediate consequence of the failure to develop a treatment orientation. It denied to Knott the only means available to him to make "strategic replacements," to establish his own inner circle of assistants who shared his orientations and were loyal to him. As it was, his immediate subordinates were men who had worked their way up through the ranks at ECI, who did not share Knott's orientation to treatment, who viewed him as a usurper of their prerogatives for advancement, and whose positions were secure by virtue of civil service. O'Toole, the assistant warden, had begun work at ECI in 1946 as a guard and had been successively promoted up the custodial hierarchy, becoming assistant warden in 1969. Smalley, the deputy warden, had also come to ECI in 1946 as a guard; and Dick White, the director of classification, had been in his position for over twelve years.

Administrative Conflict

Despite considerable difference among these three men, they frequently acted in concert to thwart Knott's programs. One example of their resistance is the area of work release. Knott openly espoused the concept of "community-based corrections," and one of the accomplishments of which he was most proud was the procurement and renovation of a cottage off the prison grounds as a residence for fifty prisoners on work release. As he saw it, this was to be the first step in the development of several such cottages. But the placement of individuals on work release required the approval of the Classification Board composed of Knott, O'Toole, Smalley, White, and one other member. Inmates were frequently denied work release by 3-2 or 4-1 votes with the result that although the cottage could accommodate 50, there were seldom more than 20 or 25 inmates on work release at any one time.

Knott might have been able to overcome such resistance had he been able to secure additional personnel similarly committed to his orientation, or if he had the support of his superiors. He had neither. His one opportunity to make a "strategic replacement" occurred when Smalley resigned as deputy warden. Knott sought to replace him with a man with whom he had worked prior to coming to ECI. This effort was vetoed by his superior, however, and Smalley was replaced by Boucher who, like the others, entered his position after fifteen years as a guard, lieutenant, and captain.

Knott's superior was Vincent Flint who, as we have seen, had worked at ECI for nearly twenty years as director of classification and assistant warden. He had close personal ties with both O'Toole, whom he had favored for warden, and White, who had succeeded him as director of classification. Knott thus found himself entrapped by a network of informal ties between his superior and his subordinates. "I'm in a squeeze between the guy above me and the guys below me, and I can't move a thing," was the way he put it.

GOAL DISSENSUS

The strain in the relations between Knott, Flint, and the others was not merely a clash of personalities but a reflection of the dual goals assigned to the institution: to protect society and to rehabilitate the offender. Both goals are granted equal legitimacy but decision-making requires administrators to accord a priority to one or the other. Knott accorded priority to the treatment goal. He characterized his correctional philosophy as "liberal, left of center, progressive," and was willing to sacrifice an appreciable degree of security in the interest of rehabilitation. Flint and the others, while not in diametric opposition to Knott, espoused a more conservative view. Flint, for example, characterized himself as a reformer. But he contended that reform programs would be destroyed by adverse community reactions if the reforms jeopardized institutional security. Thus, in Flint's view, treatment efforts had to be limited by custodial concerns.

In attempting to develop a plan of action for the prison, then, Flint and Knott were brought into frequent conflict. In these conflicts neither party had complete power over the other. On the one hand, Knott's attempts to promote treatment goals were limited by the power of Flint. On the other hand, Flint's commitment to security was limited by the investigative commissions that had strongly recommended the development of treatment programs, by the decrees of the court, by the attention of outside groups that had become interested in prison reform, and by the possible threat of inmate disturbances if changes were not forthcoming.[6] The relations between the top administrators were thus contained within a system of checks and balances; Knott was able to develop a variety of reform programs within the institution, but Flint was able to exercise a veto on any changes that in his view threatened security or that might incur an adverse reaction from the community. Among the programs implemented by Knott were the following: a vocational training program, a work release program, an inmate advisory council, the expansion of visiting privileges and a relaxation of custodial rules regarding dress, haircuts, and the like. Among the programs proposed by Knott but vetoed by Flint were the following: the expansion of the work release program into a system of halfway houses, home furloughs for selected prisoners, and an in-service training program in treatment techniques for correctional officers.

Such continuing conflicts among the top administrators created a situation of organizational drift, a situation in which the resources of the institution were not clearly committed to any goal beyond that of self-maintenance and in which administrative decisions frequently had the effect of neutralizing one another. As one officer expressed it:

> It's like having a ship without a rudder. . . . If you say we're supposed to rehabilitate people, we don't do that. If we're supposed to produce things, we don't do that either because we don't work them enough. And all these changes mean we don't punish them either. Nobody knows what we're supposed to do so we don't do anything.

As suggested by this comment, one result of goal dissensus and conflict among the administrators was an absence of policy direction that exacerbated a pre-existing state of anomie among the lower level custodians.

ANOMIE AMONG THE CUSTODIANS

Prior to 1956, the officers were "guards," and their role was precisely defined. The sole functions of the guard were to maintain security and internal order. A detailed set of rules regulated even the most minute aspects of inmate life, and a complementary set of written procedures guided the guard in his surveillance of inmate behavior and enforcement of the rules. Today the official title of the custodial staff is "correctional officers," a title that both incorporates and symbolizes the conflicting and ambiguous definitions of their current role.[7] As the term "officer" connotes, the custodians remain organized in a military hierarchy, the function of which is to ensure security and order. But the adjective "correctional" connotes an additional expectation of equal priority. In some way the officers are expected to be agents in a rehabilitative process in addition to maintaining security and internal order. How this is to be accomplished has never been, and probably cannot be, precisely defined. The only guidance given the officers are the general guidelines that the maintenance of security and order is to be accomplished in a manner consistent with the "home away from home" atmosphere that has been the goal of the reforms, and that they are to contribute to this atmosphere by being relaxed and friendly in their relations with inmates.

To a large extent, the home away from home atmosphere has been created by the abolition of specific rules regarding inmate behavior. The *Inmate Guide Book*, for instance, specifically states that "we refrain from listing a series of do's and don'ts." This absence of specific rules for inmate conduct does not mean that inmates are permitted to act in any manner they desire. Rather, while inmates are granted considerable freedom of action, it remains "understood" that their conduct will not be a threat to security and order and that behavior constituting such a threat is subject to punishment. But what types of behavior constitute such a threat? Clearly, an attempted escape or the possession of a knife does. But what about loud hollering, rough horseplay, or other forms of seemingly innocuous behavior that may nonetheless result in a fight or possible disturbance? On such matters there is no consensus. Decisions of this nature are left to the common sense and discretion of the officer, which results in considerable inconsistency in rule enforcement, as well as a sense of futility and frustration among the officers.

> That's the biggest problem today. There's no policy, no guidelines. You know I consider myself to be a well-balanced person and I try to understand what they mean by not listing the "do's" and "don't's." But you just can't run an institution without a written policy of some sort. But fantastically enough that's what we're doing. There is no written poli-

cy. . . . It's frustrating, damn frustrating. You're just never sure what it is you're supposed to be doing, and the next guy might be doing the exact opposite of what you're doing.

GOALS AND MEANS

In part, the anomic state of the custodians is a result of ambiguous and contradictory role definitions, which in turn are a function of the contradictory goals assigned to the prison and the resultant conflict among the top administrators. There is a second source of anomie, however. As elaborated by Merton, a major source of anomie is "disassociation between culturally prescribed aspirations and socially structured avenues for realizing these aspirations."[8] Seen in this light, anomie among the custodians at ECI also is the result of their continued commitment to the goal of custodial control in the face of institutional changes that made the attainment of that goal by traditional means increasingly more difficult.

The officers do not accord equal legitimacy to the conflicting and muddled definitions of their role. In the absence of treatment programs and professional treatment personnel, there has been no attempt made to convert the officers to the perspectives of modern treatment ideology. They continue to refer to themselves as guards, to view their primary function as security and control, and to hold a custodial perspective on the nature of crime and the proper treatment of inmates. In their view, crime is the result of the laziness, greed, or immorality of the individual offender. Criminals deserve to be punished for their wrongdoing. Nor, in their view, is there any conflict between the goals of punishment, custody, and rehabilitation. Quite to the contrary, these are seen as complementary and consistent goals. Punishment and custody are ensured by the strict enforcement of rigid rules. These same measures are necessary to the success of treatment efforts. An austere prison existence will instill in inmates a fear of return. By learning to conduct himself in accord with the rules of the prison, the inmate will find it easier to abide by the less stringent rules of society after his release. Moreover, to be successful, education and training programs must insist on attendance and attention to the instructional program. And finally, introducing such programs, as well as the many volunteer programs, when custodial rules are being relaxed is an abdication of the responsibility to protect the community. The increase in traffic in and out of the institution is a threat to security and order that necessitates more rules rather than less.

But in fact, as has been pointed out, as a result of the policy of humanitarian reform inmates have been granted increasing freedom, and written rules regarding inmate behavior have been replaced by unwritten "understandings." Moreover, as a result of the court decrees in 1970, the power of the officers in enforcing these understandings has been restricted. One ruling, it will be remembered, extends certain minimal safeguards of due process of law to inmates. Consequently, officers may lock an inmate in his cell only if he presents a clear and present threat to the security and order of the institution, terms which are left undefined. Further, an officer reporting an infraction must first notify the inmate that he is being reported and tell him the reason for it. He must then submit the report to his superior for investigation and be prepared to answer questions at a disciplinary hearing at which the inmate has the right to counsel. From the viewpoint of the officers, these rules are a serious infringement upon their authority and make it impossible for them to perform their duties. Further, the ruling ignores the very vulnerable position in which they find themselves — a situation in which an aggrieved inmate might easily assault them. One result, then, according to the officers, has been an increased reluctance to take action against an inmate unless absolutely necessary.

Deterioration of Relationships

The result of these intrusions upon the coercive powers of the custodians has not only been normlessness in the area of job performance, but also a deterioration of the working relationships among the custodians. Like the police in the case of the Miranda decision, the officers view the court decision as placing the law and the courts on the side of the inmate and in opposition to them. By extending legal rights to inmates, restricting the power of the officers and placing the institution on eighteen months probation, the decision makes the prisoners the "good guys." In short, the officers feel themselves betrayed and "sold out" by agencies that should support their authority. These agencies are not only the courts but the Department of Corrections itself. The nature of the court ruling was in the form of a consent decree, a compromise agreement between counsel for the plaintiffs and the Department of Corrections. The officers interpret this action as a betrayal of their own superiors.

> I'm thoroughly disgusted by the whole thing. And the main thing that disgusts me is that it was our own people that was supposed to be down there fighting for us that dreamed up that catastrophe. . . . They're the ones that wrote it. The Legal Aid Society, or whatever it was, they just read it and of course they were delighted! But it was our own people, Flint and the state's attorneys, they're the ones that sold us down the drain.

In the eyes of the correctional officers, the court decision is only the most recent example of betrayal by their superiors. Given their commitment to custodial values and the need for strong external controls in rehabilitation, the entire series of reforms has been a "sell out." As they see it, the decisions to relax controls and grant greater freedoms to prisoners have not been made in an effort to develop a rehabilitative approach. They have been made to pacify the inmates so as to protect the positions of the top administrators. In their eyes, the interests and welfare of the officers have been sacrificed to the self-interests of their superiors and the inmates.

> Flint and them other big shots, what do they care? They can't go any higher up now unless they was elected governor. So all they want is a quiet can. Their attitude is "keep it cool, boys. Don't have any trouble out there. Don't hit the papers. Keep the lid on. If you have to give a little, give a little." It keeps the inmates happy but we're the ones that have to come in here and put up with all this shit. No one gives a damn about us.

The feeling of not being supported by one's superiors pervades the entire chain of command and is fed by many daily incidents. On one occasion I witnessed an officer break up a fight between two inmates. He waded in among some twenty-five spectators and separated the two combatants. He informed each that they were to be reported for fighting and ordered them to return to their cells. At this point he was accosted by the spectators who argued that there was no reason for reporting them as it had merely been a friendly argument. Nonetheless, the officer stood his ground, reported the inmates, and returned them to their cells. Later that day, he learned that the captain had returned them to normal status, and that no Disciplinary Board was recommended, as there had been no animosity involved.

Such incidents are not uncommon. The superior officer and the Disciplinary Board confront a violation from a different perspective than the officer on the scene. Inmates hostile and perhaps violent at the time of report may be quite calm by the time the superior officer conducts his investigation. Thus, an incident that may have appeared serious at the time, and perhaps was, may appear to have been not so serious several hours later. Moreover, the investigation by the superior officer and the evidence brought forward by the inmate and his counsel at the hearing may uncover mitigating circumstances unknown to the officer who submitted the report. Such was the case, for example, of one inmate who assaulted another and was merely reprimanded. The investigation revealed that he had been unable to see the doctor that day to receive his dosage of Thorazine. Then, too, the Disciplinary Board is obliged to consider the welfare of the inmate and the effect of a disciplinary action on the general population as well as the facts of the matter. There may be evidence that segregation or solitary confinement may be unduly harmful to the physical or mental health of the prisoner, or it may be feared in some cases that a severe action may incite a disturbance. Finally, and perhaps most importantly, superior officers regard the reports of many officers with a high degree of suspicion.

There is a widespread belief among the superiors that many officers exaggerate their reports so as to ensure a punishment. Nor is this belief altogether unjustified. On one incident I was able to follow, the officer reported the inmate for "refusing an order to come down off the tier and using profanity and threatening me when I informed him of the booking." In fact, the inmate had refused the order but accepted the report without complaint except to attempt to explain why he had failed to come off the tier when so ordered.

For several reasons then, the disposition of a disciplinary report is often less severe than that deemed just by the officer submitting the report. Ideally, the officer is not expected to concern himself with the disposition of the case. His function ends with the submission of the report. In fact, officers take an intense interest in such dispositions and can relate to a questioner how many reports they've "won" and "lost" over a specified period of time. But because they are not expected to be concerned with the disposition, they are seldom informed of the reasons for whatever decision is made. The result is a general feeling that they are unsupported by their superiors, and that the disciplinary process makes them look like fools to the inmates they are expected to supervise.

> Most of the time the inmate just gets a reprimand, and a reprimand is the most menial form of punishment you can inflict. An officer can be abused to such a degree that he can't take it anymore so he files a disciplinary report and the thing gets watered down so much by the process that follows that it's insulting. . . . By the time the report is dispensed with, the officer is a laughing stock to the inmates and a sadist with a pen to the Board.

The absence of a specified set of impersonal rules in combination with the belief that one's "common sense" decisions will often be unsupported by his superiors has resulted in a deterioration of the working relations among the lower level custodians themselves. Under such conditions, to exercise custodial control is to place oneself on the line. The submission of a disciplinary report may in fact result in the questioning of the integrity or competence of the officer. Moreover, the fact that another officer may overlook or permit the same behavior, means that to enforce a rule may also draw the personal vindictiveness of an inmate. In consequence, the officers define their rule enforcement function in a highly personal manner. Each officer constructs his role in a manner so as to cause himself the least trouble. They view themselves not as a team working together to ensure security and control, but as individuals whose function is to minimize disorder and trouble in their individual areas of responsibility even at the expense of overall institutional security. One evening, for example, I was in the gym after evening recreation in the yard. Sentenced men are allowed to use the gym at this time, but men awaiting trial are to return to their wing. In the gym at the time were some twenty-five prisoners, eight of whom were men awaiting trial, conspicuous by their khaki shirts and trousers. It was inconceivable that the officer in charge of the gym, posted by the door, did not notice these men. Yet he made no attempt to remove them. Some fifteen minutes later the officer in charge of the A/T wing came into the gym, and without a word to the gym officer, set about gathering his charges. To do this meant that he had to leave a wing containing some one hundred prisoners unsupervised.

One of the areas in which the lack of cooperation in rule enforcement among officers is most evident regards the pass system. It is understood that no inmate is to be permitted to go from one area of the institution to another, say from the shop to the wings, without a pass from his supervisor, and that officers are to issue passes only for good and sufficient reason. Again, however, this is not a written rule nor are the "good and sufficient reasons" delineated. The result is that many officers are reluctant not to grant a pass. One shop officer explained:

> If there was a clear policy on it and everybody enforced it, they'd be no problem. I could just say "no it's against the rules." But that ain't the way it is. So if I say 'no' then I got an argument or a fight. So usually I just let them go. That way I don't have the argument or the fight, just the worry that he might be getting into something.

A similar response was given to me by a wing officer when I noted a number of men in his wing who should have been in the shops.

> To tell the truth, I don't care if they have passes or not. As long as they ain't troublemakers I'll let 'em in. The way I figure it is that it's the shop officer's job to know where his men are. That's what he's getting paid for. And if he let's 'em out, why should I set myself up by saying 'no.' Then he's an angel and I'm a p——k. I can do without that kind of grief.

Thus, as a result of contradictory organizational goals and conflict among the top administrators, the role definitions of correctional officers at ECI are ambiguous and to some extent conflicting. Further, the policy of humanitarian reform has stripped the officers of much of their coercive power while increasing the problems surrounding the maintenance of internal order and external security. In response to these pressures, there has developed among the officers a state of normlessness regarding their job performance that has deteriorated working relationships.

ADAPTATIONS OF THE CUSTODIANS

Merton has identified several modes of deviant behavior as adaptive responses to anomie: innovation, ritualism, retreatism, and rebellion.[9] Two of these modes of adaptation were most in evidence among the custodians: innovation and rebellion. Innovation refers to the attempt to secure goals by proscribed means. This mode of adaptation characterized the job performance of the custodians. Rebellion refers to collective efforts to modify the social structure. This mode of adaptation was manifest in the organization and the activities of the officers' union.

THE CORRUPTION OF AUTHORITY

Among the custodians at ECI innovation takes the form of a widespread corruption of authority, a pattern of relations wherein the officers seek to maintain control and minimize their personal trouble through personal ties and illicit exchanges with prisoners.[10] A central thrust of the reform emphasis has been to decrease the social distance between keeper and kept. One of the most striking aspects of institutional life at ECI is the extent to which in fact this distance has been minimized, and the extent to which officers are enmeshed in friendship relations with prisoners. On a random tour through the wings one may find one officer engaged in conversation or even horseplay with a group of inmates, and a second watching television with another group. At the same time the officer in the gym may be playing pool or Ping-Pong, and upstairs the officer in the library may be engrossed in a game of chess. Similar patterns exist in the shops where officers may provide coffee for inmates at their own expense and work alongside them. Throughout the institution officers and inmates, particularly long-term white prisoners, are on a first name basis.

Presumably such relationships are an aspect of the rehabilitative process, a means by which prisoners may be reformed through positive relationships with law-abiding citizens. In some instances these relationships may in fact serve this purpose. Most often than not, however, they are indicative of the corruption of the officer rather than of the reform of the inmates. The corruptive nature of these arrangements becomes clear in such instances as when on a hot, August day three inmates are drinking Kool-Aid® under the shade of a tree while their supervisor mows the lawn. Or, as on another occasion, when an officer aids an inmate in making picture frames and shadow boxes from state-owned lumber, for sale to other inmates, the officer is thus making himself an accessory to grand larceny. Or, as is frequently the case, information of a vital nature to the performance of custodial duties is not relayed to officers to whom it is of the most immediate concern for fear they will forewarn inmates of some impending action.* One senior captain candidly informed me:

> It's gotten so that I cannot tell an officer things that I should be telling him. I can't tell him anything serious that I might think is going down because he runs right to the inmates. And it might be in his area. . . . I'd say there's only five or six officers that I can really communicate with, that I can say watch this guy, let me know where he goes, who he's with 'cause I think he might be into drugs. With most, if I tell 'em, they'll go to the inmate and put him onto it. . . . I can't figure it out. But one thing I do know, most of 'em ain't working for me, they're working for the inmates.

In fact, according to our interpretation, the officers are not

---

*Shortly after the study was completed, four prisoners escaped from maximum security despite the fact that their plan was known in advance. One factor that facilitated the escape was the decision not to inform the officers in charge of the wing from which the escape was made, presumably for fear they would harm the inmates.

working for the inmates; they are working for themselves. Unable to secure compliance with their directives by the enforcement of a set of impersonal rules, they seek to secure compliance by means of friendship, overlooking infractions, and providing highly desired information to inmates. Their behavior is not so much a repudiation of the goal of custodial control as it is an attempt to maintain order, and at the same time to protect themselves, in the face of institutional changes that have made order more difficult to maintain and their position more vulnerable.

THE REBELLION OF THE HACKS

With reference to rebellion as an adaptive response to anomie, Merton has written:

> When the institutional system is regarded as the barrier to the satisfaction of legitimized goals, the stage is set for rebellion as an adaptive response. To pass into organized political action, allegiance must not only be withdrawn from the prevailing social structure but must be transferred to new groups possessed of a new myth. The dual function of the myth is to locate the source of large-scale frustrations in the social structure and to portray an alternative structure which would not presumably give rise to the frustration of the deserving.[11]

As we have seen, the reforms at ECI have been experienced by the officers as barriers to the achievement of goals to which they are strongly committed. The apathetic performance of their duties represents not only a response to a situation they perceive as futile, but a withdrawal of allegiance to the structure established by the mixed goals of custody and rehabilitation. While I have no direct evidence on this point, statements by officers indicate that this has long been the case, that the officers have from the beginning been frustrated by the gradual extension of privileges to inmates and the incursion upon their own authority. But the relative quietude, which pervaded the prison from 1956 to 1968, and the widespread popular support given to the reform program deprived the officers of any issue by which they might hope to generate public support for their own position. The inmate disturbances from 1968 through 1970 provided them with such an issue. In 1969 the rebellion of the officers began.

Work Stoppages

In the midst of the disturbances in April 1969, the officers staged a "sick out" and held a press conference to protest the absence of rules and regulations at the institution and to demand an improved pension plan and pay raise. In response to their protest, the legislature granted the officers a substantial increase in salary, an increase that still left their salaries considerably below those of correctional officers in other states, however. Moreover, no action was taken on an improved pension plan nor their demands for the reinstitutionalization of custodial rules. The real significance of the protest, however, lay in demonstrating to the officers that they could expect to achieve some gains by independent actions of this nature.

After the court rulings in August 1970, the officers again staged a "sick out." This time they sought the support of the state employees' union in gaining a revocation of the rulings. However, the union not only refused to support the officers but chastised them for irresponsible action. Following this unsuccessful attempt to gain union support, 116 officers resigned from the state employees' union, and a petition was submitted to the state Labor Relations Board to hold an election on prison employee representation. The petition was signed by 184 of some 240 ECI employees in the bargaining unit. The petition was granted and at an election in December, 1970 the ECI employees established their own independent bargaining unit, The Fraternal Order of Correctional Officers.

The Officers' Union

The new union immediately embarked upon an aggressive strategy to secure its interests. In the eleven months from January through November, the union organized five walkouts to publicize their demands. Each of these walkouts occurred in the wake of an inmate disturbance used to dramatize the plight of the officers and each followed a similar strategy. On each occasion the press was notified of the impending work stoppage, and the morning shift, on which most officers work, congregated on the grounds outside the prison rather than reporting to work. There, against the background of obscenities and cat-calls from inmates, who remained locked in their cells, spokesmen recounted the reasons for the walkout and reiterated demands for higher pay, an improved pension plan, more officers, and the re-establishment of written rules regarding the conduct of both inmates and officers.

On the first three issues, the officers had the support of both Flint and Knott, and the new union was successful in securing a considerable increase in salary and a special pension plan permitting retirement at age fifty after twenty years of service. But the re-establishment of written rules remained in contention until November 1971. Knott openly opposed such a policy on the grounds that it will "put us right back where we were thirty years ago." In the wake of the uprising at Attica, the officers' demands for written rules became more strident, and following an incident in which some thirty inmates refused to enter their cells one evening, the union organized a three-day walkout in November. Under pressure of this sort, Knott was forced to relent, and a five-man commission of officers was appointed to develop a set of written rules for both inmates and officers.

For the better part of the period of this study, then, the lower level correctional officers, the "hacks," were engaged in a minor rebellion. By organizing themselves into an independent union they were able to secure better pay, an improved pension plan, and most importantly a commitment by the administrators to their "myth" that written custodial policies would eliminate their frustrations.

SUMMARY

The intent of this chapter has been to portray the social situation of the custodians at ECI. From our perspective they constitute the dominant group, standing above and controlling the subordinate inmate population. As we have seen, however, the dominant position of the custodians has been eroded by several factors. First, the contradictory goals assigned to the institution along with goal dissensus among the top administrators has resulted in ambiguous role definitions for the officers and a lack of effective leadership. Second, the officers have retained a commitment to the goal of custodial control in the face of institutional changes that have stripped them of much of their coercive power, thus making the attainment of this goal by traditional means more difficult. As a result of these pressures, the administrative/custodial hierarchy is characterized by a state of normlessness and deteriorated working relationships. On the job, officers attempt to maintain order and protect themselves by allowing their authority to be corrupted. Off the job, they are engaged in a minor rebellion against the prison administration in an attempt to secure more stringent custodial regulations. Thus, not only have the resources at the disposal of the custodians been depleted by the reforms, but also their capacity to mobilize their still considerable resources has been impaired by their anomic state.

REFERENCES

1. Gresham M. Sykes, *The Society of Captives: A Study of a Maximum Security Prison* (Princeton, N.J.: Princeton University Press, 1958), ch. 3. Sykes argues that physical coercion is an ineffective means of securing compliance on a routine basis, that punishment is an ineffective measure when men are living close to allowable limits of physical punishment, and that the rewards are administered in such a manner as to be defined as punishment. The result is that guards must often sacrifice a degree of their authority in their efforts to secure compliance.

2. Emile Durkheim, *The Division of Labor in Society*, trans. George Simpson (New York: The Free Press, 1964), Book 3, ch. 1; *Suicide*, trans. John A. Spaulding and George Simpson (New York: The Free Press, 1951), Book 2, ch. 5.

3. Robert K. Merton, *Social Theory and Social Structure*, (2d rev. ed.; New York: The Free Press, 1957), pp. 132-139.

4. A second prominent use of the conception is to refer to a psychological state of isolation. See Robert M. MacIver, *The Ramparts We Guard* (New York: Macmillan, 1950, pp. 84-85; David Reisman, Reuel Denney, and Nathan Glazer, *The Lonely Crowd* (New Haven: Yale University Press, 1950), pp. 287 ff; Leo Srole, "Social Integration and Certain Corollaries; An Exploratory Study," *American Sociological Review* 21 (December 1956), 709-716.

5. Alvin W. Gouldner, *Patterns of Industrial Bureaucracy* (New York: The

Free Press, 1954), chs. 4-5.

6. For a detailed analysis of the ways in which pressure groups may influence correctional administrator, see Lloyd E. Ohlin, "Conflicting Interests in Correctional Objectives," *Theoretical Studies in Social Organization of the Prison* (New York: Social Science Research Council, pamphlet #15, 1960), pp. 111-129.

7. Role conflict here is used to refer to two or more inconsistent but equally legitimate sets of behavioral expectations associated with a single position. The problem of role conflict of correctional officers has been the subject of some study. See Oscar Grusky, "Role Conflict in Organization: A Study of Prison Camp Officials," *Administrative Science Quarterly* 3 (March 1959), 452-472: Donald R. Cressey, "Contradictory Directives in Complex Organizations: The Case of the Prison," *Administrative Science Quarterly* 4 (June 1959), 1-19; Lloyd E. Ohlin, "The Reduction of Role Conflict in Institutional Staff," *Children* 5 (March-April 1958), 65-69.

8. Merton, p. 134.

9. Ibid., pp. 141-157.

10. Sykes, pp. 52-53; Also, Sykes, "The Corruption of Authority and Rehabilitation," *Social Forces* 34 (March 1956), 257-262.

11. Merton, p. 156.

Chapter 15

IMPLICATIONS OF COLLECTIVE BARGAINING IN PRISONS

JAMES B. JACOBS AND NORMA MEACHAM CROTTY

ASSESSING the effect of collective bargaining on corrections is, at best, a hazardous undertaking. Collective bargaining is not the only force influencing the evolution of corrections in the last decade. Bureaucratic centralization of state administration, professionalization of corrections administrators, prisoner politicization, and judicial activism have all contributed to tension and change within penal institutions. The difficulty of isolating the independent effects of unionization does not mean, however, that there is nothing to say about the impact of collective bargaining. It does mean that we should approach our inquiry cautiously and that the reader should regard our observations as hypotheses that require further study.

EFFECTS ON PRISON ADMINISTRATION

The unionization of the guards and the establishment of collective bargaining in corrections has had enormous significance for the prison's system of internal management and organization. The redistribution of organizational power has brought the guards more job security, more control over their work assignments, and more say in decision-making at all levels. One effect has been to undermine the prisons' hierarchical and authoritarian system of management by creating a tripolar prison world. Formerly, prison policy was dominated

From James B. Jacobs and Norma Meacham Crotty, *Guard Unions and the Future of the Prisons* (Institute of Public Employment Monograph Number 9), Ithaca, N.Y.: New York State School of Industrial and Labor Relations, Cornell University, 1978. Copyright 1978 by Cornell University.
Editor's note: Footnotes have been renumbered.

by administrators, although the prisoners themselves often influenced events. The line staff, aligned with the administration, had little say in mapping strategy or in setting priorities. The emergence of collective bargaining immensely strengthened the rank and file's position. The union leader, the guards' spokesman, is now an active participant in the day-to-day running of the penal facility. The union is actively involved in shift and post assignments, discipline, working hours, and new programs.[1]

The redistribution of power has ended the autocratic rule of the warden and the custodial elite. Especially in states where civil service protection was weak, the warden and his top assistants previously had broad discretion in disciplining the workforce. Guards suspected of trafficking in contraband or neglecting their duties were often transferred to undesirable shifts and assignments and ultimately forced to quit. While civil service provided some protection, "problem cases" were suspended or fired.

Collective bargaining changed all this radically. Under the New York contract, discipline can be imposed only for just cause. Suspensions prior to a full disciplinary hearing are severely limited. The Bill of Rights, which precedes the enumerated articles, provides for union representation of employees at each stage of the grievance and disciplinary procedures. No employee can be requested to sign an admission of guilt for use in a disciplinary proceeding without a union representative present. No recording devices can be used during disciplinary hearings without the consent of the employee. In all disciplinary proceedings the burden of proof rests with the employer. The contract states that "no employee shall be coerced or intimidated or suffer any reprisal either directly or indirectly that may adversely affect his hours, wage, or working conditions as a result of the exercise of his rights under the agreement." Finally, work assignments cannot be used for disciplinary purposes. The net effect is to increase the guard's job security and to diminish the top administrators' ability to control the work force through sanctions. The warden must now rely more on positive incentives and better techniques of employee relations, an area of little importance to his predecessors.[2]

Collective bargaining itself, however, limits the capacity of administrators to rebuild staff solidarity. Unionization reifies the status divisions between administrators and top custodial personnel on the one hand and rank-and-file officers on the other. It has redefined the prison organization in adversary terms so that wardens are bosses and complaints are grievances. The spectacle of rank-and-file guards, through their union, suing their own supervisors (on such matters as overcrowding or the right to carry revolvers off duty) would be incredible were it not for our acclimation to similar suits by other public employees and to the generalized litigiousness of our society.

Since collective bargaining is a system of employer-employee relations imported from the private employment world, it will necessarily accelerate the trend toward "civilianizing" the prison. Shop stewards, grievance hearings, and labor-management meetings already make the prison familiar to those with experience in the private sector. How much "civilianization" can occur without losing the capacity to manage maximum-security prisons effectively is an issue to follow closely in the years to come. Throughout the history of the American prison the most obvious characteristic of the guard force was its paramilitary organization. At the apex of the pyramid stood the warden whose "orders" flowed through his captains and lieutenants down to the rank-and-file line officers. While the prison guard was the lowest member of the formal organization, every guard ranked higher than even the most senior prisoner. The authoritarian control exercised by the staff over the prisoners paralleled the control that the warden and the custodial elite exercised over the rank and file. Traditional thinking in penology required a highly disciplined work force to meet the prison's special requirements for order, discipline, and control. The guard force took its model from the armed forces rather than from organizations of industrial production.[3]

Is the redistribution of organizational power brought about by collective bargaining compatible with the prison's paramilitary structure? The union now constitutes an alternative basis for authority in an organization that traditionally demanded single-minded allegiance to those in command. The local

union presidents and stewards have more *de facto* power than
some lieutenants and captains. It seems a worthy hypothesis
that the vitality of the paramilitary regime will be undermined.
The existence of separate union locals for top officers blunts
this problem somewhat, but careful empirical research will be
required to explore the issue fully. Ultimately, collective bargaining may spell the end of the prison's paramilitary organization. The momentum which imports one feature after
another of the civilian workplace into the prison may well lead
to the abolition of rank and military uniform. The prison
regime of the future may be characterized by supervisors rather
than sergeants, security specialists rather than lieutenants, and
middle managers rather than captains.

The erosion of the local control and growth of central administration have been trends in corrections for the last several
decades. While public employee unionism is not the only force
responsible for this development, it has contributed to it. The
whole structure of statewide collective bargaining and a single
contract assumes a centralized management and a centralized
employee representative. In contrast to the previous autonomy
of individual prisons, the collective bargaining contract necessarily stamps a great deal of uniformity on the operation of a
state's penal facilities.

In New York, the Department of Correctional Services has
steadily withdrawn control over labor relations matters from
the local institutions. This was accomplished by requiring consultation with the central office on all such matters. Consequently, the warden's authority either to resist the union or to
make concessions to it is limited. Ironically, the same union
that once demanded more centralized prison administration —
in order to wrest strict authoritarian controls from local
wardens — now finds itself frustrated by the warden's diminished discretion to deal with local problems. Union leaders
frequently complain that wardens cannot make any decisions
without approval from Albany.

The key decisions affecting day-to-day prison management
increasingly emanate from Albany. Much of the corrections
department's authority has been lost to the Office of Employee
Relations, which has ultimate responsibility for negotiating the
collective bargaining agreements — an authority which some

Department of Correctional Services officials believe has been used to trade away management prerogatives for budgetary concessions.[4] In addition, the department's authority will be diminished as arbitrators are brought into the decision-making process on more issues, especially if interest arbitration is enacted.

No discussion of the effect of collective bargaining on corrections can neglect the potential of job actions and strikes for disrupting the day-to-day administration of the facilities. The Taylor Law prohibition on strikes has not prevented the New York guards from threatening to strike and from actually carrying out limited job actions from time to time. For the most part, such tactics have proven successful for the officers, who have usually achieved their goals and avoided punishment under the law. Most of the job actions have involved disputes about institutional management. The officers have repeatedly demonstrated their concerns about unsafe prisons, lack of discipline, lax controls on contraband (including weapons), and unsatisfactory staffing ratios.

Despite numerous job actions and threatened strikes, the relationship between labor and management in the New York prisons has been relatively harmonious, at least when compared with Ohio, which has experienced bitter and protracted guard strikes. Staudohar attributes the conflict in Ohio to the lack of a viable collective-bargaining framework.[5] To test his hypothesis, future research should compare those states that have experienced guard strikes with those that have not, and states with and without formal public sector bargaining. Whether or not a public employee collective-bargaining framework ameliorates labor tensions, the existence of organized employee associations, with or without collective bargaining, makes strikes and job actions possible. If the guards' aspirations and expectations cannot be met, society faces the specter of crippling strikes and reliance on the National Guard to keep the prisons running — an unhappy possibility for corrections and for American democracy.

EFFECTS ON PENAL POLICY

The charge has frequently been made that guard unions are

reactionary and pose significant obstacles to reforming the prisons.[6] We believe that this is not necessarily the case; under certain circumstances the dynamics of unionization can make it easier to introduce penal reform. Collective bargaining makes successful implementation of new programs possible through early consultation with the union leadership. The diffuse emotional opposition to new programs that sometimes surfaces among the guards presents greater obstacles to reform than the more rational opposition of a centralized union leadership open to negotiation and compromise. Surely, some unions may be every bit as strident and emotional as the rank and file, but this seems unlikely in the light of the professionalization necessary to conduct statewide collective bargaining, the platform of national unions such as AFSCME, and an objective assessment of the guards' self-interests. In New York, we have not found a single instance where union opposition defeated a major reform proposal. Future comparative studies may reveal whether New York's experience is unique.

A strong emphasis on safety and security is not necessarily incompatible with prison reforms. Most liberal prison reforms cannot succeed without a viable security system. Council 82 consistently advocates progressive reform of the prisons, but links reform to adequate levels of staffing and assurances of safety for both guards and inmates. The union strongly supports the construction of new prisons, especially a super maximum-security institution. Whether such a facility is a move toward or away from reform depends on whether one supports a moratorium on new prison construction or believes that expanding the number of beds, despite the potential for increasing the total prisoner population, is a step toward ameliorating human misery.[7] It also depends on whether one thinks that confining the worst troublemakers in a single super maximum-security facility would improve living conditions for the rest of the prisoners. In any case, it is incorrect to label the union's position reactionary.

The substance of prison reform is not always free from doubt. In inadequately staffed, vastly overcrowded prisons, it is by no means clear that expanding program opportunities for prisoners, thus proliferating inmate movement about the prison, constitutes reform. Prisoners are not a monolithic group; they are more divided than they are united.[8] Racial, political, and other factional tensions abound, and increased inmate movement without adequate security can lead to more assaults, rapes, and other brutalities. Additional guards may well be an indispensable requirement for a more humane maximum-security environment.

In 1976, Council 82* linked its interests with those of the prisoners in a federal lawsuit charging that severe overcrowding in the New York State prison system constituted cruel and unusual punishment for the prisoners and thereby forced officers to violate prisoners' Eighth Amendment rights.[9] AFSCME, asserting the rights of guards and prisoners, sought an injunction against any reduction in the number of corrections officers or in the budget, which might decrease the ratio of guards to inmates. It also requested a court order requiring the Department of Correctional Services to allocate sufficient expenditures to provide adequate, decent, and safe physical facilities.

> Plaintiffs and the class which they represent have the constitutionally protected right to be employed in a manner so as not to be unduly subjected to loss of life or health and have a constitutional right to a reasonable degree of protection from injury by inmates during the course of their duties for the Department of Correctional Services.

Although the union eventually dropped the case, the suit supports our hypothesis that Council 82 has attenuated the stridency of the guards' anti-inmate ideology. Historically, the guards could be expected to oppose various reforms simply because they were "giving too much" to the prisoners. Although the rank and file have not completely abandoned these beliefs, the union leadership is sophisticated enough to realize that the position of the guards will not improve if they oppose prison reforms, for they thereby reinforce the stereotype of the stupid, racist, brutal, and repressive guard. The union can better advance the interests of its membership by favoring de-

---

*Editors Note: Council 82 of the American Federation of State, County and Municipal employees represents New York's state security personnel, of whom guards are the largest single group.

cent, humane prisons.

The union has not hesitated to describe the guards' role as including counseling and other treatment-oriented duties. It has objected to turning over all nonsecurity functions to civilian employees. The more sophisticated the guards' role, the stronger the claim for better pay. By stressing their essential role in the implementation of sophisticated correctional programs, the guards can gain greater wages and benefits. The union's lobbying efforts may eventually produce increased funding for corrections. Certainly the union can pursue its objectives more freely and more aggressively than an executive agency.

Ultimately, the interests of prisoners and officers are inextricably intertwined. Improvements for one group are likely to bring about improvements for the other, while deteriorating prison conditions will affect both groups negatively. This fact has not escaped notice by AFSCME's Department of Legislation and Political Education, which recently stated:

> We are working with the Education Commission of the States (ECS) to devise a satisfactory reform of education and rehabilitation services in correctional institutions. The ECS will present its reforms to all state governors in 1977 as a model for community and institutional corrections rehabilitation. AFSCME will insure that this plan advances the interests of corrections employees to insure better working conditions and increasing responsibility in the rehabilitation process.[10]

Another example of the congruence of interests is the effort of corrections officers, particularly at Attica, to have the Department of Correctional Services promulgate uniform statewide regulations on such matters as what personal property can or cannot be possessed by a prisoner. The officers argue that the different rules on contraband at each facility make the guards appear arbitrary. The formulation of a uniform set of rules and procedures is in the best interests of both guards and prisoners.

The union's consistent demands for better training, better recruitment, and more professional standards are completely consistent with the goals of prison reform. The reiteration of these demands in the wake of the Attica riot was a major factor in the establishment of the New York Corrections Academy in 1971.[11] The department's responsibility to train its employees is embodied in the collective bargaining contract. To the extent that academy training has "professionalized" the work force and made individual officers more sensitive to the prisoners' problems, the union may have made an important indirect contribution to reform.

In one other instance the momentum and logic of the union movement have led to an important reform. Some penologists, most notably Dean Norval Morris of the University of Chicago Law School, have advocated the introduction of women into front-line positions in all maximum-security prisons. The New York Department of Correctional Services did not move to integrate its guard force since the majority of rank-and-file officers were strongly opposed to it. Yet the political and legal pressures from women union members forced the union to accede to their demands for bidding rights in all institutions. The momentum of unionism finally led to a change which the department would not and perhaps could not effect.

Those who maintain that the New York union chosen as our model is a conservative force impeding reform build their case on three issues: seniority, the defeat of the nomination of Herman Schwartz as chairman of the Corrections Commission, and the prisoners' grievance procedure. Each of these claims can be effectively rebutted.

First, it is questionable whether bidding by experienced officers for jobs with little or no inmate contact undermines overall institutional security. We have argued that allowing dissatisfied guards to transfer from jobs with sustained inmate contact might reduce tensions and conflicts. Rather than an obstacle to reform, seniority might be looked upon as an opportunity to recruit and train young officers who want to serve in "contact" positions. In other words, by permitting officers to choose or reject sensitive positions, seniority increases job satisfaction and alleviates tensions.

With respect to the Herman Schwartz nomination, we have pointed out that the top union leadership blunted some of the .

emotional opposition of the rank and file. The primary opposition to Schwartz came from the conservative sheriff's association and from forces in the legislature that opposed Governor Carey. The executive director of Council 82 attacked Schwartz only mildly in the legislative hearings and did not lobby against him. No doubt legislators could read between the lines.

Finally, the implementation of a prisoners' grievance procedure demonstrates that the guard union will not automatically oppose reform and may indeed make reform easier to achieve, at least when the interests of the guards are also protected. The grievance committees were originally funded by the New York City Bar Association as an "experimental inmate grievance procedure . . . providing for inmate and line staff participation [with] impartial arbitration as a final step." The pilot program was initiated at Green Haven on August 1, 1975, but did not become fully operational until February 1976. The committee consisted of two inmates, two line officers, and a chairman/mediator who could be either a prisoner or a staff member. Procedures permitted inmates with complaints about institutional matters to take them before the committee and to appeal decisions that did not satisfy them. After the initial success of the Green Haven program, the New York legislature passed a bill establishing a similar procedure at every state institution.[12] Most significant, for our purposes, is the fact that the bill passed the legislature without any opposition from Council 82, despite some criticism from rank-and-file officers.

The present system allows an inmate with an unresolved complaint to file a formal grievance. The committee has several days to attempt informal resolution; if that fails, a hearing must be held. The inmate may appear *pro se* or with a representative to present his case. If the matter does not involve a challenge to institutional or departmental policy, the committee's decision is final. If the grievance does question an institutional or department policy, an appeal lies with the warden. Challenges to policies can be carried one step further, to central headquarters in Albany. After the Department of Correctional Services makes its ruling, an appeal may be taken to the Corrections Commission, which may delegate its review authority to an outside arbitrator. The commissioner of the Department of

Correctional Services has ultimate authority to accept or reject a decision of the Corrections Commission or its chosen arbitrator, but if he rejects the decision, he must state in writing his reasons for doing so.

The very existence of this complex grievance procedure gives prisoners significant participation in prison management. It is not surprising that many corrections officers were originally opposed to the idea. They were particularly worried that the prisoners would use the procedure to bring charges against individual officers. They were also concerned that full-time service on the grievance committee might abrogate officers' seniority rights.[13] Nevertheless, the union did not block this progressive reform. Negotiations between Council 82 and the Department of Correctional Services resolved the guards' doubts and, as a result of guard participation, the grievance procedure was implemented successfully.

With respect to the scope of grievable issues, the department and the union rejected specific charges against a corrections officer and agreed that only rules, practices, and generalized complaints would be brought before the committee. With respect to seniority rights, they agreed that service on the grievance committee would count as "time served in title." The local institutions were left considerable flexibility in devising selection procedures and in setting rules on tenure for committee members.

Despite early hostility to the program, especially at Attica, the grievance committees, with the approval of labor and management, were implemented at each state prison facility. The early results were encouraging.[14] Eighty-one percent of the 8,116 grievances filed up to September 30, 1976, were resolved at the institutional level, with almost 40 percent resolved informally. In most cases the committee's recommendations were unanimous. Though skeptics said that the system would be flooded with frivolous and invalid complaints, the committee found merit in approximately 60 percent of the cases. Several long-standing policies were changed as a result of recommendations by outside arbitrators.

Implementation of the grievance procedure proves that a professional and centralized union can facilitate prison reform when the interests of the officers are taken into account and when major concerns are negotiated. Although we cannot know what the outcome of the grievance committees would have been in the absence of the union, there is reason to believe that the hostility which the program met in the beginning might have prevailed.

We conclude that the unionization of New York prison guards by the American Federation of State, County and Municipal Employees has not retarded prison reform. While unionization is certain to have profound effects on the administration and organization of the prisons, possibly requiring a new type of administrative system, it has certainly made the guard force more conscious of its rational self-interest. The pursuit of enlightened self-interest may lead the guards to accept and even advocate many prison reforms they would have rejected in the absence of the collective bargaining.

REFERENCES

1. See James B. Jacobs, *Stateville: The Penitentiary in Mass Society* (Chicago: University of Chicago Press, 1977), Chap. 7.

2. John W. Wynne, Jr., "Unions and Bargaining Among Employees of State Prisons" *Monthly Labor Review*, March, 1978, p. 16, states: "The state correctional administrator's ability to carry out his traditional administrative responsibilities is being diminished and diffused by the labor relations process."

3. See Joseph Roucek, "Sociology of the Prison Guard," *Sociology and Social Research* 20 (1935): 145-151.

4. Wynne, "Unions and Bargaining Among Employees of State Prisons," p. 15 observes that:

> The management side of the bargaining table is characterized by fragmented authority and by the possibility of internal disputes over labor relations policies, correctional programs, and political goals. In the twelve research states that permit comprehensive collective bargaining for state employees, the chief negotiator for management is part of the state's office of employee relations. Thus, he has no formal responsibility for operations in the state's correctional agency, nor is he responsible to the director of that agency. As a result, the state's negotiator may have guidelines and goals different from those that would be deemed important by the director of a department of corrections. This multifaceted structure tends to shift a measure of decision-making and policy-making authority from the state's chief correctional administrator to the state's chief negotiator, who generally does not understand the unique features in the workings of correctional

agencies. Although attempts are sometimes made to let correctional administrators contribute information and ideas to the bargaining process, communications tend to break down during the intense final stages of negotiations.
Sometimes contract provisions are entered into without adequate legislative
funding and the correctional administrator is forced to shift scarce resources
away from program needs to fulfill contract obligations. This has had particularly serious effects on the operation of many correctional agencies.

5. Paul Staudohar, "Prison Guard Labor Relations in Ohio," *Industrial
Relations* 15 (1976): 177-190.

6. Staudohar makes this point in passing but gives no reasons for his
conclusion that "the guards have been a reactionary force working counter to
what inmates may regard as their legitimate interests." Prison Guard Labor
Relations in Ohio," p. 189.

7. The National Council on Crime and Delinquency, an influential
private criminal justice reform organization, has lobbied extensively for an
end to prison construction. See NCCD policy statement, "A Halt to
Institutional Construction in Favor of Community Treatment," 1974.

8. See James B. Jacobs, "Stratification and Conflict Among Prison
Imates," *Journal of Criminal Law and Criminology* 66 (1976): 476-482.

9. Kelley v. Carey, 76 Civ. 1529 (T.P.G) (S.D.N.Y., filed April 1976).

10. Report of the President and Headquarters Department, AFSCME, AFL-
CIO, Twenty-second International Convention, Miami Beach, Florida, June
14-18, 1976.

11. See Jay Cohen, "The Corrections Academy: The Emergence of a New
Criminal Justice System Institution," *Crime and Delinquency* (forthcoming).

12. N. Y. Corrections Law § 139 (McKinney 1975).

13. Selection procedures for officers vary from facility to facility. At some
institutions the job is assigned according to the applicant's seniority. Other
facilities require every officer to serve in order of seniority. Some prisons
made committee membership in permanent assignment. The Attica local
refused to participate until late 1976 when department and union officials
agreed that officers would bid to be included in a ten-man pool for
assignment to grievance committees for three months.

14. For a review of the program see Special Committee on Penology,
"Grievance Procedures in the Correctional Facilities of New York State
Instituted under the Auspices of the Association," *Record of the Association
of the Bar of the City of New York* 32 (May/June 1977): 381-392.

A COMPREHENSIVE BIBLIOGRAPHY ON PRISON GUARDS AND GUARD WORK

Adler, H.: Ideas toward a sociology of the concentration camp. *Am J Sociol, 63:* 513-522, 1958.

Amir, M.: Sociological study of the house of correction. *American Journal of Correction,* March-April, pp. 20-24, 1966.

Athens, L.: Differences in liberal-conservative political attitudes of prison guards and felons. Status versus race. *International Journal of Group Tension, 5, 3 (September):* 143-155, 1975.

Barnes, H. E. and Teeters, N. K.: *New Horizons in Criminology.* New York, P-H, 1943.

Beard, E.: *Personal Practices Relative to the Recruitment and Retention of Minority Correctional Employees.* National Institute of Law Enforcement and Criminal Justice, U.S. Department of Justice, 1974.

Becker, A. M.: Women in corrections. *Resolution,* Summer, pp. 19-21, 1975.

Bernlef, J. and Zuyderland, S.: *Prison Weariness — A Book of Details about Dutch Correctional Institutions.* Ministerie Van Cultur, Recreatre En Maatschappelizk Werk, 1974.

Biderman, A.: Internment and Custody. In Sills, D. E. (Ed.): Vol. 8. *International Encyclopedia of the Social Sciences.* New York, Macmillian, 1968.

Bidna, H.: Effects of increased security on prison violence. *Journal of Criminal Justice, 3 (Spring):* 33-46, 1975.

Boehm, A.: Present and future situation of the prison guard service — prerequisites for changing career training in the general corrections service. *Zeitschrift Fuer Shatvollazug and Shaffaelligenhilfe, 24 (1):* 10-15, 1975.

Brady, J. C.: Evaluation of semantic differential changes in correctional training officer attitudes. *Journal of Correctional Education, 20 (Spring):* 4-6, 1968.

Briggs, D. and Dowling, J.: The correctional officer as a consultant: an emerging role in penology. *American Journal of Correction, 26 (3):* 28-31, 1964.

Brief, A., Munroe, J., and Aldag, R. J.: Correctional employees' reactions to job characteristics: a data-based argument for job enlargement. *Journal of Criminal Justice, 4, 3 (Fall):* 223-230, 1976.

Brodsky, C.: Longterm work stress in teachers and prison guards. *J of Occup Med, 19 (February):* 133-138, 1977.

Brodsky, S.: A bill of rights for the correctional officer. *Federal Probation,*

June, 1974.

———: Criminal justice settings. In Kaslow, F. and Associates (Eds.): *Supervisor, Consultation, and Staff Training in the Helping Professions.* San Francisco, Jossey-Bass, 1977.

Brooks, R. J.: The role of the correctional officer. *American Journal of Corrections, 26 (May-June):* 22-24, 1969.

Brown, B., Dupont, R., Kozel, N., and Spevacek, J.: Staff conceptions of inmate characteristics: a comparison of treatment and custody staffs at two differing institutions. *Criminology, 9 (August-November):* 316-329, 1971.

Burns, H. and Spencer, S.: General responsibilities of a correctional officer. *American Journal of Corrections, 26 (May-June):* 40-44, 1969.

Cameron, N.: Cadet training and the prison service. *Journal of British Criminology, 13:* 354-372, 1973.

———: The New Zealand prison officer cadet training scheme. *Australian and New Zealand Journal of Criminology, 4:* 35-45, 1971.

Cape, W.: In-service university training for correctional officers. *American Journal of Correction,* (Sept.-Oct.), pp. 36-38, 1965.

Carroll, L.: *Hacks, Blacks and Cons.* Lexington, Lexington, 1974.

———: Race and three forms of prisoner power: confrontation, censoriousness, and the corruption of authority. In Huff, C. R. (Ed.): *Contemporary Corrections: Social Control and Conflict.* Beverly Hills, Sage, 1977.

Change, D. H. and Zastrow, C. H.: Inmates' and security guards' perceptions of themselves: a comparative study. *International Journal of Criminology and Penology, 4:* 89-98, 1976.

Clemmer, D.: *The Prison Community.* New York, HR&W, 1958.

———: Use of supervisory custodial personnel as counselors: an expedient, *Federal Probation, 20 (December):* 36-42, 1956.

Cloward, R.: Social control in the prison. In Cloward, Cressey, et al. (Eds.), *Theoretical Studies in Social Organization of the Prison,* Pamphlet 15. New York, Social Science Research Council, 1960.

Cockerham, W. E.: Connecticut prisons weather prison guard strike. *Corrections Magazine, III, 2 (June):* 37-41, 1977.

Cox, G.: Correctional position and salary survey. *Quarterly Journal of Corrections, 1 (1):* 45-51, 1977.

Craddick, R. A.: A note on the dilemma of custodial officers in counselor training. *Canadian Journal of Corrections, 12 (April):* 117-119, 1970.

Cressey, D. R.: Contradictory directives in complex organizations: the case of prison. *Administrative Science Quarterly, 4 (June):* 1-19, 1959.

———: Prison organization. In March, J. G. (Ed.): *Handbook of Organizations.* Chicago, Rand, 1965.

Cronin, H.: *The Screw Turns.* London, John Lang, 1967.

Crouch, B. M.: *A Selective Comparison of Prisons in Louisiana, Arkansas, Mississippi, Oklahoma, and Texas.* Unpublished manuscript, 1977.

———: *Role Conflict Among Correctional Officers.* Paper presented before the Mid-West Sociological Association, St. Louis, 1976.

Daeumling, A. M. and Possehl, K.: *Self-Image and External Image of Prison Guards*. Ferdinand Enke Verlag, 1970.

Davidson, R. T.: *Chicano Prisoners. The Key to San Quentin*. New York, HR&W, 1974.

Day, R. C. and Hamblin, R. J.: Some effects of close and punitive styles of supervision. *Am J Sociol, 69 (March):* 499-510, 1964.

Darmer, F. A.: The prison officer. In Jaffray, J. K. (Ed): *The Prison and the Prisoner*. Boston, Little, 1917.

Downey, R. N. and Signori, E. I.: The selection of prison guards. *Journal of Criminal Law, Criminology and Police Science, 49 (September-October):* 234-236, 1958.

Duffee, D.: The correctional officer subculture and organizational change. *Journal of Research in Crime and Delinquency, 11 (July):* 155-172, 1974.

———: *Using Correctional Officers in Planned Change*. Washington D.C. National Institute of Law Enforcement, North Technical Information Service, 1972.

Editors: In Illinois guards have a wider role. *Corrections Magazine, 11, 6 (December):* 41-43, 1976.

Einsele, H.: *Corrections Law Reform from the Expert's Viewpoint*, from the Proceedings of the Corrections and Preventive Measures Conference. Nauheim Ferdinand Enke Verlag, 1974.

Esselstyn, T. C.: The social system of correctional workers. *Crime and Delinquency*, April, pp. 117-124, 1966.

Evans, A. A.: Correctional institution personnel-amateur or professional? In Sellin, T. (Ed.) *Prisons in Transformation*, Westport, Greenwood, 1972.

Farmer, R. E.: Cynicism: A factor in corrections work. *Journal of Criminal Justice, 5, 3 (Fall):* 237-246, 1977.

Fireman, A.: A study of the interaction between prisoners and guards. *American Journal of Corrections, 25 (March-April):* 24-30, 1963.

Fogel, D.: *We Are the Living Proof: The Justice Model for Corrections*. Cincinnati, W. H. Anderson Co., 1976.

Frongeamore, M. P., Culla, L., and Nicolai, A. M.: Women in penitentiary administration — Italy. *Rassegna Di Studi Penitenziari, 27 (1):* 37-47, 1977.

Frank, A.: Goal ambiguity and conflicting standards: an approach to the study of organizations. *Human Organization, 17 (Winter):* 8-13, 1958-1959.

Frank, B.: The emerging professionalism of the correctional office. *Crime and Delinquency*, July, pp. 272-276, 1966.

Gallington, D.: Prison Disciplinary Decisions. *Journal of Criminal Law, Criminology and Police Science, 60 (June):* 152-164, 1969.

Galvin, J. J. and Karacki, L.: *Manpower and Training in Correctional Institutions*. Staff Report of the Joint Commission on Correctional

Manpower and Training. Lebanon, Sowers, 1969.

Gill, H.: Training prison officers. *American Journal of Correction, 20 (4):* 8-11, 22-26, 1958.

Glaser, D.: *The Effectiveness of a Prison and Parole System.* New York, Bobbs, 1969.

Goffman, E.: *Asylums.* New York, Anch. Doubleday, 1961.

Goldstein, B.: *Screening for Emotional and Psychological Fitness in Correctional Hiring.* Washington, D.C., American Bar Association, 1975.

Gottfredson, M. R., M. J. Hindelang and N. Paris: *Sourcebook of Criminal Justice Statistics.* U.S. Department of Justice. Law Enforcement Assistance Administration, 1978.

Greenberg, D. and Stender, F.: The prison as a lawless agency. *Buffalo Law Review, 21:* 798-838, 1972.

Grusky, O.: Role conflict in organization: a study of prison camp officers. *Administrative Science Quarterly, 3 (March):* 452-472, 1959.

Guenther, A. and Guenther, M.: Screws vs. thugs. *Society, 11 (July-August):* 42-50. 1974.

Guenther, A.: The language of prison life. In Johnston, N., Savitz, L. (Eds.): *Justice and Corrections.* New York, Wiley, 1978.

Hammerman, H. A.: Prison guard service as reflected in empirical studies: How they got to be guards. *Zertschrift Fuer Strafvollzug und Straffaelligenhilfe, 24 (2):* 68-71, 1975.

Haney, C., Banks, C., and Zimbardo, R.: Interpersonal Dynamics in a Simulated Prison. *International Journal of Criminology and Penology, 1:* 69-77, 1973.

Hardesty, D.: *Kansas Correctional Officer Selection Study: Final Report.* Topeka, Consulting for Business, Industry and Government, 1970.

Hargan, J.: The psychology of prison language. *Journal of Abnormal and Social Psychology, (30):* 359-365, 1935.

Hawkins, G.: *The Prison: Police and Practice.* Chicago, U of Chicago Pr, p. 81-108, 1976.

Hazelrigg, L. E.: An Examination of the Accuracy and Relevance of Staff Perceptions of the Inmate in the Correctional Institution. *Journal of Criminal Law, Criminology, and Police Science, 58 (June):* 204-210, 1967.

Heffernan, E.: *Making it in Prison: The Square, the Cool and the Life.* New York, Wiley, 1972.

Heim, R.: Prison personnel: a review of the literature. *American Journal of Correction, 28 (1):* 14-20, 1966.

Henderson, R. L.: The correctional officer and the educational program. *American Journal of Correction, 32 (May-June):* 18-21, 1970.

Hogan, H. W.: A social-psychological study of prison guards. *Experimental Publication System,* June, MS. No. 407-256, 1971.

————: *A Study of Authoritarianism, Job Satisfaction, and Personal and Social Characteristics of Prison Guards and Guard-Applicants in*

Tennessee. Unpublished Master's thesis, Department of Sociology, University of Tennessee, 1969.

Hohmeier, J.: *Significance of the Guard Personnel in Modern Corrections.* From Codetermination in Prison-Resocialization as Democratization-Conference Proceedings. Evangelische Akademie Locum, 1973.

Holland, T., Heim, R., and Holt, N.: Personality patterns among correctional officer applicants. *J of Clin Psychol, 32 (October):* 786-791, 1976.

Hommeier, J.: *Surveillance and Resocialization-Empirical Investigation of the Position of Guard Staff and Inmates in Corrections.* Ferdinand Enke Verlag, 1973.

Hooper, C.: *Sex in Prison: The Mississippi Experiment with Conjugal Visiting.* Baton Rouge, La State U Pr, 1969.

Irwin, J.: *The Felon.* Englewood Cliffs, P-H, 1970.

Jacobs, J. B. and Grear, M.: Drop-outs and rejects: an analysis of the prison guard's revolving door. *Criminal Justice Review, 2 (2):* 57-70, 1977.

Jacobs, J. B. and Crotty, N. M.: *Guard Unions and the Future of the Prisons.* Institute of Public Employment, New York State School of Industrial and Labor Relations, Ithaca, Cornell University, 1978.

Jacobs, J. B. and Kraft, L. J.: Integrating the keepers: a comparison of black and white prison guards in Illinois. *Social Problems, 25:* 304-318, 1978.

Jacobs, J. B. and Retsky, H.: Prison Guard. In Leger, R. and Stratton, J. (Eds.): *The Sociology of Corrections.* New York, Wiley, 1977.

Jacobs, J.: *Stateville: The Penitentiary in Mass Society.* Chicago, U of Chicago Pr, 1977.

———: Street gangs behind bars. *Social Problems, 21, 3 (Spring):* 395-409, 1974.

———: What prison guards think: a profile of the Illnois force. *Crime and Delinquency, 24 (2):* 185-196, 1978.

Jessor, R.: A behavioral science view of the correctional officer. *Federal Probation, 27 (March):* 6-10, 1963.

Johnson, E.: Bureaucracy in the rehabilitation institution: lower level staff as a treatment resource. *Social Forces, 38 (May):* 355-359, 1960.

Johnson, J. and Care, B.: *Survey of Line Officer Needs: A Selective Inquiry Among College and Correctional Personnel,* Coordination Bulletin No. 15. Washington, D.C., American Bar Association and American Association of Community and Junior Colleges, 1973.

Johnson, R.: Ameliorating prison stress: some helping roles for the custodial personnel. *International Journal of Criminology and Penology, 5, 3 (August):* 263-273, 1977.

Joint Commission on Correctional Manpower and Training: *A Time to Act.* Washington, U.S. Govt. Print. Office, 1969.

———: *Perspectives on Correctional Manpower and Training.* Staff Report, Washington, D.C., Joint Commission on Correctional Manpower and Training.

Joseph, N. and Alex, N.: The uniform: a sociological analysis. *American Journal of Sociology, 77, 4 (January):* 719-731, 1972.

Katsampes, P.: *Changing Correction Officers through Decision Making Training Sessions.* Albany, School of Criminal Justice, 1972.

Kassebaum, G., Ward, D., Wilnes, D., and Will, K.: Job related differences in staff attitudes toward treatment in a women's prison. *Pacific Sociological Review, 5, No. 2 (Fall):* 83-88, 1962.

Kelling, G. L. and Schenk, Q. F.: Stresses accompanying professionalization of correction. *Crime and Delinquency, 17 (July):* 289-295, 1971.

Kercher, G. A. and Martin, S.: *Severity of Correctional Officer Behavior in the Prison Environment.* Presented before Texas Academy of Science, Huntsville, 1975.

Korim, A. and Johnson, J.: Line officer educational needs-concensus among correctional and academic administrators. *American Journal of Correction, 34 (5):* 36-37, 1972.

Krajick, K.: They keep you in, they keep you busy, and they keep you from getting killed. *Corrections Magazine, 1 (March):* 4-8; 10-21, 1978.

Kuethe, J. L.: Prison parlance. *American Speech, 9-10:* 25-28, 1934-1935.

Larson, J. H. and Pendleton, S. L.: *Rule Breaking in Prison: A Reflection of Correctional Officers' Attitudes and/or Inmate Adjustment Problems.* Paper presented at the Annual Meetings of the Midwest Sociological Society, Omaha, 1978.

Lundberg, D. E.: Methods of selecting prison personnel. *Journal of Criminal Law, and Criminology, 38:* 14-39, 1947.

————: *Some Aspects of the Job of Prison Guard.* Unpublished doctoral dissertation, Cornell University, 1946.

Lunden, W.: Staff turnover and tenure in the British prison service. *American Journal of Corrections, 31 (January-February):* 26-34, 1969.

————: The Prison Warden and the Custodial Staff. Springfield, Thomas, 1965.

Mangram, C.: Liability for correctional malpractice. *Youth Authority Quarterly, 30, 4 (Winter):* 8-16, 1977.

March, R. A.: *Alabama Bound.* University, U of Ala Pr, 1978.

Marquart, J. W.: *Career Contingencies of the Correctional Officer.* Unpublished Master's thesis, Department of Sociology, Kansas State University, 1978.

Maxim, P.: Treatment-custody staff conflicts in correctional institutions: a re-analysis. *Canadian Journal of Criminology, 18, 4 (October):* 379-386, 1976.

May, E.: Prison guards in America: the inside story. *Corrections Magazine, 11, 6 (December):* 3-12, 36-4, 44-48, 1976.

McCleery, R.: *Policy Change in Prison Management.* East Lansing, Mich St U Pr, 1957.

————: Communication patterns as bases of systems of authority and power. In Cloward, Cressey, et al., (Eds.): *Theoretical Studies in the Social Organization of the Prison,* Pamphlet 15. New York, Social Science Research Council, 1960.

McCorkle, L. W.: Guard-inmate relationships. In Normal Johnson, et al.

(Eds.) *The Sociology of Punishment and Corrections.* New York, Wiley, 1970.

McCorkle, L. W. and Korn, R.: Resocialization within the walls. *The Annals, CCXCIII (May):* 88-98, 1954.

McLaren, D.: Cons, hacks and educated screws — the prison politics of discipline and rehabilitation. *Canadian Journal of Criminology, 15, 1 (January):* 25-38, 1973.

Mechanic, D.: Sources of power of lower participants in complex organizations. *Administrative Science Quarterly, 7 (December):* 349-364, 1962.

Megathlen, W. and Day, S.: The line staff as agents of control and change. *American Journal of Correction, 34 (3):* 12-16, 1972.

Menard, J. M.: Preparing correctional officers and inmates for their interaction. *Offender Rehabilitation, 1 (3, Spring):* 241-249, 1977.

Miller, W.: Ideology and criminal justice policy: some current issues. In Leger, R. and Stratton, J. (Eds.): *The Sociology of Corrections.* New York, Wiley, 1977.

Mitford, J.: *Kind and Usual Punishment.* New York, Vintage Books, 1974.

Morris, N.: *The Future of Imprisonment.* Chicago, U of Chicago Pr, 1974.

Morris, T. and Morris, P.: *Pentonville.* London, Routledge & Kegan, 1963.

Motivans, J.: Occupational socialization and personality: a study of the prison guard. *Proceedings American Correctional Association,* pp. 186-196, 1963.

Murton, T. O.: *The Dilemma of Prison Reform.* New York, HR&W, 1976.

Nagel, W.: Custody and treatment — some aspects of conflict. *Prison Journal, 43 (Autumn):* 2-9, 1963.

Oswald, R. G.: Rights of correctional personnel. *American Journal of Correction, 34 (6):* 18-20, 1972.

Paddock, A. L. and McMillan, J.: *Final Report Vienna Staff Training Project.* Southern Illinois University, 1972.

Paterson, A.: Recruitment and training of prison staff. In Ruck, S. K. (Ed.): *Paterson on Prisons: Being the Collected Papers of Sir Alexander Paterson.* London, Frederick Muller Ltd., 1951.

Penfold, D.: The changing concepts of the custodial officer's job. *Canadian Journal of Corrections, 4 (July),* pp. 298-299, 1961.

Perdue, W. C.: Screening of applicants for custodial work by means of a temperament test. *American Journal of Correction, 26 (November-December),* pp. 14-19, 1964.

———: The temperaments of custodial workers. *American Journal of Correction, 28 (March-April),* pp. 16-19, 1966.

Peretti, P. O. and Hooker, M.: Social role self-perceptions of state prison guards. *Criminal Justice and Behavior, 3 (June):* 187-195, 1976.

Piliavin, J.: The reduction of custodian-professional conflict in correctional institutions. *Crime and Delinquency, 12 (April),* pp. 125-134, 1966.

Prisgrove, P.: Group structure of prison officers' perceptions of inmates. *J Consult Clin Psychol, 42 (4):* 622, 1974.

Prison Officers Association: The role of the modern prison officer. *Prison Officers Magazine*, November, pp. 1-3, 1963.

Reckless, W.: Training of the correctional worker. In Tappan, P. (Ed.): *Contemporary Corrections*. New York, McGraw, 1951.

Rice, R.: Intentions and the structure of attitudes among inmates and non-inmates. *Journal of Research in Crime and Delinquency, 10:* 203-207, 1973.

Roucek, J.: Sociology of the prison guard. *Sociology and Social Research, 20:* 145-151, 1935.

Sandhu, H. S.: Perceptions of prison guards: a cross-national study of India and Canada. *International Review of Modern Sociology, 13 (March)*, pp. 26-32, 1972.

Sandhu, H. S. and Allen, D. E.: The prison guard: job perceptions and in-service training in India. *The Indian Journal of Social Work, 32 (July):* 115-120, 1971.

Schrag, C.: Social role, social position and prison structure, *Proceedings of the 89th Congress of Corrections of the American Correctional Association*, 178-188, 1959.

Sebring, R. H. and Duffee, D.: Who are the real prisoners? A case of win-lose conflict in a state correctional institution. *Journal of Applied Behavioral Science, 13 (1):* 23-40, 1977.

Shelly, E. L.: Where counselors really counsel. *American Journal of Correction, 29 (July-August):* 30-31, 1967.

Shoom, S.: Authority: one aspect of the correctional worker-client relationship. *Canadian Journal of Criminology, 14:* 181-184, 1972.

Singer, L. R. and Keating, J. M.: The courts and the prisons: a crisis of confrontation. *Criminal Law Bulletin, 9:* 337-357, 1973.

Singleton, D.: Changing the attitudes of prison officers. *American Journal of Corrections, 22 (April)*, p. 22, 1960.

Smith, L., Merrow, W., and Harris, J.: *Prison Screw*. London, Herbert Jenkins, 1962.

Smith, R. R., Wood, L. F., and Milan, M. A.: Ex-offender employment policies. A survey of American correctional agencies. *Criminal Justice and Behavior, 1, 3 (September):* 234-246, 1974.

Smith, W.: *Some Selective Factors in the Retention of Prison Guards*. Unpublished master's thesis, Department of Sociology, North Carolina State University at Raleigh, 1963.

Sommer, R.: *The End of Imprisonment*. New York, Oxford U Pr, 1976.

Stageberg, R. W.: The correctional officer as seen by a workhouse superintendent. *American Journal of Correction, 26 (July-August)*, pp. 32-36, 1964.

Staudohar, V. D.: Prison guard labor relations in Ohio. *Industrial Relations, 15 (2):* 177-190, 1976.

Stingley, J.: Prison guards: twenty-four hour day of fear, low pay, and hatred. *Los Angeles Times*, September 6, 1971.

Stotland, E.: Self-esteem and violence by guards and state troopers at Attica.

Criminal Justice and Behavior, 3, 1 (March): 85-96, 1976.

Street, D.: The inmate group in custodial and treatment settings. *American Sociological Review, 30 (February):* 40-55, 1965.

Sutherland, E. and Sellin, T.: *Prisons of Tomorrow.* New York, Arno, 1931.

Sykes, G.: The corruption of authority and rehabilitation. *Social Forces, 34 (March):* 257-262, 1956.

———: *The Society of Captives.* Princeton, New Jersey: Princeton U Pr, 1958.

Sylvester, S., Reed, J., and Nelson, D.: *Prison Homicide.* New York, Spectrum Pub, 1977.

Tannenbaum, F.: *Wall Shadows: A Study in American Prisons.* New York, Putnam, 1922.

Task Force Report: *Correction, Task Force on Corrections.* The President's Commission on Law Enforcement and Administration of Justice. Washington, U.S. Govt. Print. Office, 1967.

Ten-Eyck, S.: The correctional officers job. *Correctional Review,* January-February, pp. 14-17, 1963.

Teske, R. and Williamson, H.: *Correctional Officers' Attitudes Toward Selected Treatment Programs.* Paper presented at the Annual Meetings of the American Society of Criminology (November) Tucson, Arizona, 1976.

Thomas, J. E. and Williams, T. A.: Change and conflict in the evaluation of prison systems. *International Journal of Criminology and Penology, 5:* 349-365, 1977.

Thomas, J. E.: *The English Prison Officer Since 1850: A Study in Conflict.* Boston, Routledge & Kegan, 1972.

———: The prison officer: A conflict in roles. *Journal of Psychosomatic Research, 18:* 259-262, 1974.

Toch, H.: *Peacekeeping: Police, Prisons, and Violence.* Lexington, Lexington Bks, 1976.

Walsh, R. T.: Researcher-participant collaboration in corrections research: a case study. *Canadian Journal of Criminology, 18, 4 (October):* 387-400, 1976.

Webb, G. L. and Morris, D. G.: *Prison Guards: The Culture and Perspective of an Occupational Group.* Austin, Coker Books, 1978.

Weinberg, S. K.: Aspects of the prison's social structure. *Am J Sociol, 47:* 717-726, 1942.

Weir, H. G.: *Conflict of Security and Rehabilitation in the 1970s —* Australian Institute of Criminology — Training Project No. 5 — Proceedings. Australian Institute of Criminology, 1975.

Weiss, C. and Frair, D. J.: *Terror in the Prisons: Homosexual Rapes and Why Society Condones It.* Indianapolis, Bobbs, 1974.

Wheeler, S.: Role conflict in correctional communities. In Cressey, D. (Ed.): *The Prison, Studies in Institutional Organization and Change.* New York, HR&W, 1961.

Wicker, T.: The other prisoners [the prison guards], *New York Times,* September 28, p. 37, 1971.

Wicks, R.: Is the corrections officer a second class citizen? *American Journal of Correction, 36 (1):* 32-34, 1974.

Wilkerson, F.: A new look at custody. *American Journal of Corrections,* November-December, pp. 24-28, 1969.

Williams, J. S. and Thomas, C. W.: Attitudinal correlates of professionalism: the correctional worker. *Criminal Justice Review, 1 (2):* 120-125, 1976.

Wittmer, J., Lanier, J., and Parker, M.: Race relations training with correctional officers. *Personnel and Guidance Journal, 54 (February),* pp. 302-306, 1976.

Wynne, John, Jr.: *Prison Employee Unionism: The Impact on Correctional Administration and Programs.* Washington, U.S. Govt. Print. Office, 1978.

————: Unions and Bargaining among employees of state prisons. *Monthly Labor Review,* March, 1978.

Yanagimoto, M.: Selection and training of personnel in Japanese correctional institutions. *American Journal of Correction, 30 (6):* 26-31, 1968.

Zald, M. N.: Power and Conflict Institutions. *Administrative Science Quarterly,* June, pp. 22-49, 1962.

Zimbardo, P. G., Haney, C., and Jaffee, D.: A Perandellian prison: the mind of a formidable jailer. *New York Times Magazine, 7 (April),* pp. 38-40, 1973.

Zimbardo, P.: Pathology of imprisonment. *Society, 10 (March),* pp. 4-8, 1972.

NAME INDEX

A

Adorno, T., 93, 95, 103
Adag, R., 40, 41
Alex, N., 288 n, 290
American Correctional Association, 195, 205
Attica, 37, 41
Austin, J., 190, 205

B

Baker, J., 21, 32, 41
Banks, C., 93, 205
Banton, M., 75, 103
Barber, B., 21-22, 29, 32, 43
Barnes, H., 60-61, 202, 205
Beard, E., 37, 41
Becker, A., 36, 41
Becker, H., 63, 98, 103
Bennett, J., 54
Bettelheim, B., 257 n
Bittner, E., 187, 205
Bohlander, E., 22, 32
Brief, A., 40, 41
Brodsky, C., 18, 39, 41
Browning, F., 21, 41

C

California Task Force on Violence, 20, 26, 35, 44
Canon, K., 291, 301
Carroll, L., 23-24, 31-32, 41, 93, 103
Carter, R., 26, 36, 38-39, 41
Cavallin, H., 9, 41, 58, 61
Chambliss, W., 23, 42
Clemmer, D., 183, 205, 274 n, 290
Cockerham, W., 36, 41
Cohen, B., 277 n, 290
Cohen, J., 278 n, 290, 335
Council of Europe, 57, 61

Craddick, R., 9, 42
Cressey, D., 9, 17, 42, 185, 192, 194, 205, 327 n
Cronin, H., 189, 205
Cross, S., 72, 103
Crouch, B., 10, 42, 64, 92, 103, 207, 223-224

D

Davidson, R., 21, 42, 66, 70, 82, 98, 103
Denney, R., 321 n
Dingwall, R., 80, 103
Downey, R., 52-53, 61
Drummond, D., 71, 103
Duffee, D., 57-58, 61, 63, 103, 221, 224
Durkheim, E., 302, 321

E

Editors, 223-224
Emerson, R., 33, 42
Esselstyn, T., 63, 103
Etzioni, A., 74, 79, 103, 216, 224
Evans, A., 53, 61

F

Faine, J., 22, 42
Farmer, R., 92, 104
Feshback, S., 291, 301
Flanagan, J., 17, 42
Fogel, D., 34, 42
Frank, B., 39, 42
Frenkel-Brunswik, E., 103
Fuller, D., 26, 34, 42

G

Gerth, H., 75, 104
Gettinger, S., 13-14, 42
Giallombardo, R., 64, 104, 222, 224

SUBJECT INDEX

A

Administrative succession, impact on guard work, 303-307
Administrators
and prison change, 32, 35, 191
conflict among, over goals, 154, 303-308
guards conceptions of, 156-158
rebellion by guards against, 318
Aggression
by guards, 93-96
under competitive prison relations, 31
under paternalistic prison relations, 28
Alabama prison system, 13
Alaska prison system, 115
Angola, 19, 31
Anomie among guards, 302, 308-316
guard adaptations to anomie, 316-320
Anticipating trouble with inmates, 83-86
Arkansas prison system, 13, 28, 32, 64, 114-116, 130
Arizona prison system, 13
Attica, 49, 52, 118, 291-301
Authoritarianism among guards, 93-96

B

"Being the Man," 72-74
Brutality, 126-128

C

California state prison, 20, 36, 64, 114-115, 123
Censoriousness, 24
Collective bargaining. See Unionization
Competition vs. paternalism as styles of guarding, 216-219
Competitive prison relations, 30-33
Confrontation, 24
Connecticut prison system, 114, 122, 127-128, 134

"Contamination" of guards by inmates, 250-251
Control over inmates
and role of personal dominance by guards, 219-221
Corruption of authority, 24, 77-78, 195, 238-243, 266-267, 316-318
Courts
and paternalistic prison relations, 30
and prison change, 11-13
impact on guard work, 13-16, 173-174, 295, 311-312
Cynicism, 92, 168, 249, 268

D

Danish prison administration, 56-57
Danger, 25-26, 114, 153, 194, 200-201, 286-288, 293
Dependence on inmates, 193, 195
Discipline of guards, 324
Discipline of inmates, 214-216, 227-231, 312-315
District of Columbia prison system, 13, 37
Division of labor in guard work, 192-199

E

Employee organizations. See Unionization
Encounters with inmates, initial, 72-74, 121-123
Ex-offenders as prison staff, 37, 51

F

Favoritism in promotions, 101, 189
Favoritism toward inmates, 262
Family concern for guards, 149
Federal Bureau of Prisons, 37, 53, 57, 61
Florida prison system, 13
Force used by guards, 251-256

351